The Tour Guide

FIELDWORK ENCOUNTERS AND DISCOVERIES

A series edited by Robert Emerson and Jack Katz

THE TOUR
Guide

Walking and Talking New York

JONATHAN R. WYNN

University of Chicago Press
Chicago and London

Jonathan R. Wynn teaches in the Department of Sociology at the University of
Massachusetts, Amherst.

The University of Chicago Press, Chicago 60637
The University of Chicago Press, Ltd., London
© 2011 by The University of Chicago
All rights reserved. Published 2011
Printed in the United States of America

20 19 18 17 16 15 14 13 12 11   1 2 3 4 5

ISBN-13: 978-0-226-91905-8
ISBN-13: 978-0-226-91906-5
ISBN-10: 0-226-91905-6
ISBN-10: 0-226-91906-4

Library of Congress Cataloging-in-Publication Data

Wynn, Jonathan R.
    The tour guide : walking and talking New York / Jonathan R. Wynn.
        p. cm. — (Fieldwork encounters and discoveries)
    Includes bibliographical references and index.
    ISBN-13: 978-0-226-91905-8 (cloth : alk. paper)
    ISBN-10: 0-226-91905-6 (cloth : alk. paper)
    ISBN-13: 978-0-226-91906-5 (pbk. : alk. paper)
    ISBN-10: 0-226-91906-4 (pbk. : alk. paper)
    1. Tour guides (Persons)—New York (State)—New York. 2. Tourism—
Social aspects—New York (State)—New York. 3. Culture and tourism—
New York (State)—New York. 4. New York (N.Y.)—Description and travel.
I. Title.   II. Series: Fieldwork encounters and discoveries.
F128.3.W96 2011
917.47'10444—dc22   2010048754

Walking, ideally, is a state in which the mind, the body, and the world are aligned, as though they were three characters finally in conversation together, three notes suddenly making a chord.

Rebecca Solnit

Through stories about places, they become inhabitable. Living is narrativizing. Stirring up or restoring this narrativizing is thus also among the tasks of renovation. . . . One must awaken the stories that sleep in the streets and that sometimes lie within a simple name, folded up inside this thimble like the silk dress of a fairy.

Michel de Certeau and Luce Giard

Public spaces are the primary site of public culture; they are a window into the city's soul. As a sight, moreover, public spaces are an important means of framing a vision of social life in the city, a vision both for those who live there, and interact in urban public spaces every day, and for the tourists.

Sharon Zukin

CONTENTS

ACKNOWLEDGMENTS

In *Here Is New York*, E. B. White wrote that the city gives a "sense of belonging to something unique" to its citizens as a "supplementary vitamin" for all its ills ([1949] 1999, 33). That anodyne was prescribed to me by many wonderful, mostly Brooklyn, folk: Joanna Bron, Susan Lott, Dan Skinner, Liz Polizzi, Robyn Goodmark, Daniel Lewis, Jessica Ruglis, Leejone Wong, Sara Yff, Jason Scher, and Jason Jeffries of Verb Café, Kara Pranikoff, Mark Shulman, and especially my favorite New Yorkers—Hannah and Solomon—to whom this book is dedicated.

This book would not be possible without Patricia Clough and Jack Katz, who provided me critical guidance and support at the beginning and end of this research, respectively. I must express gratitude to the following people for their various comments, questions, edits, and myriad influences throughout the various stages of this project: Benjamin Stewart, Alexandre Frenette, Richard Lloyd, Mary Walsh, Ailsa Craig, Marion Wrenn, Grace Mitchell, Kristin Dombek, Erin O'Connor, Jeffrey London, Jennifer Reich, Carla Barrett, Allen Shelton, Joelle Hann, Harvey Molotch, Craig Calhoun, Richard Sennett, Paul Willis, and Mitchell Duneier. I am incredibly grateful for my book group of Claudio Benezcry, Andrew Deener, Colin Jerolmack, and Ryan Centner, and the three anonymous reviewers of this manuscript. In addition, few words can describe how much I appreciate the professional staff at the City University of New York–Graduate Center, particularly Rati Kashyap and Urania Willis (who make an appearance in appendix A), and the folks at the University of Chicago Press, Douglas Mitchell and Timothy McGovern, for making both my graduate career and the publishing process as smooth as can be. Last, and most of all, I am indebted to the wonderful tour guides who so graciously allowed me to tag along with them for all these years.

On a related note, sections of chapter 4 appeared in *Qualitative Sociology* 28, no. 4 (2005) and sections of chapter 5 appeared in *Radical Sociology* 32, no. 1 (2006), and I would like to thank the editors and anonymous reviewers from those journals as well.

City Murals

Characters in the Crowds, Offering New York "Like a Native"

I walked around a lot when I moved to New York City. I was struck by its hustle and bustle, histories and cultures—the rich mix of street life urbanist William H. Whyte wrote of with verve to match. On my near-daily strolls up Fifth Avenue, from 14th Street to the City University of New York's Graduate and University Center at 34th, I would occasionally encounter small clusters of people knotting up the sidewalks around Union Square and the Empire State Building. I watched tour guides with their packs of followers as they told tales and pointed at this building or that park. On the same street I would also hear facts called out over the intercoms of red, double-decker tour buses as they barreled down Fifth. One day, waiting at the intersection of 23rd Street, I eavesdropped on a walking tour at the Flatiron Building to hear how the term "23 Skidoo" "came from this exact spot." Because of the shape of the 1902 building, the guide explained, winds swoop down and furl the edges of young ladies' dresses, and back in the 1920s police would have to tell boys who lingered in packs hoping for a glimpse of bare ankle to stop loitering. "They'd have to give 'em the 23 Skidoo," he said, pretending to shuffle off ruffians with a nightstick. The group laughed.

As I moved along myself, I wondered about the veracity of the story, but I also started thinking about the role these characters play in what Jane Jacobs called the "intricate sidewalk ballet" of cities (1961, 50). These sorts of things are the odds and ends of urban life that encourage social interactions between strangers. Whyte called it *triangulation* (1980, 94). Even if they don't join in, New Yorkers continually bump through these groups, knowing little about the folks who lead them, how they got there, and how they develop the content of their stories. Once I reached my school's library, I looked up the origins of "23 Skidoo" in Irving Lewis Allen's *The City in Slang* (1993) to find that the guide's origin tale was oft repeated, but apocryphal. Wandering further, I tread deeper into this niche of the tourism market and its history.

Tour guides, I read, have been around since antiquity. The ancient Greeks called those who showed foreigners to sacred sites *periegetari* (leaders around) or *exegetai* (explainers), and the Romans called them *mystagogi* (those who show sacred places to foreigners). At the height of antiquarian tourism, guides were at all the major cultural sites and even the smaller towns off well-trodden paths. There were so many that travelers were often suspicious of their moral bearings. The roaming scholar Varro would pray: "Jupiter, protect me from your guides at Olympia, and you Athena, from yours at Athens!" (Perrottet 2002, 6). In the first century, Athenian guides would show off the already centuries-dead culture to their visiting Roman conqueror-tourists, as well as to their fellow countrymen. And Romans were fascinated by, and proud of, their own city in a fashion that reminded me of many New Yorkers today. Jumping to the early 1900s, the Chinese in Manhattan's Lower East Side called those who brought "slumming" outsiders *lobbygow* (Chinatown pidgin for "tour guide")—characters who were, again, approached with skepticism, yet prospered due to piqued interest in exotic urban corners. Guides, it seems, have existed in the public imagination somewhere between the labels of "trickster" and "teacher": "Tour guides have always had a place—albeit at times on the lowest rung. The work of the tour guide is vastly misunderstood [and they] have been aptly called the orphans of the travel industry, somewhat hidden as they are."[1] Like Rome, New York is a city of immigrants, and vast enough to interest even the most tenured of residents. The same gaps in knowledge that lead to duplicity and suspicion also create the demand for these "explainers" to teach histories and to tell stories. Sitting in the library, I began to ask myself questions. In a way they are educators and cultural translators, but how do they learn about and share this information? How is their work conducted and, furthermore, what do they contribute to city life?

The answers to such questions lie in the sheer breadth of experiences and interactions New York City has to offer. Block by block, there are dizzying amounts of cultures and histories. Mid-century, E. B. White said there were three New Yorks: the one of the born-and-bred local, the one of the commuter, and the one of the migrant (1949); Colson Whitehead recently wrote that there are millions of versions (2003). The city of the commuter who retraces his daily steps from suburban Long Island to Wall Street will be different from that of the West African who lives in Harlem and sells fake Gucci watches on big blankets in Battery Park. The city of the Columbia graduate student will be different from that of a Brooklyn retiree. There are thousands of locals and travelers who are eager to learn those perspectives, and guides provide that service. They teach the minute details, hidden histories, cultural topographies, neighborhood flows, and how to spot a good cheesecake. City knowledge—about the Stonecutters' strike, the story behind Chumley's Tavern and the term "86," the best way to get from the Waldorf-Astoria Hotel to the Cloisters, the history of East Harlem, or the true origin of "23 Skidoo"—is a kind of currency. Perhaps because of such a mosaic of people and cultural goods, in the ensuing years of studying walking tours I found more participants from the shores of Astoria, Queens, than from Athens, Greece.

As I left the library and hit the sidewalks for research, I found dozens of street-level interrogations of my new city.[2] Save for all of them being short, two-hour walks, the commonalities between tours seemed to stop there. "Wildman" Steve Brill offers tours about the edible flora of Prospect Park. Bruce Kayton gives ones on the radical-left history of Central Park. Bill Brown focuses upon the surveillance cameras of Chelsea. A member of the Micmaq tribe leads one on the Native American history of Lower Manhattan. There are *Sex and the City* location tours, actors who offer a "Literary Tour and Pub Crawl" of Greenwich Village, Harlem cultural tours, Queens food tours, and there are even "vampire tours" that I haven't had the nerve to take. (I did, however, take a tour of the Green-Wood Cemetery's catacombs, becoming one of the first public visitors inside for decades.) Then there are artists like Janet Cardiff, Andrea Frazier, and Sophie Calle who use walking tours to make art out of public spaces,[3] and the activists who tour to transmit their ideological beliefs to an audience. There are institutions that use tours as a part of their programming, including the Central Park Conservancy, the Museum of New York, and the National Italian-American Foundation, and many of the large business improvement districts (BIDs). The Municipal Art Society developed a walking tour for jurors on their lunch breaks, and hip New York health club Crunch offers walking tours to "work out the mind and body." And whether they are on their own or a part of one of these groups, guides take on a variety of topics. Some specialize in a theme or one geographic area while others pride themselves on their breadth; some guides give tours for free while others design a tour around any group's special interests so long as the price is right. There is a certain *joie de New York* to it all. The names of guides' businesses and the tours themselves invite you to have an "Adventure on a Shoestring" or "Rent-a-New-Yorker." You too can do New York "Like a Native."

These guides are a loosely tied, informal group. They are a diverse community as well, varying in styles, content, backgrounds, and levels of participation in the field. Because of this heterogeneity, an illustrative moment occurred in June 2003 when New York City's Department of Consumer Affairs (DCA), headed by Commissioner Gretchen Dykstra, initiated a new set of licensing regulations and redesigned the Sightseeing Guide Licensing Exam. It was a move that at once nullified current licenses and proved to be so difficult that it had a 36 percent pass rate. The DCA (in one form or another) has licensed guides since 1937 and the modern framework—which requires passing the multiple-choice test and paying a fee—was put into place in 1980. The moves, however, radicalized guides, and drew enough protest to oblige the city council to schedule a hearing. Presentation of this event provides an opportunity for introducing some of the issues guides face. Many who figure prominently in the field were in attendance, and it was where I received my first understandings of how complex the world of the informal tourism labor market really is. The following ethnographic fieldnote (along with a second one that appears later in the introduction) describes the moment, as well as the social context of the walking guide.

The Fight over the Test (New York City Hall, June 2003)

I crane my neck to look at the mural above, *New York Receiving the Tributes of the Nation*, for a few moments. Spanning the city council chamber's ceiling, it was installed around the same time the five boroughs merged in 1898. It is the image of New York personified, not filled with a blasé swagger but with humility. Seated at a throne, Europe gives a kneeling New York a diploma, placing him among the world's great cities. I sit on the periphery of the hall. The room's musty smell gives me the incorrect impression it was cracked open this morning. To my left two men are analyzing the clothing details of a life-sized plaster sculpture of Thomas Jefferson, an original sketch for the monument on the Washington Mall. One of them, I overhear, dresses

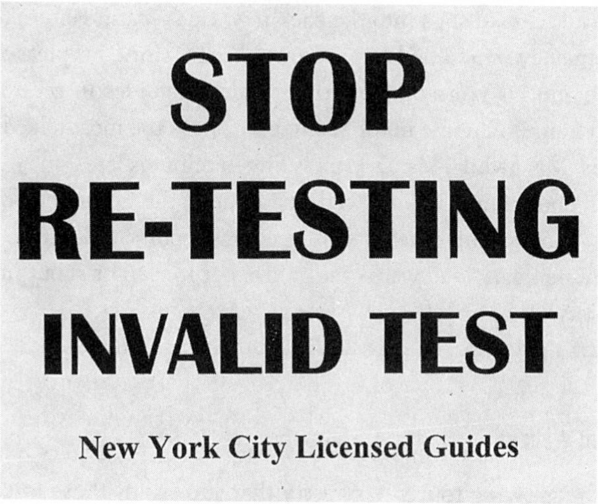

STOP RE-TESTING INVALID TEST

New York City Licensed Guides

Figure 1 A sign passed out for the City Hall hearing, 2003.

as Abraham Lincoln for his work and has the beard for it. A few people mill around, taking pictures of the paintings, the dais, the balcony. Folks shake hands, circulate through the seats, and queue up for a list to testify. Someone is passing out yellow "Stop Re-Testing—Invalid Test" signs. The bustle picks up; there's laughing, joking.

I sit alone and take notes, but soon Seth Kamil, owner of Big Onion Walking Tours, sits behind me. I reintroduce myself—"I'm Jon Wynn . . . the sociologist"—and wait a beat as he realizes he had granted me full access to all of his guides and tours a few months ago. As soon as he places me, he's more than cordial, whispering into my ear throughout the proceedings. Seth explains that most guides cannot recall an event that has raised more tension than this test. He is slightly amused at the ado, saying fellow guides are tested in San Antonio, Washington, D.C., and New Orleans, and that for London's "Blue Badge" guides undergo eighteen months of training and eight written and practical exams.

Overhearing our conversation, the guide seated next to me explains that he was once an employee of a now-defunct tour bus company, and that they were instructed, on the rare occasion when a DCA officer would come to verify a guide's license, to just take off his uniform and pretend to be one of the tourists. They were notorious for hiring "anyone with a heartbeat." The exam might "clean up" the industry, he tells me, since "just about anybody could be a guide."

As the rows fill with over eighty guides, quietly and in his usual bow tie and jacket, a man slips into the back row. He is Justin Ferate, the man who wrote the new, embattled test. Despite his hard work, his pleas and concerns over it, and his years of mentoring dozens of guides in the room, few approach him. Bonhomie in the room drops; he is the most talked-about guide in years. Meanwhile, Ms. Dykstra is fifteen minutes late.

City Councilman Phillip Reed, chairman of the Committee on Consumer Affairs, hammers his gavel. The proceedings begin without the commissioner and Councilman Reed warns the guides not to clap or shout in response to testimony.

The Work of Walking

Despite the growing tourism industry that surrounds these folks, the world of guides themselves has garnered very little academic attention.[4] Perhaps as an epiphenomenon of antiquated and romantic notions of the noble traveler, these texts focus upon the solitary tourist: a postmodern protagonist arriving at a set of cultural objects and activities without aid. Guides are also unaccounted for in the studies of major organizations, like the World Travel and Tourism Council and the World Tourism Organization, and in more academic accounts of tourism, which favor statistics on airline tickets, hotel rooms, and amusement park visits as indicators of the industry.[5] In fairness, they are a relatively difficult group to grasp in any quantifiable way. The work is seasonal and informal. There are no accurate measures of this sector of the industry along racial, class, age, and gender lines; nor is there any sense of how frequently guides give tours or how much money they earn. Furthermore, with a menagerie of actors in, and influences on, the city it may be challenging to see guides as pivotal actors on the urban scene: they are not venture capitalists able to summon investment money or politicians able to make speeches or shape zoning laws; they do not erect sculptures or buildings; they are considered neither cultural nor scholarly elite. Indeed, those who filled City Hall on that June day are difficult to categorize into any conventional "occupation."

It is precisely for these reasons that these "orphans," the ground troops of the travel industry, are a curious group. Their nuanced work—a blend of teaching and entertainment, interaction, and experience—has a relative impact on their participants and the city fabric precisely because their work operates between the varied cultural and municipal institutions, and between the physical spaces of built structures themselves. In these places, guides present historical nuggets, bits of wisdom, and whimsical stories tied together in order to make abstract concepts tangible and subjective meanings practiced in a way that coheres into a loosely constructed narrative of a community, a neighborhood, a city. Walking tours locate people within a vast physical and cultural landscape. At the same time, guides also bind a group together into a community of learning, if only for a few hours. The guide is part historian, part cultural critic, and part city booster. And when I ask about their work, they tell me teaching visitors and locals out of doors and in New York's public realm is a special contribution to the city, and that walking tourism is valuable because it "provides mobile stories" and "a kind of education on foot." This aspect was reinforced repeatedly in my conversations with guides. As self-taught walking guide Eric Washington told me, "It's one of the fun things about doing tours: you're really experiencing what you don't get looking through a bus window." And as Justin Ferate explained it: "For a couple of hours, you're getting this concentrated focus on this particular acreage that you are covering on foot, and you are really able to have a discourse, you are able to raise your hand and ask questions." Eric and Justin are just two members of a passionate group of for-hire urbanists, historians, and activists who offer an array of perspectives about history and culture in public spaces.

There are a number of precursors to today's walking tourism: the Peripatetics ("the ones walking about," a term given to Aristotle's followers, as well as those philosophers who do not have a fixed academic home); the religious pilgrimages of the Middle Ages; the seventeenth-century trend of sending young noblemen out to see the world on a Grand Tour; the *Wandervogel* (an 1890s German youth movement founded upon the pairing of nudity and nature hikes); the European youth hostels after World War I that offered packaged tours as an inexpensive way for teenagers and young adults to entertain themselves; and the post–World War II Situationist method of the *dérive*.[6] The New York walking guide is perhaps the latest incarnation of engaged stroller, set within a complex constellation of social and cultural forces. The guides I spoke with were still struggling through a massive constriction of their industry after September 11, 2001. Guides also work within overarching trends of rising commodification and tourism, shifts in the postindustrial labor market, and fading local neighborhood histories. They serve as a small-scale counterpoint to the perceived "Disneyfication" of cities, specifically of places like Times Square, which guides and scholars alike describe as becoming too packaged, commodified, and predictable.[7] In this context these urban characters re-enchant neighborhoods and blocks, and create experiences, offering a sort of magical urbanism, but they are not alone in this endeavor. Others shape the city in a similar fashion, counter to the corporate, Disneyfied city: "found art" artists who take scraps from the sidewalks and reassemble them into studio art, Green Guerrillas who reclaim deserted lots for gardening, the graffiti artists who electrify the city's walls, the homeless recyclers and sidewalk vendors who burrow through the city's refuse to resell it, and street thespians and sidewalk buskers who set up shop to reinvigorate the sidewalk with prose and song. Like these characters, walking guides engage with city dwellers and travelers, using what Gerald Suttles described as the "vast, heritable genome of physical artifacts, slogans, typifications, and catch phrases . . . most appropriately called collective representations" to alter New York's fabric (1984, 284). In so doing, they become what Jack Katz has called "urban alchemists," characters who emerge from densely populated urban scenes that create the conditions for the "sometimes wild, sometimes even frantic, often ingeniously innovative effort to appropriate an almost magical kind of public good that could be taken to define cities" (2007, 4; see also 2010). Urban alchemists use the free matter, the hidden and supplementary cultural goods produced by the city, and refashion them into something significant for the metropolis and for themselves.[8]

The licensing exam illustrates the tension between a loose group of urban dwellers who shape New York culture and the larger forces at work in cities, as the exam codifies relevant urban history and culture, while also serving as the prime instrument through which the DCA attempts to professionalize an informal labor market. Guides' reaction to the exam focuses on their feelings about the city itself as much as on the quality and content of the work. The struggles over the licensing exam can be seen within this context. The DCA commissioner's efforts to bolster the city's tourism industry as an engine for post-September 11 growth, and the resultant fracas, brought some attention to the field, from the local *Gotham Gazette* to national coverage on Fox News and NPR's *All Things Considered*. The *New York Post*, for example, sent a reporter to take the exam, and a few newspaper articles were published in the weeks surrounding the meeting. Many guides felt Commissioner Dykstra had more self-serving purposes, but she explained how it was great for the city. When appearing as a guest on Brian Lehrer's WNYC morning show on April 4, 2003, Ms. Dykstra told the audience that a "harder test would instill pride among the guide corps and confidence among tourists." As a fun way to get listeners to think about the kinds of information guides know, Lehrer and Dykstra played a game with callers entitled "Test Your NYQ." They offered the following question:

Q: Considered to be Britain's "last romantic poet," Dylan Thomas (1914–1953) was a conundrum as a writer. He was a Welsh poet who could neither read nor write in Welsh. Having become an intrinsic part of the bohemian scene of Greenwich Village, Dylan Thomas lived only to the age of thirty-nine. The end came after a binge of almost monumental proportions. He said, "I've had eighteen straight whiskies. I think that's the record." Then he collapsed. At which noted Greenwich Village watering hole did this take place?

A: 1.) The Lion's Head; 2.) Chumley's; 3.) The White Horse; 4.) The Corner Bistro.[9]

Intended to exemplify the test and stimulate interest, public relations events such as this one quickly irked guides. Letters were sent to city council, and emails flew across guides' listserves. The Dylan Thomas question led to one guide's comment, "What does a drunk poet have to do with what I do?" The problem, test writer Justin Ferate explained to me, was that the released questions were used in these venues because they were too flawed or just not worthy of being included in the exam, but "representative enough." Not explicitly stated as castoffs, these questions were understandably scrutinized by guides hoping to divine clues to the exam. Such concerns over community, information, and government oversight, and resulting protest led to the event at city council, which we can return to now.

Testing Your "NYQ" (New York City Hall, June 2003)

The commissioner arrives. She walks in quickly and with authority, joining Justin Ferate and two others I do not recognize at the witness table. She begins her testimony with an apology, saying that she was told that the meeting was a half hour later. Ms. Dykstra's testimony runs at as fast a pace as she had walked in on. Expressing astonishment over the protestations, the commissioner says she repeatedly asked for the city council's support and input in the matter and decided to move forward only in the absence of a response. She mentions that when she first came to the DCA, she found dozens of letters from guides complaining about the old exam. She reads a few aloud. Some of these concerns, she explains, came from the Guides Association of New York City (GANYC) itself. When I asked, the guide next to me explains that GANYC is a loose, nonprofit guild of guides founded in 1974, and has an executive board that was pushing for a "professionalization of the field."

Dykstra's answers are curt and defensive. She explains that she decided to rewrite the mandatory test because it was outdated and too simplistic. She testifies that guides found the previous exam to be unchallenging, incorrect in places, and largely inconsequential. One question, for example, asked, "What is the name of the pair of buildings that are the tallest structures seen in this photograph?" "The revamp," she explains, "was necessary." She echoes the DCA promotional material, claiming that the new exam includes questions "ranging from historical facts about New York City neighborhoods, immigration patterns, landmarks, and architecture to identification of ethnic foods, vital transportation information, and how to greet the city's throngs of visitors."

She then explains how the Grand Central Partnership and the Times Square BID (two of New York's major business improvement districts), and NYC & Company (New York's Convention and Visitors Bureau) provided financial support to tap Justin Ferate for the rewrite. She introduces Justin as a twenty-year veteran of the industry who received AAA's "Best Walking Tour in New York" award and was described by New York governor George Pataki as the "most engaging tour guide."

Reading from a prepared statement, Justin's voice shakes despite decades of speaking to crowds in the streets. He says he wanted to write with a committee, circulate it with ten guides, hire a lawyer, do a series of trials, and have multiple versions—things he believes to be proper protocol for test administration—and each was denied by Ms. Dykstra. Going above and beyond his mandate, Justin wrote 300 questions for two versions of the exam and an additional 100 to be released to the public as "sample questions" good enough to be used for radio and print promotion.

Finally, the other two individuals at the dais, representatives from NYC & Company and Gray Line (the largest tour bus company in the city), testify in support of the exam. While neither claims direct involvement in the process, the former describes an industry that has over 300,000 jobs, generates $3 billion in city and state taxes, and can benefit from a stronger exam. The latter states: "Guiding is truly a job for professionals."

Through the statements, guides chuckle and suck air through their teeth. Tsk-tsk-tsk. Once dismissed, Dykstra, Ferate, and their associates file out the back door. But they were just the beginning. They miss a parade of guides who queue up for their turns at the microphone, and the proceedings become animated. There is shouting and clapping, and the chairman's gavel falls for order again and again. Guides repeatedly preface their remarks with comments about how Justin had been a strong advocate and mentor and was worthy of respect. All prepared statements, however, pivot on a "but . . . "

The testimony became a Greek chorus in my notebook: "It is insulting to our abilities and achievements!" "There's no need for it." "Why have a test if our clients weed us out?" "The questions are long and convoluted."

It is raucous, and through the haze of yellow signs and salty testimony, a picture emerges in my black notebook. I write, "Originally welcomed by most, then subjected to city bureaucracy, the exam seems to be the unpleasant result of compromise." The test had become such an issue with the guides I was studying that I decided I had to take it.

The Walking Guide, the City, and This Book

As I began my research, queries over the exam elicited the full range of emotions, from anger to bewilderment to approval. In one interview, an autodidactic guide, Harry Matthews told me, "Actually, the most common question I get is 'Where's the toilet?' I think that's something they should put on the exam. 'You're at such and such intersection, where is the nearest public toilet?' [laughs]." Jane Marx, a twenty-eight-year guiding veteran, said on a radio program, "You know what is not in the test? How do you keep eighth graders interested? . . . You can't test humor, warmth, kindness, presentation of information, silliness. And that is the essence of a good tour." All these concerns over "untestable" elements are easy reminders that small-scale social interactions are what give walking tourism its character and the work its distinctive shape as much as any particular story or fact.[10]

The qualities these guides exhibit may be difficult to measure via a multiple-choice exam but they are worth our attentions. Ethnographic work, furthermore, is well suited for such a study. This book focuses upon the urban character of walking guides, their work, and this social world. Rather than examining "the tourist," I wanted to come at these issues of urban cultural experience from the other side of the interaction. To do so, I found an interest in urban and workplace ethnographies of other characters, a tradition that spans from early studies on the hobo, the taxi-hall dancer, and the professional thief, to contemporary studies on sidewalk vendors, blues musicians, doormen, and boxers.[11] This book adds to the mosaic of urban characters by describing and evoking the patterned social relations of individuals who are explicitly engaged with the cultural histories and physical spaces of cities, who work in a central node of the largest industry in the world and maintain this life by constructing a postindustrial, informal career path. Grounded in this tradition, *The Tour Guide* illustrates the nature of this actor by analyzing and re-presenting *in situ* participant-observation data to elucidate how connections are created among their clients, their labor practices, and the fabric of the city itself—its communities, histories, and cultures. I began to realize that a study of tour guides is as much a story about the working conditions at the edge of the leisure and tourism supersector of the labor market as much as it is about cities, urban life, and how everyday folk participate in public culture.

Their transformative qualities, and the postindustrial careers they piece together in order to engage in this kind of life in public spaces, make walking guides an ideal first study of the concept of the urban alchemist. The contrasting forms of the licensing exam and the urban alchemist are only the opening salvo for discussions that are provided in the following chapters, wherein the major struggles within the field are unpacked through the figure of the city tour guide as an unconventional intellectual. The first chapter explores the history, cultural forces, and tensions in the field. The second and third chapters chart out how a guide maneuvers through a career and considers the social relationships he or she forms. The fourth and fifth chapters deal with the particular tricks of the trade guides use and the affects these interactions have on their senses of self. The sixth chapter is about the tales they tell, and the final chapter explores why the collectivity of those stories is an important part of urban living and cultural life that differs from the popular notion that cities are becoming overly Disneyfied.

To explore this world, I interviewed 78 individuals within and around the social field: 43 guides, 20 tour participants, and 17 people who work in and around the industry (see appendix B for a "Cast of Characters"). I selected guides through theoretical sampling—aimed at a diversity of tour topics, geographic foci, and positionality in the social field (e.g., freelance guides as well as institutionally affiliated guides, guides who give tours for free and guides who make their living at it, guides who regularly tour and those who do not)—and made contact through public advertisements and listings. Research was conducted in a way that satisfies a four-cell research design—wherein data was collected, and is presented, on one guide in one site/tour, one guide in multiple sites/tours, multiple guides in one site/tour, and multiple guides in multiple sites/tours—to provide rich description and more informed assertions, rather than having to rely upon guides' interpretations and claims alone. Overall, I took 67 tours in New York City from September 2001 to March 2006 and May 2008 to June 2009, for over 157 hours of walking (appendix C). After reading about Kusenbach's pairing of interviewing and "going along" (2003) and Marcus's description of multisited studies that "follow the thing" (1998), I was inspired to conduct over 200 hours of interviews with guides at various stages of their careers, and before and after they had led their tours to check "what they say" with "what they do" in practice. I have secured waivers to use the real names of every one of the guides named within (indicated in appendix B). Last, as in another tradition in urban ethnography, a reflexive section (appendix A) addresses my own participation in the field further, including taking the licensing exam and leading a tour myself.

The chapters privilege guides' personal stories as well as the product of their craft—the tour. Extended ethnographic narratives are woven throughout the text so that the reader can "follow the thing" along with the researcher. Each chapter includes two sections that highlight a particular walking guide and his or her tour. In these segments seven guides are profiled. They are selected not to represent the racial, ethnic, gender, and political dynamics of the field as a whole but for their affinity with the themes of the chapters they are presented within, for the geographic and topical diversity they demonstrate, and for the social interactions and struggles they evince. For example, a retired civil servant who dresses in a top hat and coat and speaks in a vaguely British accent in order to give a "Gangs of New York" tour is paired with the chapter that introduces issues of historical and cultural trends in the tourism industry; a self-taught African American guide who gives tours of a forgotten neighborhood and hopes to teach classes at a local college illuminates a chapter on the social networks of guides; an office worker who in his free time gives radical-left history tours is highlighted within a discussion of how guides attempt to weave together a meaningful life through their careers; an aspiring Ph.D. student who gives tours for a guiding company and talks about her struggles with her persona is introduced in the chapter on the tensions between education and entertainment. As such, these sections are parts of a larger whole and are key to understanding this world. This method of re-presentation makes this book a walking tour about walking tours.[12]

The Guiding World

From the Colossus of Rhodes to the Statue of Liberty

Tourism has been around for millennia. Everett C. Hughes once intimated that the first tours were religious pilgrimages, wherein travelers crossed vast distances to experience hallowed grounds and spiritual rituals, and Thoreau notes that the term for someone who *saunters* is derived from *Sainte-Terrer*, or "holy-lander."[1] Historical texts show striking similarities between antiquarian and contemporary tourists. Author Tony Perrottet's travelogue, *Pagan Holiday*, proves as much by juxtaposing the paths of those ancient wanderers with his present-day adventures. Detailing that early wave of tourism, he writes:

> Across the entire Mediterranean world, an elaborate tourist
> infrastructure, anticipat[ed] our contemporary version. . . . The
> ancient sightseers visited lavish temples—the equivalent of
> our modern museums, crowded with wondrous artifacts—and
> handed over hefty donations to shyster priests for a glimpse of
> a Gorgon's hair, a Cyclops's skull, or Ulysses' sword. Just like us
> they sought out celebrated historic landmarks like the Parthenon
> and the Pyramids (2002, 6).

On a sunny summer day, outside one of the two Starbucks on Astor Place, Tony and I chatted over coffee about how the ancient tourist hordes were just as desirous of the well-beaten path and commemorative tchochkes as today's travelers. Only the destinations have changed from the Colossus of Rhodes to the Statue of Liberty. Tony told me how ancient Romans felt that they had seen the world once they had gazed upon each of the world's Seven Wonders—perhaps the original best-of list devised by an unknown scholar in the third century BC—long before Dean MacCannell made his famous complaint of late twentieth-century tourists' obsession with "sets" of experiences. Travel and tourism—from Roman tourists to medieval pilgrimages to the Grand Tours of the French and Italian elite in the eighteenth century—flourished in the modern era with the sightseeing trips of Thomas Cook. Taking hundreds of people from Leicester, England, to Loughbourough and back, Cook's mid-nineteenth-century business aimed to bring tourism, which had once been the privilege of the rich, to the masses. Prefiguring the powerhouse industry to come, his standardized junkets to Egypt followed the exact route Romans took in 19 AD to the Seven Wonders (Cocks 2001, 109). Just like the ancient Romans, many post-Revolution New Yorkers went sightseeing in their own city, observing the struggles of commoners. While the richest and most notable would often hire police escort, the fascination with the nearby exotic world drew waves of "rubberneckers" led by hucksters and pseudo-experts, as early as the 1890s.[2] It was, in fact, quite fashionable to venture into the Bowery or the Tenderloin as part of an evening's outings, as George Chauncey details in *Gay New York* (1994). The desire for brief, controlled exposure to the other half inspired "slumming parties" where "normal men" would pay to rub elbows with the "fairies" of the Lower East Side.

Tony echoed many of the stories I heard from guides as he eagerly shared the tale of perhaps the most infamous of those early *lobbygow*, George Washington "Chuck" Connors. It is a classic story of New York City tourism, best described in—and often cribbed by guides from—Luc Sante's *Low Life* (1991). Around 1900, Connors brought well-to-do residents to areas of ill repute, mostly around Five Points (what is now the Lower East Side) and Chinatown. Having grown up in lower Manhattan, the child who made fun of his Chinese neighbors first grew to like them (or at least to collaborate with them) while he made work as a Bowery boxer. Later, Connors exploited his unique relations with locals and knowledge as a guide, pointing out a notorious gang member here, or a Chinese slave wife there, as his listeners closely followed in rapt amazement. The climax of his tour was a particularly salacious opium den, in which shocked slummers would find white women lounging, smoking opium, and being seduced by Asian men. The men would then start acting crazily and, invariably, get into a knife fight. But these were nothing more than lucrative hoaxes set up by Chuck and carried out by friends and employees. His fame swelled, and he was alternately referred to as "the White Mayor of Chinatown."[3] Early expeditions like these were fonts of misinformation.

One of the earliest tours I took, in fact, was on the very streets Connors made infamous. My guide, Mark Levy, is a raconteur who grew up in the Bronx and the Upper West Side and speaks proudly of the 1904 Flatbush Brooklyn Victorian house he and his sons now live in. He has worked a series of different jobs over his forty years of employment, as, alternately, a civil servant, a tenant organizer, a low-income housing manager, and a nonprofit magazine publisher. He also worked in damage assessment and construction management at the site of the World Trade Center after September 11, 2001. Touring this area allows Mark to blend historical information with the old haunts he used to work in. He layers stories about the rise of street gangs and social reform movements between the nicknames of government buildings he picked up while working here (e.g., "the Tombs" and "Darth Vader's House") and his experiences at Ground Zero. He took early retirement to try to make a living as a guide in early 2001 while pursuing his master's degree at Hunter College. Mark initially worked as a bus guide, and this tour is his move into the walking segment of the market. He founded a company, Levy's Unique New York, as a family endeavor that includes his sons and a few friends.

Acting Parts in Chinatown (Five Points Tour, May 2003)

Despite the usual bustle of Canal Street on the weekend, my guide is easy to spot. Standing outside of Starbucks, Mark Levy is sporting a top hat, topcoat, and a cane. A thick beard is not enough to hide his wide smile as he glad-hands participants. On the dramatic side of this trade, he is, as advertised, in costume as the notorious nineteenth-century gang leader Bill "The Butcher" Poole. After I announce myself to him, Mark introduces me around to the group and to his two sons, who appear to be joining us. One participant says, "Ah, you're the one who's writing the paper." I thought it strange: how does he know who I am or what I am working on? Why does Mark know everyone so well?

Handshakes complete, we cross the street, and Mark acts as if we have walked through a time portal; he stands up straighter and bellows out a starting line: "Ladies and gentlemen, good citizens of this land. . . . Welcome . . . to the Five Points District of New York." Mark works to have us believe we have been transported to the most notorious slum of the late 1800s. "The Butcher" sweeps his cane through the air like a carnival barker as he de-scribes—in the present tense—how the complicated forces of immigration, the collapse of the apprentice system, and the lack of jobs have led to the rise of this neighborhood's gang culture and its crime rate, allegedly the highest in the world. Participants smile broadly. Local Chinese Americans weave be-tween us. Neither group pays much mind to the other. The tour heads down the block.

The tour's first stop, however, focuses on recent history. Mark drops out of character to talk for a moment about a small memorial for three court officers who died in the rescue effort on September 11. But back into "The Butcher" role, he moves us to a nondescript corner, the curb of which was once the shore of Collect Pond. Full of fish, then choked off by carcasses from nearby tanneries, the once-bucolic fishpond became a major vector of disease—so much so that one-third of all cases in the 1832 cholera outbreak occurred here in the city's poorest and most crowded district. The pond was eventually drained, then filled in, but "just like the dirt below," Mark contin-ues, "the neighborhood slowly filled in with the city's darker social concerns." A park named after the pond is all that is left. While talking about hidden borders, poverty, and plummeting land values, he points to the caved-in side-walk at our feet. "The area's still sinking. . . ."

Everyone chats as we walk. I wonder: Are the other participants some office group on a weekend retreat? Are they New Yorkers? The group is ac-tive. They're asking questions, telling stories, and joking around. A few blocks away, a participant tells the group a story about the former police headquar-ters on Centre Street, but stops himself to say, "I'll give this one to you for free," before describing how the Edwardian baroque building has been con-verted into high-end condominiums and mentioning a few of its famous resi-dents. The participants bicker a bit over the year it was built. Later, as we work our way up through Little Italy, two participants walk up to a woman dining at a sidewalk café on Mulberry Street to tell her she shouldn't leave her purse near the railing with her billfold hanging out. And participants keep sidling up to me, asking, "So, you're writing about tourism?" Putting it all together, I realize that everyone in the group is a tour guide except me. After asking, I find out that Mark offered this tour to the public but also to fellow guides as a dress rehearsal. Walking while writing, I scribble: "Is a lo-cal guide on a walking tour a tourist?"

The Rise of New York Guiding

Immigrants and gangs weren't the only folk walking through the streets of Five Points. Because of muckraking and social reform efforts by people like Jacob Riis, government agencies targeted this area for municipal policy. Tour guides were pivotal to early New York City policymaking, in fact. At the turn of the last century the Committee of Fifteen—an influential citizens' group against gambling and prostitution—used two local guides, Wong Aloy and Wong Get, to provide their window into the Five Points area for their efforts to instigate urban reform (a move that was oblivious to how deeper gang connections and rivalries shaped these guides' own perspectives).[4] And over time, interest in these areas led to increasingly packaged tours not unlike those of Thomas Cook. "Rubbernecking wagons" traveling from uptown's lofty mansions to downtown's lowly tenements were precursors to the red double-decker buses I saw clogging the Fifth Avenue entrance to the Empire State Building 100 years later. Hotels supplanted slumming parties, genteel travel writers replaced Chuck Connors, and more comfortable rail travel fed New York's tourism industry. By 1915 urban tourism became profitable as "a growing number of tour agencies, railroad passenger departments, guide-book publishers, and city business organizations served and promoted pleasure travel in American cities" (Cocks 2001, 5–6).[5]

Until 1937, very little was required to lead such adventures. A *New York Times* editorial (1938) stated that the "sole equipment of most of the barkers is a hat, a paper sign that reads 'sightseeing' and a line of patter"—and there were 500 sightseeing guides and eleven "major sightseeing companies." With success came regulation and the city (through one agency or another) began licensing guides from that point forward. The rise and fall in how many guides were licensed over the decades has been impossible to track, since guides are issued the same type of license as other street vendors, and there undoubtedly have been hundreds who were never licensed in the first place. Walking tours eventually rose to significance as an organized activity for local and visitor consumption in the 1950s, particularly due to their importance for cultural institutions. The Municipal Art Society's Director of Tours, Robin Lynn, claims their organization gave the city's first organized walking tours in 1956 by pairing up architectural historian Henry Hope Reed and painter E. Powis Jones. According to historian and walking guide Francis Morrone, "Reed basically invented the New York City architectural or historical walking tour" (2005), and his powerful and passionate tours are credited for helping to found New York's Landmarks Law and the resultant Landmarks Commission in 1965. By 1960 the *New York Times* called walking

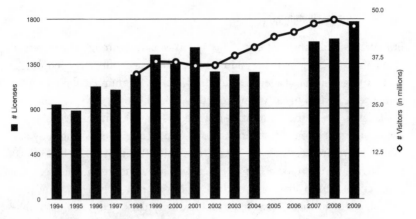

Figure 2 New York City sightseeing guides licenses as compared to New York City
visitors (data for 2005–2006 licensing not available). *Source*: NYC & Company (2009).

tours "Manhattan's newest outdoor sport" (Kellogg 1960). The Museum of
the City of New York made tours a regular part of their public programs in
that decade, and the 92nd Street YMCA began developing its own programs
in the 1970s. Justin Ferate, who came to New York and the industry in the
1980s, started out at the YMCA facing overwhelming crowds: "Some weekends 300 people would show up, and we would just have to divide them into
groups of 50 for each of us." An increase in the number of guiding licenses
(only recorded systematically 1994–2004 and 2007–9) mirrors the mid-
1990s tourism boom: in 1994 there were 949 licensed guides, and by May
2009 there were over 1,780 (see fig. 2).

While discussing his book, Tony Perrottet and I marveled at how, from
its modest and loosely connected origins, the tourism industry has become
nothing short of a global juggernaut worthy of the kinds of regulation represented by the Department of Consumer Affairs licensing exam. The ancient
tourist infrastructure, built upon a loose network of guides, hoteliers, boat
captains, religious pilgrims, and thieves, has been replaced by a bulwark of
venture capitalists, savvy corporations, cultural institutions, and federal and
municipal governments. In the world economy, this industry offers jobs to
natives and immigrants, skilled and unskilled workers, men and women—
from black-suitcased souvenir peddlers to red double-decker bus drivers,
hot-dog vendors to destination management companies, and pickpockets
to Department of Consumer Affairs commissioners. New York City—the
gateway to Emma Lazarus's "New Colossus," and even the city's copper-clad
centurion herself—are symbols of the might of municipal, national, and
international tourism. According to the World Travel and Tourism Coun-

cil (2009), today's tourism trade surpasses $7 trillion of economic activity, producing over 9.2 percent of the world's economic output and supplying 9.2 percent of global employment (one out of 12.3 jobs in the world market, or approximately 235 million jobs). In the United States, the tourism and travel industry accounts for over 21 million jobs (one out of 9.3 jobs), and contributes $1,633.5 billion to the nation's economy (9.4% overall).[6] New York City is a pivotal node. In 2009 an estimated 45.25 million domestic and international visitors came to the city (surpassing Orlando as the number one destination in the United States) spending $28.1 billion, which in turn supported 313,997 tourism-related jobs with over $17 billion in wages.[7]

As the world's largest industry, tourism is seen as a panacea for urban centers in need of rejuvenation and local economies wrought with the deindustrialization, unemployment, and epidemic disinvestment beginning in the 1970s.[8] In New York City, even the most 'blighted' neighborhoods, histories, and cultures are increasingly excavated for some kind of cultural profiteering: from AOL Time Warner's investment in Harlem to the attempt to reenergize the struggling waterfront of South Street Seaport. In the latter example, the shipping motif melds history with commercialization into an alloy of purchasable seafaring symbols, meanings, and experiences to commodify not only urban space but history itself. From the planning stages to its opening, three-fourths of the Seaport's museum space was reassigned as commercial space—"obscur[ing] the city's actual history."[9]

Economic incentive has led to large-scale prospecting for heritage and cultural diversity in a manner similar to that of those old, standardized, and commodified rail tours. Following the success of places like Times Square, city planners have been quick to pitch (and critics quick to decry) developments in Potsdamer Platz (Berlin), Canary Wharf (London), Universal Studios' CityWalk (Los Angeles), Fremont Street Experience (Las Vegas), French Quarter (New Orleans), and Faneuil Hall (Boston) as the rise of "corporate culturalism" and the ossification of urban culture.[10] The repetitious tour-bus patter, the static language of the tour book, or the ersatz and "Disneyfied" areas like Times Square and the South Street Seaport are derided in the popular and academic presses as nurturing a tourist populace that has been called the "epitome of avoidance," the most "acquiescent subject[s]," and "barbarians" in search of "sanitized razzamatazz."[11]

A century after Chuck Connors's infamous excursions, and 118 blocks uptown from Mark's Five Points tour, a scene unfolds that encapsulates the collision of this stagnant and packaged corporate culturalism and walking tourism. Ron Barrett, a middle-aged African American guide, grapples with these issues on a March 2006 tour of Spanish Harlem given to a class of college students sponsored by a major nonprofit cultural institution. From my fieldnotes:

Our multiethnic group is yelled at as we walk through a housing project on our way across East Harlem. From a few stories up, we hear, "Get out of my neighborhood white people! We don't fucking want you here!" One of the students giggles and turns to her friend: "Aren't you from Peru?" She replies: "Aren't you Chinese?"

On the nondescript corner of 114th and Pleasant Avenue, we stand outside a shuttered eatery. There is little to indicate that this is a famous restaurant. While the white letters, "Rao's," are unassuming, this place is known for its glittery patrons and its no-reservations policy—the tables are "owned" by clientele that one has to know to get a seat. This group of 20 college students keeps their cameras and pens ready. Our guide tells us that not many tours come around here.

Ron uses the Italian restaurant as evidence of the ethnic history in this now-predominantly Puerto Rican area. The original Rao's was gutted by fire and has been rebuilt as a newer, almost sanitized version. Known for its mix of local politicos, Hollywood actors, and real-life Mafioso, Ron contrasts the fictional glitz with the real-life conditions of the neighborhood. The co-owner, Frankie Pellegrino, has a recurring role on *The Sopranos* as an FBI chief, Scorsese cast six regulars in *Goodfellas*, and the diners still pack heat: two years ago Louie "Lump Lump" Barone shot connected Al Circelli off his barstool over a lady's honor, events that later became a *Law & Order* television storyline. The place is tucked into a building with newly developed high-priced condos on an otherwise dismal-looking block. While it still stands as a monument to the neighborhood that once was, in the 1930s, "probably the largest Italian community outside of Italy." Our guide tells the group: "I almost wish they would move instead of keeping this Disneyfied version. . . . It's worse than a movie set."

When I looked into aspects of the tour afterwards, I found out that Rao's owners hired a set designer to "improve" the ambiance, contrasting starkly with the once-brutal landscape depicted in Philippe Bourgois's *In Search of Respect* (1995). These are the contradictions inherent in urban tourism. Urban corporate tourism strategies may garner a lot of attention, but walking guides like Ron Barrett and Mark Levy ferret out discrete connections to larger themes of neighborhood change and ethnic tension. The larger processes of tourism and urban culture shape the landscapes of the city and impinge upon the way guides approach their craft, profoundly affecting their interactions and relationships with clients. Guides, for example, clearly profit from the newfound interest tourists have in these corporatized areas: one told me that prior to Scorsese's *Gangs of New York* you "couldn't get a dead cat to visit" the Five Points area, but it is now bustling with guides. Even the local newspaper, the *Village Voice*, lamented these changes by posting a billboard advertisement that read, "Welcome to McHattan" (see fig. 3), on the Bowery—an area that is both geographically and culturally proximate to Five Points.

Guides like Ron worry these new trends reinforce a sort of racial voyeurism, and several express concern over tourism in Harlem—what some call "whites on safari."[12] And Justin Ferate echoes similar concerns on the sidewalk. In an interview, he tells me that "some people want to know where to get a fruit smoothie and 'We're outta here.'" And another Big Onion guide describes for me his more historical approach, something he feels separates him from what he sees as pop culture. "We do historical walking tours," he tells me, "and what that means is that we don't do nostalgia tours." Although it sounds disparaging, he is quick to add, "I've taken those tours and I like them. I have nothing against them. I'm just letting people know what we do is putting things in a *historical* perspective."

Tony Perrottet suggested to me that the ever-present struggles of translation and potential duplicity, of exploitation and use, of history and fruit smoothies evidenced by these tours have led to a series of contrary ideals and emphases that resulted in tourism getting a "weird reputation." "It's fashionable to regard it in contempt," he continued, "[now] you've got this weird snotty academic thing going on; total ignorance of the tourist experience, because no one really likes to admit that they are going on a tour. Academics included, obviously." He reminded me, "it was once an honor to show people around." The guides I spoke with, in fact, feel they are valuable to the city and contrast their work with the broader, more commodified urban culture. Guides feel that by depositing participants into the rich melee of fast commuters, vocal street vendors, and surly locals they provide a unique experience. One guide, Mark Shulman, described this broader disposition:

> At the heart of it, in order to be a guide, you're naturally an inquisitive person, you're probably mostly intelligent, you've got a liking of people, you have some sort of presentation skills because if you didn't, it would be mortifying to try to stand in front of [a tour group]. You are probably a quick thinker. You have to, naturally, have more facts on hand than you

Figure 3 "Welcome to McHattan." *Village Voice* advertisement on the Bowery. A land-mark music venue, the Bowery Ballroom, is to the right. Photo by Jonathan Wynn, 2008.

are actually presenting, because that's the nature of it. . . . You're not in it for the fifteen bucks an hour, or whatever you might be pulling in. The key characteristic of these people is the willingness or desire to pass this infor-mation along. And then under that, I think, how you do it and what you say and the enjoyment that you want to see back from your audience.

As such, guides see the city with different eyes, as compared to the hotel magnate, the corporate CEO, or the venture capitalist. They seek to illuminate the history and culture just behind the façades, re-enchanting the everyday, or tracing out the long dead shoreline of Collect Pond. Quoted in the *New York Times,* Justin says, "I walk down a street in New York, and it is as if I am surrounded by old friends" (Hedges 2003), and Mark Levy, as shown in the next fieldnote, quite literally surrounds himself with friends for his more pop culture tours, still providing a taste of the whimsical and revelatory magic found in other tours.

Part Tour, Part Repertory Theater (Five Points Tour, May 2003)

Despite the swirling presence of other guides in the Five Points area, Mark feels his company offers the unique service of "entertaining and performance-based" tours. As part of that endeavor, he instructs his two sons—who until now have been tailing the group—to take pictures and hand out fliers to passersby. One is in his early twenties and the other is in his mid-teens, and both are charming but disengaged.

As we all cross Foley Square, through gorgeous government buildings (and more than a few in the "brutalist" style), "The Butcher" tells us about the different jobs young women held in the 1890s. "As one would expect, there were not many choices women had to make money other than prostitution or thievery, but one of the finer jobs was that of a 'Hot Corn Girl.'" Just then, a young woman comes up from behind me. In full period costume, she stands to my left and sings a tune:

> Hot corn! Hot corn!
> Here's your lily white hot corn.
> All you that's got money—
> Poor me that's got none—
> Come buy my lily white corn
> And let me go home.

She speaks in a vaguely English accent, holds a wicker basket of wrinkled and burnt corn, wears a strapless dress, and has a live off-white rat leaving red scratches on her shoulder. "The Butcher" introduces us to "Becky." Keeping her blonde hair clear of the rat, she gives us a description of how she makes a living: "A lass don't have other waysa supportin' 'erself, save for, well . . ." As they both go through a little patter, she smiles and curtseys. Moving the rat from one hand to another, she asks if we want to pet it. Laughing, a few guides take her up on it and I keep my hands occupied by taking notes. I cannot help but feel a little embarrassed for her, but just like the historical composite she's playing, Becky has to make a living, I suppose.

The event makes a splash. This area is flooded with civic workers during the week but is now awash with tourists, increasingly curious of our little performance. It's an odd scene. Tourists are gathering to gawk at a group of guides. Mark's sons leap into action, circling around the new crowd, one passing out fliers and the other clicking his camera.

As we bid farewell to Becky and Foley Square, the group is aflutter. Mark is proud of the stunt. A guide asks how he orchestrated her entrance, and it turns out he had tipped his hat as her cue. "She's great, isn't she?" The Levys met her at a Renaissance fair. Mark hopes to create a distinctive "part guild, part repertory theater" by weaving together acting and tourism, and Becky is just the first step. "She even came with her own rat!" he says.

Two stops later the eldest son, Matt, takes the stage of the street to talk about the Bowery and its historical relationship with the down-and-out. Midway through, he stumbles on a date, gets frustrated, and, even though the guides prod him with a few questions to help him along, his dad bails him out and quickly wraps up the rest of the story. Discouraged, Matt scratches the back of his half-shaved head and parts company.

As the three Levys and I reconvene over Chinese food after the tour in Columbus Park, the elder admonishes Matt for not studying, his top hat resting beside him. In the post-tour interview, they talk about how Matt's shtick is material he is developing for his own tours. Matt explains that, while he was at college a few years back, he was a part of a group that would give free and impromptu two-hour performances of poetry on Boston street corners. Part of their current business plan is to have Matt run his own line of tours, focusing upon New York's punk and poetry scenes. Like his father's costume, Matt's tattoos, piercings, mismatched socks, and asymmetrical haircut are an apt uniform as well.

"There Are Many Guides, and Only One Test"

Mark Levy's move from bus tours to walking tours reveals a need for further definition of this field. Tour guides come in many forms: bus guides, weekend guides, guides who give tours in only French, guides who give only food tours, and so on. Such diversity led Andy Sydor, the shop steward for Gray Line's Union—a section of Transport Workers Union Local 225—to focus his criticism on any exam's ability to adequately gauge that miscellany. He told me in a later interview that he has "*nothing* against Justin," who was a mentor and friend to him, "but, there are many kinds of guides, and only one test." How is one exam supposed to evaluate the expertise of all guides? Should it? Should the guides who only give tours of Queens be required to know Staten Island? Should the guides who only give tours in Russian be tested in English?

There are similar kinds of work across the tourism, culture, and leisure sphere. The innumerable docents in New York City's ninety-two museums are institutionally bound and often comprised of volunteers (see Goodlad and MacIvor 1998). There are also Big Apple Greeters, which is a more formal organization of volunteers based around the same idea: Begun in 1992 as the brainchild of a former Manhattan Borough president (and aspiring mayor) Ruth Messenger—designed to match business and leisure visitors with volunteers who, according to their promotional materials, "love New York"—over its first thirteen years, greeters spent approximately 23,000 hours with 7,000 visitors. Its stated purpose is to promote New York as a friendly, inviting, and manageable place, to bolster tourism and economic development, and to "create opportunities for New Yorkers to show pride in their city." The over 300 volunteers in the program—a group described as "lawyers, artists, writers, business owners, utility employees, and teachers"— do not need to be licensed (Fried 2006).

But the real distinction is between those who have a greater commitment to the tourism field, particularly with those who give bus tours. Bus tours are very different from walking tours, and many in the industry see the former as cultural fast food. The repetition of material seems to be the most lamentable aspect; while holding a modest level of freedom of content, bus tours are tied to a specific route, and guides must rattle off the same things two or three times a day. As Andy described it to me:

> Double-deckers are skimming. You can't go into detail. At the same time, you are more able to construct a narrative, or a kind of relationship between neighborhoods—a walking tour can't cover that much ground. . . . The buses are jammed with sixty people who really don't care what you are saying; they just want to go to certain locations. It is basically: herd the people in and get them to the Statue of Liberty, and gab a bit on the way. *It's not serious.*

According to many, a bus job is described as "just a job" and "simply something you do to make a living." Andy told me this negative reputation—held by bus guides as well—stems from years of questionable practices of bus companies. In the 1980s companies were known for their fleet of unsafe vehicles, and a former bus guide, Timothy Levitch, told a reporter his bus company treated tourists as "cadavers," wanting little more than to avoid giving a refund (Oder 2005). One guide, when discussing the new exam, exclaimed, "If these idiot bus companies hire guides who don't know what they're saying, and they don't make [an] effort at quality control, why penalize me?" More recently, Andy told me that their work is so undervalued Gray Line Bus Tours attempted to fire all its guides and replace them with a tape-recorded script a few years ago, allegedly with the blessing of the DCA. It was a move thwarted only through worker mobilization. Today there are 175–250 guiding positions at the two major bus tour firms, CitySightsNY and Gray Line Bus Tours, depending on the time of year. At those numbers, these more conspicuous members of the industry are, at best, only a tenth of the licensed tour guides in New York City.

Walking guides, meanwhile, are perched atop the "intellectual food chain" (as Andy called it). This level of engagement in the industry allows guides to be more autonomous and entrepreneurial, gives them the chance to make more money as well as delve deeper into topics of their choosing. Many find these qualities highly desirable.[13]

There are plenty of gradations and variations within this distinction, however. There are, for example, "step-on" guides, whose services are included in ubiquitous travel agency brochures promising a "Fabulous Three Day, Two Night Stay in New York City" (which might include a Broadway show, meals, a trip to Ellis Island, shopping, and a walking tour). For guides, this niche of the business provides quick, relatively easy money that often includes a meal or two "but," according to one guide, "it is less being a 'tour guide' and more a 'people wrangler.'" Similarly, school tours are a large segment of the market. Like Ron Barrett's stroll through East Harlem, these are attractive gigs because the contacts can be used from year to year and the pay is good. The most desirable, and most difficult to garner, are corporate clients, who pay better than most; a company may welcome new employees to the city with a tour or make a tour part of a business junket as a reward. Furthermore, there are differences in modes of transport. Guides have told me of tours conducted in taxis, boats, helicopters, subway cars, and on bicycles.[14]

To make sense of this spectrum, a few distinctive, but not exclusive characteristics of the walking guide can be identified beyond the broad understanding of a walking tour taking an hour or two of time. First, guides' tours are likely to highlight *specialized* content—whether it be of a geographic

Figure 4 Big Onion guide Jeffrey Trask on a "Before Stonewall" tour. Note the Gray Line tour bus approaching in the background. Photo by Jonathan Wynn, 2009.

region (e.g., Brooklyn Heights or Ellis Island) or a theme (e.g., culinary or architectural tours)—rather than a generalized topic. Second, unlike the bus tour, the walking tour necessitates *engagement* between guides and their audiences, and with the city itself, and is, therefore, often conversational, improvisational, and more attuned to the participants' interests and character. Third, while buses have a predetermined loop, walking tours are infinitely *changeable*—either because of the guide's own intentions (e.g., one guide boasts 12 different tours of the same geographic area) or unpredictable conditions (e.g., inclement weather or unexpected crowds). Fourth, walking guides will often *broaden* their repertoire in the hopes of attracting returning clients, whereas it is less likely that a bus guide would have the same client twice. Fifth, walking tours are *multifaceted,* as they are given by professional tour guides as well as artists, professors, and activists like a few who are highlighted in this book. Last, *locals* take walking tours, and some guides rarely have an out-of-city tourist, whereas bus tours cater to visitors. Identifying these qualities is, of course, just the first step to understanding the walking guides' world.

Seven Tensions

In his study of New York doormen, Peter Bearman writes that one can best see the social grammar, the "unspoken rules that organize social interactions, shape decisions, and motivate behavior [by] focusing on tensions and contradictions in interactions that appear when viewed from multiple standpoints, typically across levels" (2005, 4). In the context of the walking guide, these underlying rules can be understood as a set of seven constitutive struggles that arose repetitively in my fieldnotes and interviews with those in and around the industry. In the context of this book, they can provide a heuristic framework, a set of signposts that are introduced here but will open up the world of the tour guide for the reader through the following chapters. They are briefly introduced here, in the order that they arise through the remainder of the book.

One of the first tensions has already been highlighted, but is also featured prominently in chapter 2, is a tension between guiding as a *profession* and as a *hobby*. While the head of Gray Line Bus Tours stated at City Hall that "guiding is truly a job for professionals," not all are in agreement. In a survey of their own members, for example, 91 GANYC guides responded, with 77 voting against retesting of guides, 10 voting for it, and 4 abstaining. A quiet minority was thrilled at the perceived move to professionalization, while many would agree with independent guide Brendan FitzGerald (who will be highlighted later), who told me, "I think that it's fun to have a hobby that pays . . . I've had the freedom to pick and choose because I've never felt obligated to the industry." As flexible, autonomous, part-time, and semiseasonal employment, guiding is an activity that fits into a number of different biographical trajectories, and chapter 2 describes what kinds of careers guides hold, their struggles to make a living, and the rationales they give for working as tour guides.

As a part of negotiating the tension between hobby and profession, some guides hold affiliations with companies, cultural institutions, schools, business improvement districts, and the like, necessitating a delicate balance between a second tension of *legitimacy* and *autonomy*. Guides enjoy the freedom of the work but still covet the amount of authority that comes from being connected with a particular institution. Justin Ferate (highlighted in chapter 4) is affiliated with cultural institutions and business improvement districts, while, on the other hand, a politically motivated guide like Bruce Kayton (highlighted in chapter 2) proudly claims his fervent independence from affiliations, which serves as legitimation in its own right. Chapter 3 details the kinds of working relationships guides have, both at the level of individual interactions on tour and the local, cultural institutions.

Chapters 2 and 3 also mine the issues around a third tension, between guides who work as *independent* freelancers or at the behest of a *company*. GANYC is a guild and advocacy group mostly comprised of freelancers like Mark Levy.[15] They have a rotating and voluntary board of directors that organizes events and educational opportunities, and hosts a public Web site where any of its over 270 members can post their tours and contact information. It is a diverse group of teachers, public servants, actors, writers, retirees, architectural historians, and history buffs, and boasts tours in over twenty different languages. Some have been doing tours for a few months and others for decades. There are several small walking-tour outfits—the most prominent being Big Onion Walking Tours (BOWT). Founded and led by Seth Kamil, BOWT retains thirty-five to forty Ph.D. student-guides. Chapter 3 traces the interpersonal and organizational connections that a guide uses.

The distinction between independents and company guides relationships can match up but does not necessarily correspond with learning practices and guiding dispositions, which develops a fourth tension that I would draw between those guides who are more *academically inclined* as compared with those who are more *autodidactic*. Many freelancers, in fact, do possess the skill to conduct careful analyses of historical topics and give tours as a public or community service. As Eric Washington, a self-educated historian, describes it:

> There are a few academics out there who give very good tours, and you could probably count them on your hand because most academics have duties that preclude them from having the time to do walking tours. And they are dependent upon professional guides or interested parties, who are synthesizing their research into something coherent that serves to educate people on the subject. So while many history tour guides know a lot about their subject, they are not historians per se. And I don't think that they should be expected to be.

Seth Kamil, on the other hand, fancies Big Onion as an "academic department without the university." There are also a few academics who give tours on the side of their collegiate duties, like Jack Eichenbaum, who is a professor of urban geography and has been conducting tours for years. Autodidacticism is a key concern in this book because the majority of guides enact what Bourdieu called "an art of living which provides them with the gratifications and

prestige of the intellectual at the least cost" (1984, 370). This majority illustrates a mixture of experiential learning and more conventional, historical
work that will be detailed in the learning strategies and storytelling practices
that occupy the contents of chapter 4.

Earlier, Andy Sydor mentioned how bus tours are seen as being "unserious"
and, echoing similar concerns, Big Onion's owner, Seth Kamil, talked about
the strain caused by a fifth tension, between *education* and *entertainment*:

> It's very complicated. What I say to people is that Big Onion guides take
> their history very seriously. But we have a lot of fun doing what we do. So
> we may take our history seriously, and we may be serious historians, but we
> know that this is not a graduate lecture, we know that this is meant to be an
> engaging, entertaining, and informative experience. Engaging *first*.

Moreover, just as there are many academic and independent historian-
guides, there is also a contingent of aspiring or out-of-work actors who are
attracted to the flexible schedule (which allows for auditions and rehears-
als) and the harmony between the activities of acting and guiding (e.g.,
memorizing lines of a script, projection, use of props, working an audience,
adlibbing). In addition, the Levy family nurtures the theatrical, as does Stan
O'Connor, the guide who costumes as Lincoln and recites famous speeches
on tour. While building off of tensions between academics and autodidacts,
this tension is primarily discussed in chapter 5, on how guides' perceptions
of self are shaped by the tour, and how tours are shaped by guides' performed
personae.

Along the lines of sharing information, it is curious that folks whose very
purpose is to speak in public—even giving trial tours to other guides, as was
the case with Mark Levy—would also jealously guard their tour material.
This gray area creates a sixth tension, between *public interests* and guides'
own *private* ones. On the one hand, many are happy to distribute some of
their tour content, even passing out bibliographies to get their information "out there," and also artists and activists freely provide tours that anyone could sign up for that would provide a similar experience albeit with a
different kind of content. On the other hand, because turning a profit is a
necessity for most, guides do feel propriety over the information they present. This relationship is crucial, as it draws attention to the fact that guides
transform the public goods of space and culture and fashion it into their
own product. The use of public spaces and how guides educate clients is the
subject of chapter 6, wherein Bill Brown is highlighted as an overtly political
guide, who shares all his information on his tours and his Web site.

We then come to the issue of who it is that they are giving that information to. The literature on tourists is based upon the notion that they are folks who travel from afar, and yet New York walking tour takers are more likely to be locals than visitors, which raises a seventh, and final dynamic.[16] Tour guides are often conceptualized as the couriers of unfamiliarity—indeed it is an ancient maxim that, as Lao-Tzu wrote, "The farther one goes, the less one knows"—but tourism within the urban context provides a problem: the unknown abounds.[17] We can think of E. B. White, who wrote, "many a New Yorker spends a lifetime within the confines of an area smaller than a country village. Let him walk two blocks from his corner and he is in a strange land" (1949, 36) to really get at the heart of the matter here. According to Seth Kamil, walking tours are great because you can learn something "whether you are fifty years old and have lived here all your life, or you are an eighth-grader." We should, then, think of touring as an *activity* and tourist as a *role*. This distinction resets a common perception and provides us with our final tension: someone from out of town is a *visitor* and not a tourist, and a *local* can easily be the latter.[18] This is a strong thread in the final chapter, as it concentrates on the issues guides face in tourism and how the social interactions of the tour bind a group together, attempting to transform the visitor into a local.

These are seven tensions, not categories, and particular guides and particular tours operate somewhere within them. Mark Levy, for example, started at a bus company, began working for himself by building his own company, but still goes back to bus tours sporadically to make ends meet. As such, each of these issues are woven through this book and, although they are primarily addressed in particular chapters as indicated, their applicability is hardly exhausted within them (e.g., guides' struggles with *entertainment* and *education*, and how it affects their senses of self is dealt with in chapter 5 as well as chapter 6, and the tensions between *profession* and *hobby*, *tourist* and *local* are addressed in chapter 2 as well as chapter 7). These common and re-occurring themes draw out the similarities and differences between guides across all levels of engagement, and generates what Ulf Hannerz calls a "consciousness of kind" (2004, 155) of the group as a whole.

An Untidy Career

After the Rush

Many of the guides in this book rode New York's 1990s tourism boom. This growth generated millions of informal careers: seasonal, part-time, flexible, low-wage, low-benefit jobs for both women and men across the globe and in New York City.[1] The notion of guiding as being a job for professionals touted in the media and at City Hall belies vastly different levels of participation in real life. When starting out, some guides maintained their office work and gave tours as a hobby, while others transitioned from another part of the industry. Once in the field, some, like Mark Shulman, decide to give tours four or five times a year while others, like Bruce Kayton, maintain a regular schedule. What they get out of the experience varies as well: a retiree may tour to make money on top of his pension, an activist might look to get her message heard, while an actor might want to hone his repartee in front of an audience.[2] Taking the exam, in other words, is just one part of the process.

The untidy condition of this labor market shapes the variety of commitments guides hold to it and brings us to the tension between guiding as a hobby and as a profession. Making enough money to live as a full-time walking guide, for example, is quite difficult. And many do not want to work full-time in the first place, finding it to be a good job on their way to another career or to gain additional income by capitalizing on some existing skill set (either as a performer or novice historian) without taking on a more formal part-time job. The factors for consideration are fluid enough to reach incoherence, and issues that relate to this flexibility (including the search to carve out a life for one's self), places guides in a condition similar to other postindustrial culture workers (e.g., graphic designers, new media workers, musicians) (see Ross 2003). Understanding how guides enter tourism, how they face challenges and construct their own career paths, and how they justify the choices they make to do the work they do requires a better sense of the stages in their careers—specifically how these workers negotiate this industry and, more generally, of how cultural workers find a way to participate in the informal sectors of the economy. This perspective provides a picture of the different levels of engagement exemplified by the walking guide.

Considering all the ways guides participate in this field, the pressures and connections outlined so far, and the informal conditions of the business itself, an exploration of a guide's career actually finds a relatively limited number of paths. This chapter will show how guides develop their chaotic careers: how people get into guiding, what strategies they use to negotiate their informal working conditions, and the ways guides explain their ongoing commitment to such a challenging life.[3]

Deciding to "Make a Go of It": Getting into Guiding

In the pre- and post-tour interviews I conducted, I learned about guides' backgrounds, what they did before getting into the business and how they came to think of tour guiding as a part of their lives. When I asked one about why he entered the field, he expressed a general distain for the monotony and pressure of more formal jobs, answering my question with another question: "Why *wouldn't* I be a tour guide? It beats a desk job." It is hardly that easy, however since guiding is informal work and almost universally requires hustling to make a steady, and often meager, income. With these conversations in mind, I was able to identify four main avenues through which the majority of guides entered the business: as a move from a parallel field, as a place for a fresh start, as one of several gigs, or as an on-going side project. No one I spoke with gave walking tours as their first and only step to a full-time career. One becomes a walking guide incrementally. Beyond this caveat, further distinctions are required.

The guide highlighted in the previous chapter, Mark Levy, personifies the first path in which one can become a walking guide. Like many of his colleagues, Mark transitioned from another sector of the industry by working at Gray Line Bus Tours. This job provides relatively steady income and accustoms guides to working with tourists and operating within the industry, and, as Mark described it, provides them with key stories and facts about the city (what he calls the "run up"). Mark did this for two years before deciding to strike out on his own to offer tours like the one in Five Points. Tom Bernardin, as another example, started his adult life teaching English as a second language, but he lost his job when the city almost went bankrupt in 1976. A friend who knew he collected Statue of Liberty memorabilia suggested he look for a job at Ellis Island. Because it was still pre restoration, he "just wanted to get a job in maintenance or something." But when they found out he had a background in teaching immigrants, Human Resources suggested he join the interpretive staff at Ellis Island as a National Parks Service ranger. While there, Tom was trained in New York and immigration history and he saw the recent rise of tourism firsthand. After the 1990 reopening he noticed the tour guides bringing their groups in and mimicking his work as a parks ranger. As he told it to me: "I'm looking at these guides giving correct or incorrect information and I'm looking at thirty people, and I'm saying to myself, '$10, $20, $30, $40. . . . Shit, I can do that.'" He then approached a guide and described his work background. The guide told him, "You have to immediately get your guiding license, join GANYC, bill yourself as 'Mr. Ellis Island' and you'll make a lot of money." That is exactly what he did. Even though being a bus guide or park ranger can provide a steady wage and benefits, guides like Mark and Tom turned to walking tours in a search for a greater sense of autonomy in their work life.

Another way to enter the business is by being forced to look for another job. Harry Matthews worked at an advertising agency, writing press releases and doing copyediting work. Jane Jacobs's books and Ada Louise Huxtable's articles on architecture in the *New York Times* piqued his curiosity, and when he wanted to learn more about neighborhood history, he started taking walking tours. Harry went every week for a while and thought it would be "great fun" to do it, but knew it was a tough job. "Everyone I asked," he told me, "explained that it was difficult to make a living at it; hence my reluctance to simply quit my day job and make a go of it." Guiding only became an option when his company, in his words, "decided to get rid of the 'old timers.'" They offered him a generous severance package, which he describes as "not a gold parachute, maybe a silver-plated one." He was unsure of his options, since he felt he was "too old for most jobs in advertising and marketing, [and] publishing jobs were disappearing fast." But with the opportunity and a little bit of a financial cushion, he "decided to make a go of it in 1997." Similarly, Alfred Pommer retired after twenty-five years of city government work and, at sixty-three years old he talked to me about how he still needed supplemental income and used his newfound free time to start a second career: "I worked for the city and I did something I didn't like [and] now, I'm doing something I like. It is much more a relief to be responsible for your own stuff, not somebody else's." Be it forced or voluntary, a portion of the population looks to guiding to make money after their primary careers have ended and they wanted to, as Justin Ferate described it, take a "second crack at [finding] a job they feel proud of."

A third group is comprised of other folks who were attracted to guiding because it was flexible enough to fit with other part-time gigs they already had. The commonality between these guides is that they tend to come from a more theatrical background. Jane Marx provides perhaps the best evidence of this. Like Tom, guiding was not on Jane's radar as a possible career, even though her late brother was a tour guide who wrote his Harvard dissertation on guiding books. She came to it only after an unexpected confluence of events. While working as a waitress and taking acting and writing classes, she was given an assignment for her women's writing workshop on "What does 'work' mean to you?" She described her reaction to me.

> Why did I have severe discomfort every time I had any job? All the work
> so far never fit my character and natural rhythms, so I wrote about how I
> hated being inside, and that work pulled me out of real life. I realized that I
> wanted to engage with people, to work in real life and in real time, and that
> I have a message to give to people.

Hearing her read her essay to the group, one of her classmates recommended she try being a guide. Surprised and interested, she looked into getting a license, and received her first bit of advice only a few days later, from the kind of sidewalk interaction that she would nurture in her future career:

> I was walking down the block and passed a tour bus company. I saw "Coffee-
> light-two-sugars" on the sidewalk. (I knew all my customers by their or-
> ders.) I said, "Hey, Coffee-light-two-sugars, what are you doing here?" He
> told me that he was working at the tour company. "What a coincidence, I'm
> just going to take my licensing exam." He told me that I had to walk on a
> few tours first. So I did.

She started guiding on June 1, 1980. It was only though the additional experiences of her brother's history as a guide, her writing workshop, and bumping into one of her customers on the street that Jane arrived at that point. Like many of these guides, Jane may have had an antipathy to 9-to-5 work but, unlike the last group, she never really sought out a career in tourism before others suggested it.

The last path into guiding is taken by those who work in a different industry and start giving tours on the side. Joyce Gold, for example, started guiding only on weekends. She believes her experience is common, stating that it "almost always starts out as a side project." Joyce was working as a systems analyst at the Federal Reserve Bank in 1975 when she picked up a 100-year-old book offering the local history of the area and read about how her office was the location of the Battle of Golden Hill in 1770. It was an epiphany: "It made the neighborhood I worked in much more interesting." In talking to a few people, she told me she "realized nobody around me knew anything about the layers of history, so I just kept reading." She realized that she wanted to tell others about these hidden histories by guiding and developed a few tours for fun while still working at the bank.

Seth Kamil's start in the business was slightly more deliberate. While he was in graduate school at Columbia University, he began giving tours along with his colleague, Ed O'Donnell, because they were both looking for a way to pay for their education and also capitalize on their historical knowledge. According to Seth, "Big Onion allowed me to get all the way through Columbia without additional loans." They started giving tours to small groups on the weekends in 1990. They laid out a formal business plan for a tourism company run by historians a few months later, spurred on when the *New York Times* called to ask if they had any tours so that they could highlight them in an upcoming article. Seth started wondering about academic life and decided he wanted to develop BOWT rather than chance ending up as a professor "in some small town in rural Ohio." BOWT's cachet—academically trained guides—doubled as a built-in applicant pool. When Ed moved on to a faculty position, Seth started hiring fellow students, which he continues to do today. As he describes it, "We have a system that works: phenomenally brilliant, highly trained, energetic, wonderful guides that lead tours that last approximately two hours that go approximately a mile and a half that cost $12 a person, rain or shine." For those like Joyce, Seth, and Big Onion guides, the money and, perhaps, a little added value to their lives led them to include guiding as a part of their weekly routines.

None of these paths guarantee financial success, and most guides, again, cannot make guiding a full-time career as Joyce Gold and Justin Ferate do, even if they desired it. The struggles to stay in the field comprise the remainder of the chapter, but this is a good point to bring in Bruce Kayton, whose guiding illustrates the importance it can play in a person's life, even if it means juggling multiple jobs to do it. Bruce is forty-nine years old and a committed activist and amateur historian. He offers "radical history" tours on the days he has off from his formal office job, and his beginnings as a guide show how the city's sidewalk interactions provide the color, content, and even the impetus for giving tours: He used to stroll around with friends, telling stories about an event or a famous left-leaning New Yorker but, one day in the East Village, a crowd of five people gathered around to listen and everyone ended up discussing it all as a group. Like Jane's and Tom's first experiences, it was because of this sidewalk interaction that something clicked for him. "I was amazed and thought this was my *calling*," he told me, "I [realized I] loved doing this." He started assembling his notes by geographic and topical areas and has conducting weekend walking tours for the fourteen years since. He describes his weekday work as being a "one-man library" for a Midtown Manhattan research company, but, as evinced in the following fieldnote, he zealously serves up a wealth of information on radical left history as if it were bottled up all week long.

Radical, Central Park (Central Park Tour, June 2003)

This June has had a horrible stretch of weather for guiding, oscillating from a soaking week to four blistering hot days. But today the heat has broken, and I wait for the tour, listening to a jazz trio start up with a song from Dexter Gordon's *Go*. I walk slowly over to the meeting point on the southwestern corner of Central Park at Columbus Circle, under the *Maine* Monument, built in 1913. The monument's pedestal is topped with a rather garish gold statue of Columbia on a half-shell-shaped chariot pulled by three seahorses. There are twelve people, and three arrive later.

In the shadow of an oak tree, the group gathers around a man wearing a Mets hat and a T-shirt that says "Celebrate Community, Honor Diversity." Bruce gathers us closer to release a litany of facts: the two-mile-long park opened in 1859 and is home to 270 species of bird, 150 acres of water, and 120 miles of pipeline. It took 166 pounds of dynamite to carve the park and almost five million cubic yards of soil and rocks to shape it; of the more than 20,000 workers only two were women and none were African American; and five workers died on the job. Bruce's tour is data heavy, and he rattles it all off from memory.

Joining me are five people between the ages of 25 and 35, one over 60, and the rest are in their mid-40s and 50s; all are locals. There are three couples. The man over 60 is wearing a brown fisherman's hat and carries two plastic, inside-out Zabar's bags through which I can see folded-up newspapers and a pink paperback copy of *Valley of the Dolls*. One khakied participant, a producer for WBAI (New York's noncommercial radio station) and apparent friend of Bruce, becomes the assigned straight man, with dead-pan jokes bouncing off him every stop or two.

After going over the basics, Bruce offers introductory remarks to frame the tour as covering the history of New York that he sees mainstream television and newspapers, and college classrooms leave out. As he does, he gives out a packet of literature to everyone. Flipping through, I see a short bibliography, an inventory of his other tours, a flyer for a documentary on the Weather Underground, a list of "Groups, Bookstores, and Activities in NYC," a poem titled "Revolution Is Not an AOL Keyword" (a riff on Gil Scott-Heron's 'The Revolution Will not be Televised'), a few flyers for events, and clippings from the *Times*.

He pulls out a copy of his 2003 book *Radical Walking Tours of New York City* (the picture on the back cover shows him wearing a T-shirt that says "Earn Big Money: Become a Historian" above a picture of Karl Marx) and a labor history map of the city, and he tells us they cost $14 and $10 respectively. He mentions that if anyone wants to know more, they could buy the book. Implying that even a Marxist like himself still needs to make a living he trails off by saying, "This is America after all . . ."

To wheedle the group a bit, he says, "Like a TV newscaster's face, Central Park is almost completely artificial." He talks of how the Central Park Conservancy was established in the 1980s for the upper classes to protect their real estate investment and explains that, even though it is only the fifth-largest park in the city, the Conservancy collected over $250 million between 1980 and 1988 without giving a dime to parks in the outer boroughs. He also informs us that, since Vaux and Olmsted's plans were not even submitted 150 years ago, this year's "150th anniversary of Central Park" is a completely fictional fundraising device. Bruce claims Olmsted's personal connections helped him to beat out thirty-three competing plans and that he called his workers slobs and loafers. Bruce also says that Vaux and Olmsted's aversion to working-class life coincided with the plan's own middle-class partiality, forbidding marriages, civic processions, and public speaking to take place within the park.

Right from the beginning, Bruce uses the *Maine* Monument, which commemorates the deaths of the 260 sailors who died in Havana Harbor, to talk about William Randolph Hearst's "yellow journalism." He also relates that era of American imperialism to the present political climate. He then uses *West Side Story* to talk about how Lincoln Center offers hundreds of cultural events never attended by the hundreds of Latino-American residents that its construction displaced or the sorts of folk who take his tours.

Working as a Guide

Now that we have seen how guides enter into guiding, we will turn to the different ways they position themselves in the field as they begin and sustain their careers. In the spirit of Everett C. Hughes, who pressed sociologists to pay attention to occupations and the "crises and dilemma" of the roles people take as they pass through them (1958, 120; see also Becker and Carper 1956, 290), this section first introduces a few of the challenges guides like Bruce face when entering the business and then presents four methods they use to negotiate their untidy careers.

The Fragility of Guiding Work

Like many in the service industry and other informal labor markets, guides are exposed to a host of challenges. Scholars agree that the working conditions in tourism lag behind all other sectors, displaying all of what have been described as the "hallmarks of a bad nonstandard, post-industrial service job": they "pay poorly, lack health insurance and pension benefits, are of uncertain duration, and lack the protections that unions and labor laws afford."[4] Wages are obviously an important issue. At the 2003 City Council hearing, Councilman Reed asked the group, "What is the income of the average tour guide?" Among all the muted chuckling, no one in the crowd offered a figure back. Finally, he asked, "Above $60,000?" Instantaneously and univocally the audience roared, "*No!*" But, again, it is very difficult to generalize because of the varied levels of involvement and beyond pay are factors that complicate matters even further.

Sheer logistics make guiding difficult. Just as a musician might be able to put together a gig or two but not sustain a career, many guides have difficulty stringing together enough work to live comfortably: there are plenty of things to talk about in a city like New York and plenty of customers to be hired by, but the cost of living is very high and the pay can be meager. Aside from the seasonal ebb and flow of the industry, the market is flooded. More established guides were hoping the tougher licensing exam would dissuade newcomers, but, according to a prominent guide, there are still too many competitors willing to "offer tours for next to nothing" because they are starting out, desperate, or are just in the business for their own amusement and can offer tours for free, all of which this guide sees as "pulling down wages."

The uncertainty of tipping raises yet another level of economic concern. Tips are an elusive and erratic quarry and usually generate a thoughtful pause from guides. Aspiring actor and guide Darryl Reilly sighs dramatically: "*Well*, Jon, you bring up a whole other realm to the world of the tour guide: the whole tip matter." He divides the collection of folks on tours as those "who are going to give a tip no matter who is giving the tour" and then those for whom "it doesn't matter what you do for them—it's just not in their consciousness." He is grateful that the organization he works for pays him $75 per tour, and that their brochure includes a line that reads, "THE FEE DOES NOT INCLUDE TIP FOR THE GUIDE." In the end, he knows there is only a tenuous link between his effort and his tips, saying, "you have to learn to get over that." According to BOWT guide Jeffrey Trask, the issue is wrapped in other concerns about education and tourism:

> The issue of tips is an interesting thing. It's weird, right? We want tips. But on one level that's inconsistent with this idea that it is not a service [job]. It is, sort of. . . . It can be very exhausting doing tours, and some more than others. Sometimes you want a little something at the end. It's probably also a reflection of gratification—knowing that you've provided something that was enjoyable, useful, informative, interesting.

Furthermore, there are legal concerns that guides, like other self-employed and informal workers, must contend with. Tax and insurance rates, for example, are prohibitive and daunting. According to one, "It is frightening, because self-employment is a logistical nightmare." As Seth explains, few guides are insured:

> My guides are covered on my insurance, unless they are negligent. If a guide leads a tour into traffic against a light, they're on their own, okay? But there is a level of protection. Very few guides are incorporated. I think it's absolutely crucial to maintain a business. If someone trips and falls, they will sue the storeowner who is responsible for the sidewalk, they'll sue the city, and they'll sue me. I have enough insurance to pay for the lawyer, who is on retainer, to make that go away.

When I asked a well-known guide why his colleagues were not very forthcoming about their profits, he said it was "because many don't report their entire taxable income to the government." Another mentioned guides who have frequently been in trouble with the IRS for not reporting wages.

There is one last thing that demonstrates the fragility of the field. As I began interviews and participant observation in the summer of 2001, guides were in their salad days, but larger geopolitical forces quickly shook the city's labor market and brought intense pressure on the industry. As Harry Matthews told me, "September 11th was such a disaster for everyone, especially since 2001 [had been] such a boom year; and then it just all went away." While many had found their uncertain economic condition tolerable enough, and even desirable, the attacks halted ten-year gains. By the summer of 2002, there were 16,000 fewer jobs in the overall tourism industry—some of which many guides relied upon for other sources of income—than there were at that time the year before. One million fewer international visitors (who tend to stay longer and spend more money) came to the city in 2002 than in 2001, and two million fewer came in 2003. Twelve hundred members of the Local 6 Hotel and Restaurant Workers Union were laid off in the two weeks after the attacks on New York and Washington, D.C., and by 2004 it was estimated that 30,000 of the 230,000 jobs across the city's entire tourism industry were lost—roughly 13 percent of the sector's workforce.[5] Individual guides and tour companies I interviewed saw a 50–90 percent drop in business between August 2001 and March 2002. Walking guides were left particularly vulnerable. An owner of a small tourism company told me a lot of businesses like his were slowly bought up in the 1980s, and those that survived the 1990s "were ready to jump out the window after September 11th."

The effects continued for years. Tom Bernardin's tours of Ellis and Liberty Islands were nearly at a standstill when I interviewed him in early 2003. "And now this fucking war starts," he explains, "It's a bad time to be a guide. It's terrible for me. 'Hi, I give tours at the most dangerous spot in America.' It has a bull's-eye attached to it." Still, a few handfuls of tourists came, although student tours did not recover for two years. Even local school groups avoided taking tours. Big Onion, for example, has a robust foundation of school clients, but lost 80 percent of their overall business after September 2001. Seth Kamil didn't let a single guide go, preferring to spread tours equally, and didn't cut himself a check for seven months, although a few guides reported that he picked up some tours rather than have to pay guides.

Andy Sydor spoke of how he and his colleagues, like many New Yorkers, wanted to help the city in a time of trouble. Speaking for his union, he stated the following in his City Hall testimony:

When the attack on September 11th occurred, several of our members were already on the road; one of our buses passed literally underneath the flight path of one of the attacking jets. Later that same bus stopped to take on people fleeing the site, helping them back to mid-town. Since our buses are garaged in Hoboken, those buses were later pressed into service ferrying refugees from Weehawken to the Hoboken Train Terminal. I myself did voluntary service on one of those buses for several runs. I did this for no pay, and not knowing if I was ever going to work as a guide again.

Three days later, we were back on the road giving tours. We were back not because the company thought there was enough potential business. They were, in fact, planning to lay off most of our staff (and illegally attempt to cancel out our health plan).

No, we were there because the city asked us to reopen, as part of its "business-as-usual" strategy. So we went off, pointed our buses off towards a cloud of asbestos and carrion and tried to figure out how to give a tour of this city in the middle of the worst trauma in its history. We did this with no guidance from the city, and with really no help. We had to deal with up-to-the-second changes, and unpredictable challenges. We had to change some discourse on routes that took us from a Times Square full of American flags to trailers by Bellevue filled with body parts. We had to make some comprehensive sense of that, and relate it to strangers. And we guides had no guidance in doing that, but we did it. No guidance, and no real reward, save for being able to continue in a profession that we loved, and thought we would lose.

Again, we did this because we were asked by the city to do so. But in this past year and a half we have not heard anything back from the city, no thanks, no response, no reward.

While some had secretly harbored the hope that both developments would thin out the competition, many guides echoed Andy's feelings that a more rigorous exam was an added insult to injuries inflicted on September 11.

"Keeping the Work Coming In": Four Career-Bolstering Strategies in an Informal Market

Guides use at least four strategies in order to face the recurring issues and unique events that shape this unstable and flexible labor market. They attempt to maintain their careers by developing a wide social network of interpersonal and institutional connections (which is introduced here and developed in greater detail in chapter 3), advertising in the media, addressing their tour content, and diversifying their employment. All have used one of these methods; many use all of them in order to ensure that, in the words of one, they are "keeping the work coming in for as long as possible."

Few guides need no assistance starting out. Joyce Gold, for example, was isolated enough to be unaware that she needed a guiding license until five years after she gave her first tour. For the most part, though, guides work hard to make connections early in their careers. When Harry Matthews decided to enter the business, he already had a few connections from taking tours, and he contacted two guides whose tours he liked the most. Both happened to be very important and connected figures in the industry, Gerard Wolfe and Justin Ferate. Gerard is a long-time, well-known guide. When he retired to Milwaukee, Justin ascended—in many people's estimation—as the senior member of the industry, the "dean of guides," who mentored guides like Harry and Eric Washington. Harry told me, "Justin is one of the few experienced guides who takes pleasure in encouraging others." At the time Harry began his tours, Justin was running an adult education program and hired Harry as an assistant. In the process, Justin introduced him to friends and colleagues, sharing the ins and outs of the business. There are informal groups like SNYCH (the Society for New York City History, which ran from 1983 to the early nineties) and the New Amsterdam Antiquarian Chowder and Marching Society (which would meet for dinner at Donahue's Restaurant, often for public historian Barry Lewis's colorful tales).

Guides and groups of guides aren't the only components of a social network that help to position oneself in the field. As Harry's story indicates, one's interpersonal connection with a guide may lead to ties with a larger organization, be it a business, government agency, or cultural institution. There are hundreds of travel, tourism, and cultural institutions in the city. To make sense of that expansive network, guides will often rely upon the *Official NYC Travel Planner*, a free booklet of information for travel professionals, with listings of 1,700 businesses, including dozens of pages for guides and tour companies, published by the New York's Visitors and Convention Bureau (called "NYC & Company"). Similarly, the Manhattan Chamber of Commerce provides Web advertising and a listing of member businesses at a rate of $195 a year for freelancers and $250 a year for businesses with fewer than 25 employees. From these sources, a guide can compile a mailing list. One explains how she pieces these sources together:

> You can't start a business [from any single source], but you get a little bit here, you get a little bit there. I got to reach out to a lot of little places. . . . What [NYC & Company] gives you is a shitload of information every month

of companies that are sending people to New York. And I get all my stuff to those companies.

Because this social network is so important—to guides and to our understanding of their world—the following chapter will provide greater analysis on how these individuals and organizations affect the guide's work.

In addition, guides need to publicize on their own, either through developing mailing lists or by placing a listing in the local media. This is the second way guides bolster their position in the field. The *New York Times*, the *Village Voice*, *Time Out New York*, *New York* magazine, and others offer sections for guides to advertise their upcoming tours for free. The *New York Times*, for example, regularly features tours in the Spare Times section of its Friday edition. There is far too little space for tours, however, and in most publications tour listings are the first to be jettisoned in favor of advertising space. Many guides will send in their information, spend a week preparing and polishing a tour, and open the Friday *New York Times* Arts section to find their tour was not added because of a last-minute editorial decision by the paper. As one guide describes it, "You are at the mercy of the paper. Unfortunately, there doesn't seem to be a better way of disseminating information. . . . When I do a straw poll of where people got the information, almost everybody got it from the *Times*." A woman who works at one of these periodicals told me, "Oh, yeah, on more than one occasion I've been yelled at over the phone by some guide who'd been counting on a listing."

If a guide or company has been lauded by a publication, such credentials are often cited on their Web sites and in their materials. Justin and Big Onion have been listed as *New York* magazine's "Best Walking Tour," and Bruce Kayton promotes his tours as one of the top five tours in *New York* magazine. Bruce also gets exposure from invitations to be on WBAI radio often (which is why a member of the station was on his Central Park tour) and sporadically on WNYC radio, the local NPR affiliate. Guides think of press manipulation as a mysterious art form.

A third way guides attempt to solidify their position is by addressing their tour content. Some specialize, which allows them to differentiate themselves from their colleagues. No one else does what Bruce does. He is *the* "Radical Walking Tour Guide of New York," not necessarily because of his extreme views. Bruce became a specialist in radicalism by becoming a generalist in its subvarieties. Over the course of a few years, he was able to develop tours in different left-leaning political topics and in particular areas around the city, conducting "all-woman," "all-Black," and "all–gay and lesbian" tours from Greenwich Village to Harlem. Several tours overlap, which, he knows, "doesn't make a lot of sense from an economic point of view, but the idea is to get the information out there." He offers two public weekend tours a month, and thirty to forty private tours a year. Bruce isn't alone in specializing. Tom Bernardin markets himself as *the* guide for Ellis Island, and Eric Washington carved out his own niche in Harlem and has been called "Mr. Manhattanville" by guides like Justin. Then there are others who diversify their expertise. It is very common for guides to claim the ability to take on almost any theme, particularly with enough lead time. According to one, "I have my bailiwick and that's what I focus on, but I'll do *anything* if I have enough prep time."

A fourth approach to establishing yourself is to have another job. This is common since, as mentioned, very few rise to the level of being a full-time guide and most do it in their spare time. According to Harry Matthews, almost everyone in the business "has something else they do, even if it is collecting a pension," which allows them to still give tours when they can. He, for example, will occasionally dip back into the skill set from his old job, writing ads, brochures, and articles in local weeklies. As a joke, he likes to differentiate himself from his colleagues: "I often explain, I am not an unemployed *actor*/tour guide, I am an unemployed *writer*/tour guide." Other jobs held by the guides mentioned in this book are taxi driver, freelance writer, substitute high school teacher, adjunct college professor, security guard, bank greeter, translator, copyeditor, actor, voice-over actor, location scout for the film industry, and member of the Landmarks Commission. Others make similar attempts to supplement their income by writing vanity or small-press books, like Tom Bernardin, who even distributes Ziploc bags of cookies on tour in order to promote his cookbook on immigrant recipes.

Different people use different strategies, and guides adapt over time. Joyce Gold was able to guide on the side by keeping one foot outside the field until she was able to achieve the rare status of being a full-time guide. After three years of offering weekend tours of the Financial District and Greenwich Village, she decided to leave her job to work as a tour guide and a real estate agent. The flexibility of these jobs worked but, as she told me, "being a realtor just gave me access to all these old buildings, and that just further confirmed my interest in history." When her guiding business took off, things changed: "In those years, I started making enough money to do less real estate, and I looked at my finances and realized that I could make it work just giving tours, which is what I preferred doing in the first place." In the spring of 1980 Joyce offered a course called "Manhattan History: Pre-Indian to the Brooklyn Bridge." It was a success and she has been offering roughly three noncredit courses a year at the New School and NYU since then. Being a guide and teaching allowed her to complete her master's degree in metropolitan studies at NYU and write two books. Bruce Kayton also exhibits many of the practices discussed here—selling his books and radical history maps, keeping his day job, offering tours to institutions like the Tenement Museum, local colleges, and unions, and as a guest on WBAI—in order to give tours like the one I took in Central Park.

Excavations in the Park (Central Park Tour, June 2003)

Bruce uses objects in the park to connect to larger comments about the class structure of New York. We curl around the southwestern edge of Sheep's Meadow, which today is packed with sun worshipers and a confetti of bathing suits, and rest next to a hot-dog cart. He extrapolates from the cart to make the point that, to the tourist these kiosks may appear to be the be a good opportunity for immigrant workers to start a small business, but that "the truth is these spaces are all rented out by the city," and only "big businesses" can afford renting them out to put a cart there. The most expensive site, at the Metropolitan Museum of Art, goes for $411,000 a year.

Twenty feet from the cart is a whole other flavor of dining establishment—the Tavern on the Green. Bruce says it is one of the most profitable restaurants in the world and pays only 3 percent of its profits to the city, despite being on public land. This is an upscale result for what was once, starting in 1870, the fold for the herd of sheep that served as the park's natural lawnmowers. "Twice a day, the sheep would cross the street to 'mow' the lawn." At this, Bruce's friend interrupts with a comment about how infamous New York City Parks Commissioner Robert Moses didn't like them holding him up on his ride to work, but Bruce looks at him askance and, annoyed, says, "I've got a joke coming up, if you wait. . . . I think he got rid of them because he couldn't charge them a toll as they crossed the street." Moses moved them to Prospect Park in 1934, the same year he replaced a five-person committee to become the sole head of the Parks Commission, a position he kept until 1960.

While I've noticed how other tours try to cover more ground, Bruce is happy to stand for twenty-five minutes at Sheep's Meadow. He talks about the concerts played here, and folds that into a discussion of the protest history of the park. Barbara Streisand and James Taylor are mentioned, along with Martin Luther King's 1967 march on the United Nations and the first

Gay Pride March, sparked by the 1969 Stonewall riots. He weaves it back to the present, noting that today is this year's Pride march, and he claims it has become far too commercial and mainstream.

Just north of the Tavern on the Green, we get to two playgrounds built aside one another. Drawing extensively from Robert Caro's biography of Moses, *The Power Broker*, Bruce demystifies the most powerful unelected official in city history, mostly by citing his disinvestment in public transportation and antipathy to minorities and lower classes. Bruce passes around a torn sheet of paper with all of the public works that Moses had a hand in, saying, "If you took a car here today, chances are you crossed over one of his projects." As we watch kids play, Bruce tells us how a neighborhood resident found a scroll of paper that turned out to be a set of construction plans to expand the Tavern on the Green's parking lot. Within a day, dozens of affluent and connected housewives were protesting the construction. Eventually, despite winning a court ruling, Moses got such bad press (including having the poor taste to cut down trees on the week of Arbor Day) that he built a playground there instead, a few feet from a preexisting one, claiming that was his intention all along.

Farther north, we curl into the Ramble, a part of the park that was carefully engineered to look completely natural. He says such environs have been perfect for two activities at cross-purposes: bird watching (since it serves as a sanctuary for migratory birds), and gay sex (since the dense vegetation provides reasonable privacy). Assumedly referring to the latter group, Bruce tells us, "Because the area was frequented by what he called 'anti-social' people, Moses wanted to pave it over and put a retirement home here." Bruce talks about police harassment and how championship ice-skater Dick Button and future radical Harvey Milk used to frequent these woods.

At the end of the tour, after four and a half hours of walking, we make it to Central Park's Great Lawn. Sometimes his tours reach six hours in length, but Bruce doesn't mind that he might lose participants along the way. On this tour, only his WBAI friend left, and that was just because he had to get to the station. Here he winds down with the early African American and Irish American establishment called Seneca Village, noting that "the history books like to say that there was 'nothing' on this site," and wraps up with the later, Depression-era settlements of homeless, called "Hoovervilles," and the Million Person March supporting the United Nations Special Session on Nuclear Disarmament. He pulls out an old newspaper photo, pointing a few inches off the page to indicate where he stood.

Harmonizing Work, and Other Rationales

It is unsurprising that someone who talks a great deal about class conflict and labor rights on his tours is also thoughtful about his own working conditions. Bruce Kayton doesn't intend to leave his formal workplace, where we sat for an interview. Behind a clean desk with a dingy window looking out to Midtown Manhattan and a computer screen humming behind him, Bruce is soft-spoken and less animated than he is on tour. A few neat stacks of paper sit in front of him. His Marx T-shirt is replaced by a white button-down. I ask him about his tradeoffs. While relatively unsatisfying, he tells me, this job provides the health care and consistency guiding could not, but that his "intensive and intellectual" tours lend him "an importance, a purpose," as well as some added cash. He keeps the jobs separate, but every so often he'll give a tour for his company, just as a favor. On those tours he admits to toning down his political content, focusing on artists and buildings more, insisting that, otherwise, he'll "never compromise anything."

Bruce's description of his balancing act is commonplace in a field known as rarely providing a full-time career. Only a few, like Justin, Joyce, and Seth, gain what Robert Faulkner called, in his study on musicians, a "career foothold" (1973, 337) and what Becker and Carper called a clear "occupational identity" (1956). Guides who have been unable or unwilling to gain such career traction will describe themselves as "just scratching along," or "juggling jobs," reflecting what scholars have pointed to as the "collage-like" experiences of a postindustrial career. This condition is not altogether negative. Guides talk about the harmony between their multiple endeavors often and cite the untidy nature of the tourism industry as a strong attraction.[6] The fact that a guide can pick up a tour or two every month for a little extra money is only part of the appeal. In regard to piecing together her career, Katia Howard, an autodidact who was at one time an aspiring actress, told me that she finds it "fun to figure these things out." Rather than begrudging the fragile and chaotic character of their work, these cultural entrepreneurs enjoy not only the modest financial gain, but also the autonomy and significance it lends to their lives. From the fragility of the business to the strategies for establishing oneself in the field, the last two sections of this chapter detail the primacy guides like Bruce place on seeking harmony among their various activities and their off-sidewalk lives.

To understand an informal field like the one guides live within, one must learn the ways workers explain and justify their ongoing participation in such a difficult labor market. For guides there are clear, though modest,

financial benefits. Aspiring academic guides, for example, need the money
to help pay for graduate school. As one told me, "I do two tours a week at 100
bucks a pop for a total of $800 a month for eight hours of work with little to
no prep time, doing something that I love. What's the downside?" And with
over 300 tours behind him, Erik Goldner explains his choice: "A colleague
asked me if I wanted to join, and in the end, it was very simple: I needed
the money." For most guides the ratio of labor to income is reasonable, particularly among those who have a background in history and need a flexible
schedule. But with such a variety of strategies and provisional gigging across
the field, my interviews revealed strong evidence of the importance of guiding work beyond the more mechanistic explanations of scheduling or bringing in money on the side. In addition to the financial gains, guides give three
overlapping explanations for their commitments to the field: guiding har-
monizes with their other endeavors, it develops a creative outlet or uses an
already existing skill set, and it nurtures a personal connection with their
city and other people.

Perhaps the most pervasive rationale guides offered was that touring allowed them to juggle several jobs while working toward being an actor or
academic. These two aspiratory groups enter the field and are positioned in
different ways, but share similarities in what they perceive as the benefits of
the work. Katia, for example, explained why there is a high number of aspiring actor-guides like her: "they get to guide when the work comes up and
when needed, which then leaves time for auditions [while being proximate
to] New York's entertainment industry." Guiding is, as Jane explains it, an
ideal synergy between her talents, her hopes, and her need for a job. Aspiring actor Darryl—who touches his chest and looks to the sky when describing himself as an "*ack*-tor"—explains how his skills work in both realms:

> One cannot be shy. You are the leader. People asking questions, using one's
> voice. You know, on the stage we always worry, "Is it loud enough?" This
> and that. When several times a week you are with people out on the street,
> you are going to be heard amidst the traffic or other people talking. So, by
> the time you get on the stage [for an audition] . . . it is a continuous per-
> sonality. When you are trying to be an actor and you are working 9-to-5 in
> a law office, filing or doing clerk-like things, you're not using your body, or
> speaking, or your reflexes, you are just vegetating in a way. And [it would
> be difficult] to suddenly be dazzling on stage, or meet someone in an inter-
> view. Meanwhile, if one's a tour guide and if you're good at that, you've
> been doing all that all day.

Over the years, Darryl has worked in what he calls a number of "off the wall" jobs, such as a greeter at a bank and as a bus guide, but he talks about how whatever guiding lacks, "[I] like it so much I cannot abandon it for full-time employment that would give me stability," because to do so would limit opportunities to take that next acting gig. His strategies for establishing himself includes working with a Times Square cultural institution every Tuesday and Sunday and spending the rest of his time on other jobs and auditions. If he lands an acting gig, he drops guiding and picks it up again when necessary. Guiding, for Darryl, "coexists" with his aspirations: not as a hobby, but not as a profession, either.

But academic guides hold similar appreciation for the work. Seth Kamil explains how he encourages graduate students to join Big Onion. Just as it keeps an aspiring actor's theatrical chops up, Seth sees it as "job training":

> People are getting paid—yes, they're working—they're getting paid extremely well, to advance their professional careers. . . . They are public intellectuals who have a track record. Everything is about getting about getting it out of the classroom these days. . . . The skills that my guides learn being tour guides can work anywhere. And they are taking it—the [former BOWT guide] up in Dartmouth is giving walking tours of that city. So, this is what it's all about. . . . I had dinner with [him] last week and he told me they hired him because they knew Big Onion. He hammed it up a bit, I'm sure. But that makes me feel good. I don't want anybody making a life-term commitment to me. You know?

Specifically, he sees touring as a way for students to hone their teaching skills, develop an ethic of public engagement, capitalize on their own research, and pay their bills along the way. Seth takes care of the logistics and says his guides "just need to know where to be, what to say, [and] worry about being a historian on the street." He provides lots of material and they don't have to be concerned with the struggles of establishing themselves, handling mailings and promotion, gaining entry into historical sites, or maintaining personal and institutional connections in the industry. Erik Goldner, after talking about his financial considerations, offered further rationale for being a guide: "It was a chance to do history—which is what I want to do with my life—and I thought it would be a challenge to do it outside with random strangers and try and get them interested." As is the case with aspiring actor guides, if a BOWT guide's schoolwork needs to take priority for a semester, Seth will assign fewer tours and give more when a semester's workload eases up. And just as for aspiring-actor guides, this work sits between a hobby and a profession for the students.

Harmony is not everything, however. Guides also find that conducting tours serves as a creative outlet or development of a set of existing skills. Those who mention this in their descriptions of why they tour are often less concerned about their success in the field. They enjoy that guiding either provides a venue for some otherwise untapped or suppressed aspect of themselves or allows them to fashion a meaningful side project. As one declares, "It is an intellectual exercise. I really don't expect to make money on it. It's a way for me to grow, and learn more."[7] Such a statement may appear to be an ex post-facto rationalization, lending additional meaning to a practice that has little chance of viable success, but the sheer number of guides who show little interest in pecuniary concerns does challenge such a hypothesis. For example: Brendan FitzGerald—a guide who gives "privately owned public spaces" tours and is highlighted in chapter 7—is uninterested in becoming a full-time guide. Sometimes he only offers tours to friends. "It takes a lot more time than you think," he tells me, "but it's fun, like a hobby." "[For a leisure activity] a lot of my friends are in bands," he says. "I do walking tours." In the words of another guide, getting paid has little to do with it: "I've never looked at it for the money. If I ever tried to make money off of it, I'd immediately despise it." While some are like aspiring musicians—willing to work in unappealing jobs to pursue their music career[8]—these guides are akin to the office worker who plays in a jazz quartet every Sunday night to enrich himself in a way that his "regular" day job cannot. Another way to look at this significance to guiding is to consider the number of guides like Bruce who turned to the business as a way to tap into a pre-existing interest, long dormant throughout a more formal career. An elder statesmen of GANYC reminded me that activism and teaching are not the only skill sets guides have the chance to utilize: He found guiding to be a perfect second career after twenty years of working the city beat for a local paper. He told me it is "a good way to use my different set of skills as a journalist." There are others who embrace the eclectic nature of their peers, eschewing a clear "occupational identity" and proudly referring to members of their group as "jacks-of-all-trades."[9] Harry Matthews claims that his eclectic, liberal arts education from Williams College taught him to be an "aggressive generalist" before and after his career in the advertising business, and sees this lifelong disposition as key to his success and happiness as a guide.

I found an overwhelmingly enthusiastic engagement with the city and its dwellers as a third explanation for why they fit the work into their lives. A *New York Times* article developed the image of guides and their close bond with their city, describing guides as "Licensed Know-It-Alls," one of whom states, "Some people get a high running the marathon. . . . I get a high greeting visitors." There were further glimmers of such a rationale, even in the industry's lowest moments, as another *Times* article profiled a man who told the paper, "I got my sightseeing license on the first anniversary of 9/11. . . . I woke up, and it seemed the only way to deal with the day" (Eisenstadt 2003). In a similar fashion, Mark Shulman, came into guiding after breaking his leg. Being stuck inside for weeks made him realize that he "was in the middle of Manhattan and missed it terribly" and he began giving tours once his leg was healthy enough. He holds his sightseeing license as a symbol, a proud badge, of that connection with the city—despite the fact that he now makes a living as a children's book author and rarely gives tours. The close tie to the city courses through many of the stories mentioned earlier, and it is through the interactions within the city and with city dwellers that these characters realized they can and should be tour guides.

Beyond the Sidewalk

The importance of guiding is not left behind on the sidewalk. Rather, these rationales are held in other spheres of guides' lives, even after more formal commitment to the sidewalk is over. It is a reminder that, through the work, these folks craft themselves as people as much as they craft the tours they lead. Jane Marx, for example, sees it as far more than a job: It is her main connection with other people and, she contends, with city life itself. She demonstrates how the density of urban life provides not only the content of tours but also her own biographical trajectories, since she was assisted in finding her career by a chance meeting with a guide on the street. It continuously feeds into her other pursuits. With theatrical blood running through her veins, she has developed a one-woman play called "Living on Pitch," detailing how she juggled acting and guiding with taking care of her late mother, who suffered from dementia. Guiding, she tells me, "serves as a key theme, not just in the play, but my life. It is where even in the most miserable moments—and living with my mother in the final stages of her life *was* depressing—I am able to find joy and purpose." And Eric Washington, as we will see in chapter 3, transformed himself from a part-time waiter and freelance journalist into a public historian and neighborhood booster by becoming a walking guide.

Big Onion Walking Tour guides told me how guiding illuminates their off-the-sidewalk lives as well. Erik Goldner owes much of his current success in the academic realm to being a guide. Certainly the historical content is of prime importance. He is able to easily fill out a lecture with a specific story culled from his tours. "Even in a Modern Europe survey course," he tells me, "I use the example of Ellis Island to illustrate the difficult passage that many Europeans encountered when they emigrated in the late nineteenth and early twentieth centuries." Beyond the content, Erik feels he *talks* differently, too: "When I'm lecturing in class, I find that it's much easier to form coherent sentences and even whole paragraphs without referring to my notes. It has helped me to speak off the cuff coherently." And for fellow BOWT guide Jennifer Fronc, guiding allows her to "try out" the archival research she was working on for her dissertation, to see if her issues and arguments could be communicated clearly and effectively. Since college classes are frequent tour groups for BOWT, she is sometimes literally speaking to her peers and paving the way for a heightened comfort level in expressing her ideas clearly on the page, in the classroom, and at conferences:

> Guiding forced me to get over my shyness and reticence to speak in public, and over time, with the positive feedback that I received from people who came on my tours, I think it gave me confidence and a sense of my own authority, a lot earlier than a lot of new professors do, who get thrown into a big lecture hall and have to learn how to engage a room of 150 students. That's never been an issue for me.

Jeffrey Trask also envisions his part-time guiding as connected to his more scholarly endeavors, an ongoing component of his life because he sees it all as "public education." Everything has use for him. He incorporates his tours into his courses and says it will "always be a part of my work." "The same way that I examine documents in a class," he explains, "I would use the city as a document. I don't see them as two separate tracks." As "a very tight-knit group," Erik Goldner told me, BOWT guides all share these experiences and the information, and that camaraderie has spilled into their professional networks. As Jennifer explains her intellectual community:

> I was at [the American Historical Association conference] and I saw a bunch of former guides and we were talking about how lucky we were to meet people beyond our own grad programs and seminars, to interact and talk about our dissertations with each other. Of my good guide friends, all were working on NYC-based topics and we formed reading and writing groups, helping each other navigate archives and sources, etc. The acknowledgments of my book give big props to my Big Onion friends. I absolutely think it has shaped me professionally.

Like many BOWT guides, Jennifer thinks guiding has deeply shaped her professional life.

The informal nature of guiding work makes for a variety of interwoven occupational paths. Detailing guides' trajectories in and through the field and offering the ways it works for them both on and off the sidewalk provides the foundation for an understanding of the business. The social meaning of their work also entails the wide social network guides use to do their work. These two levels are interconnected as well, as we will see.

The Guide-Centered Working Ecology

Guiding Relations

On the shores of ancient Troy and Athens, a crowd of interpreters, craftsmen, portraitists, and guides would wait for boatloads of tourists to arrive from across the Aegean Sea.[1] In some ways, modern tour guides are parts of a community that is just as informal and loose as those of their ancient counterparts. Unlike those early guides—and those in many other cities today—New York *periegetari* must contend with a few new constraints. All Gotham's guides need to be licensed, and it is illegal for them to solicit business on the street.[2] The job would be a great deal simpler if a gifted storyteller was permitted to stand on the corner of 125th Street with a sign that said "Tour guide for hire: $10 per hour" to cajole a group together.

Though the informal, autonomous practice of guiding may have been an attraction for some, ethnographic vignettes have already shown how guides must maintain a network of dozens, even hundreds, of social connections. As the Italian proverb says, the wise man will "prefer to have friends on the marketplace than money in a chest" (Braudel 2002, 30), and guides can log hours of letter writing and emailing, setting up meetings and distributing advertising, before a single one of their stories is told. Guides can gain information, pick up extra work, and find support, advice, camaraderie, and mutual understanding from the people they know, and status-boosting affiliation from the variety of organizations they associate with. Career trajectories must weave through this changing web of individuals and institutions, a changeable ecology, both on the sidewalk and off it. These relationships inform both how guides work and the content of the tour itself. Guides try to shape their occupational world to suit their informal work conditions; it is a changeable ecology, but one that is largely designed and maintained by their own social connections.

Bill Kornblum's *Blue Collar Community*, a study of a South Chicago steelmill neighborhood, is a classic demonstration of the relationship between the organization of labor and the social lives and urban communities of workers. The informal, postindustrial world of guiding has little in common with that more bounded midcentury industrial landscape. Devoid of a conventional workplace, and without the dense system of taverns, unions, and political associations that made South Chicago a tight "neighborhood ecology" (Kornblum 1974, 69), walking guides must create and maintain an informal network of relationships on their own. Urban ethnographies like Kornblum's often center upon a central setting or set of places (e.g., a take-out shop, a street-corner, a jazz club, an athletic club) that serves to locate the examined social world. Data from the last chapter indicated that guides often piece together work from disparate associations with individuals and organizations often unseen in conventional urban and workplace ethnographies, and this chapter is divided into two layers that reflect this loosely connected ecology: the first half illustrates the guides' own community in terms of interpersonal relations to larger guiding groups, while the second half examines the organizations guides work with to gain legitimacy and attract a broader clientele. The chapter concludes with a discussion of how these relations shape the field through what guides feel as a conflict of autonomy and legitimation, the third tension mentioned at the end of the first chapter.

Someone who personifies these connections and their resultant tensions is Eric Washington, a guide who primarily offers tours on the Manhattanville section of Harlem. Eric is a well-traveled, middle-aged black man, and during our first talk he spoke easily of his background. Growing up in Staten Island and feeling an intense lack of African American culture in school, he told me he looked out onto the Manhattan skyline and felt it was enchanted "like Oz." Moving to the western edge of Harlem in the late 1980s, Eric worked in an array of jobs: waiting tables, landing a few acting roles, and doing a little freelance journalism and photojournalism. He was successful at juggling gigs. One of his articles, for *Out Magazine,* won him a first place prize by the National Association of Black Journalists. He then landed a job assessing St. Mary's Episcopal Church, Parish House and School for designation by the Landmarks Commission in 1998, and it was at this point that his interest in urban history and culture was ignited. As a part of his research he uncovered "Manhattanville," a name he had never heard of before. Concurrently, he wrote a freelance article about Central Park walking tours for *Time Out New York.* Putting his interest in historical preservation and the article topic together, he told himself: "No one is giving a tour of this neighborhood, but I can!" He gave his first tour on the area in 1998.

From his work on St. Mary's Eric expanded his research to the history of the neighborhood and put together a book, *Manhattanville: Old Heart of West Harlem* (2002). The book gave him recognition in the guiding community and among those who work at places like the Municipal Art Society, and through building that reputation Eric began to see himself as a public historian. Both fieldnote sections for this chapter evince how his connections with organizations explicitly inform the tour, but also impact how a guide like Eric develops a sense of self through the process.

Beneath the Pavers, the City (Manhattanville Tour, March 2004)

Eric Washington has reason to be in a bad mood. Yesterday's Friday *Times* didn't publish his advertisement for today's tour on Manhattanville, a forgotten corner of Harlem, this morning's sky threatened rain, and very few people showed up on his last tour. He didn't expect a crowd. And yet, he is all smiles as he approaches our group, because the Municipal Art Society (MAS) sponsored the tour and listed it on their calendar of events, and he has twenty-eight people gathered under McDonald's golden arches for his tour. Even the sun has come out, greasily reflecting off the red awning.

Standing on the curb, with his back to the fast food joint, Eric welcomes us. He's wearing a red baseball hat over his salt-and-pepper hair, and his Sightseeing Guide License hangs on a red and white strap around his neck. A representative from the MAS is circling around the group, collecting $10 from members and $15 from nonmembers. Eric introduces her and tells everyone to pay her, not him, for the tour.

Eric starts by talking about the name of the place itself. This section of Harlem has been targeted by Columbia University and renamed "Morningside

Heights"—sparking a hotly contested and ongoing battle over the area's history and culture. "Before Morningside Heights was ever dreamt of," Eric says, this neighborhood was a transportation, work, and residential hub for over a hundred years. Founded in 1806, Manhattanville was disconnected from Harlem (founded to the east in 1658). "The City" slowly crept northward. In recent years, few residents know about Manhattanville; the only reminders seem to be the name of the post office and Eric's tours. He is fond of saying it is "hidden in plain sight."

The 1/9 train (known in decades past as the IRT line) runs overhead from 122nd Street to 135th on an elevated trestle called the Manhattan Valley Viaduct. It rumbles through this once-placid valley. Pointing to the structure, Eric tells the group: "Most of the buildings you see were built in 1905, right after this station opened up the area in 1904." On cue, a train rolls above, *ka-clunk ka-clunk ka-clunk*, editing his talk on the ethnic fabric of the community. He carries on, but from the back all I hear is, "Harl-[ka] Dutch-[clunk] Belg-[ka] Irish-[clunk] Ashkena-[ka] Je-[clunk]."

Halfway down the block, we stop at a building that is, like many in the area, owned by Columbia University. It was once the Sheffield Farms milk-bottling plant. He talks about how the now-gray terracotta was originally sparkling white, supposedly denoting the purity of their product. Eric starts walking backwards while talking, prompting the group onward.

Walking west on 125th Street to 12th Avenue, we gather under the massive Riverside Drive Viaduct. Another overpass, but with heavy afternoon car traffic rumbling above us this time. He directs our eyes, however, down to our feet, where a layer of cobblestones and rail tracks peek up from beneath the smooth asphalt, like muscle and sinew under skin. "What do you see?" Readily, someone points out a marking that says "3rd Ave." "Right," Eric says. "You see Third Avenue, and look around and see that we're on Twelfth Avenue." He tells us how, in the late 1800s, the powerful Third Avenue Railroad Company used this area to turn its trains back downtown. Eric says that the artifact serves as a "wonderful window into transit history, commercial history and, by extension, racial history. You've all heard of Rosa Parks, right? Well . . ." Eric tells us of the lesser-known story of Elizabeth Jennings and a hotshot twenty-one-year-old lawyer (and future U.S. president), Chester A. Arthur. One hundred blocks down these tracks, and 150 years ago, Ms. Jennings was kicked off a Third Avenue car. She hired Mr. Arthur and won: for $225 and the desegregation of all New York streetcars.

"There is so much history," he tells us, "that goes unseen."

Connecting with Other Guides

Guiding, as Eric Washington explains it, can be a "lonely business." "On the one hand," he tells me, "it's nice because you don't have to answer to anyone. You keep clients happy and it's fun. But, on the other hand, it means that you are out there alone all the time." For Eric, interacting with guides, whether it is in comparing notes or just socializing, is "simply to have a chance to be re-assured that I'm not the only one out there." As mentioned earlier, autonomy is a significant draw but guides still maintain various relationships.

Eric was fortunate to benefit from Justin Ferate's mentorship. When I asked about it he recalls a specific moment when that advisory role helped him. Seemingly out of nowhere, the program director at the Brooklyn Historical Society contacted him to give a tour and he was unsure whether or not he had the credentials to do it. When he called Justin for advice, much to Eric's surprise Justin told him that he had recommended him for the job. Justin's mentoring helped him realize that he had a place in the field. "If you do research," he assured him, "you're a historian." Eric describes it with a chuckle:

> I gave no indication that I would be able to give a tour of Brooklyn, but that's how this business works. If somebody needs something—they don't know exactly what they need, and they'll see somebody who's a tour guide, and they'll just assume that they do anything. "Don't be lame," [Justin] told me, "Always say yes. When's the tour?" and I gave him the date, and he says, "Well, you have two weeks to bone up." And he helped me out and gave me material, and I boned up and I gave a great tour.

Eric explains, "[Justin] showed up on my tour, just to give a fresh ear. How boring must that have been to somebody who's taken so many tours. I'm surprised that his lip wasn't bleeding by the end of it." Such mentorship is rare, and Eric is fortunate, but interactions of guiding collegiality, like the tour featured in chapter 1, happen periodically.

Sometimes guides collaborate, an effort designed to build conversational debate into the tour structure itself while maintaining some control over the discussion. The Literary Tour and Pub Crawl is one example of this. Sometimes guides will set up the relationship between each other as a "debate," as was the case with the Municipal Art Society's first tours, an orchestration designed to educate, spark discussion, attract participants, and offer a polyvocal experience. Justin has done dueling tours on the "Jewish Rialto" (a section of Second Avenue in what is now the East Village) and other tours with an architectural bent. He describes the second tour's set-up with a colleague:

> I'm more nineteenth-century, he is a kid of the sixties. He's Mr. Modernism, I'm Mr. Non-Modernism, and we speak to two different worlds, with similar levels of appreciation. [W]e would start doing the "I don't agree with you" routine. Back and forth. But the nice thing was that it made people realize that there's more than one way of looking at the world.

Bruce Kayton once gave a series of "capitalist vs. communist" tours of Wall Street, with one of his compatriots. As he explained it:

> It was hysterical. A lot of fun. We did nine of them for about two years, he did the conservative side, I did the radical side. And we fought over Wall Street, which was perfect. . . . It was really well choreographed. I'd talk about how a third of the founders were slave owners, and all the protests at the Stock Exchange, he'd talk about how this is "great," and how anyone can make money, and blah blah blah, what a great institution, free market. I'd talk about all the corruption scandals, and brokers getting arrested.

These relationships worked well, but Justin and Bruce both admit that sheer economics limit the chance of two guides coordinating preparation work yet dividing profits. For that reason alone, they only do it sporadically.

Then there are what sociologists would call the "affiliates." Some guides keep a backstage crew—to use Erving Goffman's well-worn dramaturgical model (1959)—that takes phone calls, orchestrates scheduling, designs Web pages, even financially backs the business. Most spouses or partners have participated in some way.[3] Seth Kamil, for example, readily admits that in difficult times he and Big Onion benefited from his wife's steady office job. In turn Seth is a backstage character to his guides, describing himself as "hands-off, within reason," although he still moves to the front stage regularly, picking up tours occasionally, "just to keep on my toes." And then there are folks on tours who join in on the tour, but who aren't guides. The Literary Tour and Pub Crawl, not only demonstrates the dueling style (in evidence earlier), but also has explicit relationships with the owners of bars like Chumley's and the Minetta Tavern. On our tour the manager of the Minetta gave our group a little history of the place while our group members ordered drinks. For their 'foodie' tours Katia Howard and Seth Kamil both develop relations with specialty shops, and encourage participants to taste food from the Dominican Republic, China, and Italy, to buy their edibles and speak with employees. Nurturing these symbiotic relationships works on multiple levels: tour participants may get free or discounted sundry and get to meet colorful local bartenders, priests, rabbis, concierges, baristas ("The out-of-towners," Katia tells me, "love meeting locals"). Proprietors enjoy the added business and the chance to frame their establishment as an important cultural and historical landmark, and guides get to add some interaction and different perspectives to the tour without having to cede control of the tour entirely.

Then there are more formal groupings of guides. For-profit businesses provide a measure of stability. Bus tours—again, one of the major ways people enter into the market—offer a base salary from around $25,000 to $35,000 a year (Lee 2002) with the understanding that, according to Mark Levy, "the tips can get upwards to $250 on a good shift." Gray Line Bus Tours also provides insurance and has a union (the Transport Workers Union of America Local 225). When their walking tour business slumped after September 11, many, like the Levy family, returned to the constancy of bus tours. Still, as one guide told me, "bus guides are paid so little, I don't know how they survive." There are other businesses guides can work for as well. Destination management companies (DMCs), for example, provide the logistics (including catering, temporary staffing, transportation, entertainment, and so on) for organizations having meetings, events, and conferences in the city, or even package various groups together to get discounts on charter buses, dinners, entertainment, or something else the group desires. Their size can range from a large national organization with dozens of franchises across the country (like Briggs and American Tours International) to smaller mom-and-pop outfits with, as one described his early stages in the business, "little more than a listing with NYC & Company and a fax machine." According to one of the smaller owners, the big DMCs cover three-quarters of the tourism market and can broker for better deals on transportation, entertainment, and hotels for visitors.

Then there is the Guides Association of New York City, the largest group of guides, which operates more like a guild.[4] Joining the 270-plus members of GANYC requires having a current sightseeing license, paying a $70 fee, and coming to a few meetings to get a sponsor. There are important benefits to membership. The group maintains a Web site where members can post their tours and credentials, advocates on behalf of guides (lobbying the DCA to make it illegal for companies to hire nonlocal guides for tours in New York), and coordinates events that give members entrée to sites that the public does not have access to (e.g., "behind the scenes" tours of St. John's Cathedral, Macy's, Temple Emmanuel, and the Steinway piano factory

in Queens). An example of the importance of this group was on display after September 11. Harry Matthews described to me how one particularly
persistent member fought through government bureaucracy to discover the
"Disaster Relief for the Self-Employed" program and gave detailed instruc-
tions at association meetings and through GANYC's newsletter, *Guidelines*,
on how to receive emergency funds.[5] While having a business address in the
southern region of Manhattan was originally required for assistance, guides
learned they could make a case that their business was on the sidewalks of
Lower Manhattan even if their address wasn't.

Information can be shared, and mentoring can occur—particularly through
sponsorship—but GANYC membership is not purely beneficial. Like all
such guides associations, it is a loose guild of members who are essentially in
competition with each other for a piece of the industry. One member offered
his negative opinion of the group: "it is full of strong-willed, egocentric,
and chronically insecure people. Most of us choose to work on our own."
A particularly relevant dynamic is that new guides often hold board positions because, according to one member, "candidates often run unopposed
and are new to the industry, have more time to commit to it, but less experience." This guide suspects that the 2003 executive board's initial enthusiasm
for the licensing exam could be blamed on inexperience, which also led to
their resignation after having to face the ire of more seasoned guides.

Associating with other guides is only a part of the guide's social network.
The second set of relations will be discussed below.

Hidden in Plain Sight (Manhattanville Tour, May 2004)

Eric Washington tells us that the next two stops will evince Manhattanville's
religious mixture. The first is the Old Broadway Synagogue on 126th Street
and Old Broadway—a two-block street just east of Broadway. "We don't really
have time to talk too much about this," he says, but adds that this is one of
the last remnants of a once-large Jewish enclave. As if staged, two Orthodox
Jewish men walk by; one waves to Eric and turns to the other and says, "I actually know that guy." Eric points to a cable that stretches across the street.
"That isn't a utility cable, but a symbolic border called an *eruv*," the marker
of an area within which Jews observing Shabbat can participate in activities
that are otherwise only allowed at home. We then curl over onto West 126th
Street to St. Mary's Episcopal Church, founded in 1823, which is the oldest
continual church in the city. Inside, Eric introduces us to "his good friend,"
Reverend Koopercamp. The long-haired reverend, dressed in a purple T-shirt

is amiable and gives us a talk about the historical relevance of the parish. Eric realizes that we are behind schedule and he hurries us out.

Up Amsterdam Avenue, we quickly pass a beer brewing company, an art gallery called Triple Candy, and a nondescript building that serves as the storage space for the Metropolitan Opera's scrims. People have questions and some of the older folks start lagging behind, but Eric needs to get to the last stop on the tour. Walking up a hill, we walk past the old site of the Convent of the Sacred Heart, which turned into Manhattanville College before the campus moved upstate in 1952. One woman on the tour turns out to be a current faculty member there, and tells Eric she was motivated to come of the tour to find out the origins of her school.

The final stop is at the top of the hill: an exhibit at City College Eric curated in conjunction with the Urban Planning program—largely comprised of his vast personal collection of letters, official documents, maps, building plans, postcards, magazines, and photographs of the area. His favorite tag line is the title of the exhibit, "Manhattanville: Hidden in Plain Sight."

I think about the opening reception for this exhibit a few months earlier, where Eric gave a short speech, opening it by saying, "Manhattanville hasn't looked this sexy in years!" The first three or four rows were filled with fellow guides, whom he called on by name during the question-and-answer period. The group asked about the area's boundaries ("Roughly between 122nd and 135th, the Hudson and what is now St. Nicholas Avenue. It is a valley, but it is not restricted to that"), where the name comes from ("No one knows for sure"), and why "Harlem" won out as the moniker for the area ("My hypothesis is that 'Harlem' was older and had more institutional names attached to it, leading to a kind of permanence of the name"). He ends by telling the group: "No place, and no person, is without its history."

He is still on stage in the walking tour, and once we reach the exhibit, he backs off again to encourage us to roam freely. We all sign the guestbook before viewing the texts, timelines, reproductions, and ephemera. The chief librarian, Pamela Gillespie, welcomes the group, tells us how proud the college and local community are to have the exhibit here, and invites us to walk around. "Please," she tells us, "ask Eric or I any questions and we'll be happy to answer them for you."

The majority of the title cards of the letters, photos, pins, and lithographs say "From the Collection of Eric K. Washington." The impressive compilation offers a rich understanding of the neighborhood. At both the opening exhibition and the walking tour visit, people bump their noses against glass cases, trace maps with fingertips, and point to old magazine covers. Eric cycles around, elaborating on particular items. It is hard to tell which is more his element: the library or the streets. In truth, he's ecstatic about both, giddy about primary sources as well as the terracotta on an old milk-bottling plant. The group moves around slowly before fading off into the book stacks. In a half hour, they're all gone. The hum of interaction resonating from group's presence gives way to the mute stacks of dusty books.

Wrangling, Promoting, Connecting: Working with Organizations

Harlem has served as an important research site for many scholars interested in understanding how institutions and corporations serve as engines of urban cultural growth, creating the symbolic structure for an urban area.[6] Such processes can be seen as powerful forces in the neighborhood's ballyhooed mid-1990s renaissance. This history serves as the backdrop for the story of guides, whose work is partially informed by negotiating relations with these groups, and their small-scale re-presentations of neighborhoods are, in turn, saturated with such relationships. For example, it turns out that a guide who gives a "Immigrant Foods of the Lower East Side" tour (illustrated in chapter 5) attempted to organize a visit with Katz's Deli and was rebuffed, which led to the tour emphasizing two delis a few blocks away: Yonah Schimmel's and Russ and Daughters. Both eateries were happy to host the visit and talk to tourists, even though the guide claims that "honestly, I think that Yonah's knishes can be hit or miss."

But the uptown location of Eric's tour is particularly apt, as it is a reminder of how individual culture workers seek to nurture their organizational ties. The MAS, for example, sponsored his tour, and his story was anchored by a variety of neighborhood institutions past and present: a church, a synagogue, an art gallery, two light manufacturing plants, and two colleges. On another tour, offered only a few blocks away, Jane Marx stood under the famous Apollo Theater marquee on 125th Street and emphasized the arrival of the William J. Clinton office building, AOL/Time-Warner's investment in the Apollo, and the Magic Johnson Movie Theaters down the block and their role in the revitalization of the neighborhood. Both guides spoke to me afterwards, underscoring how these institutions have shaped Harlem, and how both tours were influenced by these organizations by extension, since such connections provided "frontstage" touchstones and tour content as well as "backstage" income and clientele. With this understanding, this section builds from earlier discussions to introduce these organizational relationships.

Organizations affect the tour in four ways—through content, hiring, attracting participants, and working behind the scenes. The first, most dominant effect institutions have is on the content of the tour. It is commonsensical to state that every institution has some sort of agenda, but in examining the work of guides one must be very sensitive to this fact. Some organizations use tours as a way to expressly advance their mission, which means they are the impetus for the tours themselves. Take, for example, New York's New Museum of Contemporary Art. In 2004 the museum began its process of moving from its posh SoHo surroundings to the more rough-hewn neighborhood to its east, the Bowery. This latter neighborhood has a strong history of being the city's Skid Row, a seemingly odd choice for a shiny contemporary museum. Much like the way Harlem is being transformed by commercial and government interventions, the museum is at the forefront of shaping the community and, in order to facilitate that process, it commissioned six contemporary New York artists to create site-specific installations that were paired with six neighborhood businesses, including a martial arts studio (wherein you had to use the code name "Gert Fröbe" to access a secret room that housed the artwork), a restaurant, and the 125-year-old Bowery Mission. Each project was featured on the museum's free tour, called "Counter Culture." The guide, curator Melanie Cohn, told my tour group that these "art interventions" were the museum's way to "integrate the museum into the community through art." (It is also an example of how an institution that may be disengaged in the tourism industry might still use the practice of a walking tour. The guide did not have, or need, a sightseeing guides license.) From my fieldnotes:

Our final destination brings us to one of Manhattan's last single-room occupancies, the Sunshine Hotel, which sits directly next to the museum's future location. It is located on the second floor of the building, and a bright yellow set of duct pipes winds down to what looks like a little callbox on the sidewalk. Called "Can You Hear Me?" and created by Julianne Schwartz, this installation was designed to facilitate communication between passersby and the hotel residents via a set of embedded mirrors. Tour participants were encouraged to place their heads into the callbox to catch a glimpse of the hotel, and to talk with residents. The guys in the hotel did more of the talking, asking participants where they were from. Most of the tourists were eager to find out what the men thought of the art object itself. "I've talked to more people in the last two weeks," one says to a tourist, "than I have in the last three years."

Such an explicit connection between the tour's content and the sponsoring organization's mission is rarely so obvious as to be traced out by a set of bright yellow tubes: curated by the museum, the expressed goal of the tour formed the content, which then shaped the interactions participants had as a part of the experience, in this instance, by connecting tourists with marginalized people.

This installation and the interactions it provided were as apparent as they were ephemeral, only lasting for a few weeks. There are more enduring connections, however. The "Broadway Open House Tour," for example, has offered weekly exclusive peeks in and out of a dozen Broadway theaters along the Great White Way for years. The Broadway League (formerly the League of American Theaters and Producers), the official trade association for the commercial theater industry, is perhaps best known for putting on the flashy TONY awards and also sponsors these smaller-scale walking tours. Costing $25 a person, the content is entirely promotional, and even crassly commercial, as was evident at the tour's conclusion:

After an hour and a half we arrive at the famous Shubert Alley, and our guide, Darryl, turns and says, "This is where the tour—sponsored by Visa, Marriott, and the Helena Rubenstein Foundation—comes to a close. Now is the time to see if you all have been paying attention and have a three-question quiz for some fantastic prizes." And after a bright, slightly overzealous ten-year-old answers all the questions and receives a pocket flashlight (which elicits an audible groan from a crowd that had been hoping for complimentary theater tickets), the guide tells us, "But everyone's a winner, because you all get a 15% off coupon for lunch at the Marriott."

Other cultural institutions that use walking tours as a part of their programming include the New York Historical Society, the Brooklyn Historical Society, the Central Park Conservancy, the New York branch of the Smithsonian National Museum of the American Indian, the Museum of the City of New York, and the Museum of African Art. The organization that that sponsored Eric's tour, Municipal Art Society, is a century-old private, nonprofit organization that looms large in the field, as it hosts dozens of planning and preservation commissions and offers hundreds of different events annually. The MAS operates 300 walking tours, including free tours (with a suggested donation of $10-15) of landmarks like Grand Central Terminal and tours of off-the-beaten-path places like an abandoned concrete plant in the Bronx that the city transformed into a public park (the MAS organized members of the local activist group Youth Ministry for Peace and Justice to be the tour guides), Sunset Park, Brooklyn, and Jersey City, New Jersey. About 80 percent of the MAS tours are on the sidewalks, and the other 20 percent are based in particular buildings or interesting behind-the-scenes locations like the exclusive University Club of New York. When I asked the director of tours at the MAS, Robin Lynn, about how this disposition affects tour content she insisted she doesn't want to focus on "touristy" sites but rather places of interest to New Yorkers.[7] Citing one of the less-developed sections of the city, she asks with a laugh, "Would a commercial tour company take you to Bushwick?" She cites other examples of nontouristic tours, like one on the conversion of vacant buildings into sustainable buildings. She says these tours reflect the Municipal Art Society's perspective on the art, history, and culture beyond Manhattan and the mainstream. While freelance guides are paid per client, cultural institutions usually pay whether two or fifty people show up for the tour. The MAS, for example, pays $200 a tour.

The aforementioned nonprofit Big Apple Greeters carries a clearer promotional bent. Volunteers told me a frequent gig would be to show businessmen and out-of-towners around the transit system. In a slightly jaded response to advertisements for the Greeters program suggesting these guides are just friendly locals who love to show off their town, a guide who has not worked with them, and must compete with their free tours, told me, "Yeah, sure. They are showing you around like a *good friend* . . . you just *happen* to be in Chinatown [laughs]."[8] Some, like Mark Shulman, were disappointed when they felt pressure from their supervisors to be very pro–New York and pro-tourism rather than being encouraged to develop their intellectual skills. As Mark explained it, "We not only had to present the city in a certain way, we'd have to highlight and focus on certain achievements," he explains. "It was like an organ of the city government that I wasn't interested in being one pipe of." Many guides are wary of this group because they are seen as giving away the proverbial milk that they are so desperately trying to sell.

No discussion on urban culture and institutional affiliation would be complete without mention of business improvement districts (BIDs). As Mitchell Duneier tells it, the overall influence of BIDs on cities cannot be overestimated. I have found that they play an enormous role in shaping urban culture through using guides as a part of this power.[9] A member of the Grand Central Partnership (GCP) told me their contract with the city "specifically identifies tourism services as one of our staple and core functions." Established in 1988 the GCP covers a fifty-three-block area and over 72 million square feet of commercial space, spends the $10 million it collects every year

by providing services similar to other BIDs (e.g., redesigning streets, controlling pedestrian walkways), as well as operating information kiosks, lobbying
city and state government, renovating the terminal, and touting a 60 percent reduction in crime in the area through their security force (MacDonald
1996). In addition to these efforts, they have been offering free tours—like
the one highlighted in chapter 4—every Friday since the early 1990s. The
34th Street Partnership, the Times Square BID, the Union Square BID, the
Lincoln Center BID, the Downtown Alliance BID, and the Lower East Side
BID now offer weekly tours as well.[10]

Even if cultural institutions or businesses do not operate a walking tour
program themselves, they may still shape tour content in less recognized
ways. Two examples of this less-formal relationship arose in the course of my
research. First, there are "fam" (short for "familiarity") tours, which tend to
be walk-throughs of businesses or institutions around the city offered to people in the tourism industry to encourage them to bring in tour groups and
visitors. Indicating the climate and interest in such events, an attendee of a
complimentary walk-through and buffet at the Museum of Sex told me: "It
was packed. It's a dangerous place, between a GANYC guide and free food."
"They're pretty effective," she tells me, "because I get a sneak peek into spaces
and meet the contact people who actively *court me* for my tours. It's win-win. I
ended up bringing a Kansas tour group to the Museum of Sex and it was great."
A second, more rare example involved Miramax Films, which approached Big
Onion to give "Gangs of New York" tours of the Five Points district, the historical site where the movie was supposed to take place. According to Seth:

> They asked us to create a history tour based around the time period of *Gangs
> of New York*. We were able to preview the film before it was released and
> basically made a deal with them that we would do a tour about the history
> of New York, and the issues surrounding the film. It would not be about the
> film, and they could not control what we say. And the tour is about New
> York in 1830 to 1870. It is not a tour about Martin Scorsese. It is not a tour
> about the movie at all.

Despite this stated independence, he told me he and his guides chose to
"draw references from the film and the book to give a broader sense of the
history. We did that at [Miramax's] request."

While content is crucial, there are three more ways these associations
alter the field. The second has to do with hiring. Earlier, we saw how an institutional tie could help a guide establish him- or herself, but here from the

organization's perspective, there are other considerations to that relationship. The MAS, for example, informs the field via its employment practices. Robin Lynn told me she tries to have guides who "focus on the built environment, and that's where, I hope, our guides match our mission." An employee of the Lower East Side Jewish Conservancy told me the organization hires guides who are "staunch about their Jewishness, staunch about their history, and [who see walking tours as] their way of giving back." Other examples of how an organization's outlook shapes the field through hiring include Big Onion's exclusive use of Ph.D. students to maintain their academic cachet, the Broadway Open House Tours hiring from a large pool of aspiring actors, and BIDs providing the most stable tour jobs in the city.

The third way organizations shape the field is how these connections work behind the scenes. The tight links between organizations can be powerful. The background of the licensing exam, for example, traces out one such set of associations that directly affected guides: Gretchen Dykstra was the founding president of the Times Square BID before becoming the Department of Consumer Affairs (DCA) commissioner, and the Grand Central Partnership joined the Times Square BID, NYC & Company, and the DCA to fund the licensing exam overhaul, hiring one of the guides most tightly tied with the GCP (and the MAS), Justin Ferate, and representatives from each came to support the exam in front of the city council. To indicate this network's investment in shaping the field, the DCA's Web site posted a statement regarding the 2003 licensing exam, which included a quote from the president and CEO of the GCP, Fred Cerullo:

> We run a localized tourism program that assisted more than one million neighborhood visitors in 2002. We recognize the importance of equipping the citywide tour guides with the knowledge to answer any reasonable question, cite relevant facts, and serve as a general expert on our ever-changing city. DCA's updated exam will help to ensure that.

And a fourth, final way these institutions shape the field is through drawing particular kinds of participants to the tour itself. Eric's tour demonstrates this: He was grateful that his affiliation with the MAS attracted participants when his *New York Times* ad didn't run. Independent guides, as compared to Big Onion guides, tend to draw an older crowd due to their connections with, and promotion through, cultural organizations like MAS and the YMCA (both of which have listed dozens of Eric's tours). Big Onion gets out-of-town visitors in part because of their relentless Web presence and vast mailing list,

as well as their affiliations with business improvement districts. Those who
work at Gray Line or freelance for a destination management company can
expect out-of-towners exclusively because they are often "meet and greets"
(so-called because guides welcome visitors at the airport), requiring guides
to make sure a group gets from the airport to the hotel to the restaurant to
some touristic site like Ellis Island, and then back to the hotel, which, in
turn, makes it less like guiding and more like *wrangling*. As such, these DMC
jobs shape the participants and interactions, lacking in even the most basic
intellectual challenge many guides are looking for. According to one of the
owners of a smaller DMC, some of these tour packages "are made to be as
inexpensive as possible, and they're boring [to do] because you are more like
Julie on the Love Boat." (More on these interactions and how they shape the
tour and the tour guide in the following chapters.)

" . . . But They Also Use Our Name to Market Themselves"

These relationships have their costs and benefits and reflect one of the key
tensions described at the end of chapter 1: Between legitimation and autonomy. MAS tours director Robin Lynn makes plain that the public sphere itself is an arena wrought with both promise and contestation, and all who are
involved hold a stake in its formation:

> The city streets have their own managers and agents of change now. You
> think that that's a public street? It's really not. Sometimes it's in a BID area.
> Sometimes it's within a historic district. Sometimes it's in a cultural district.
> And everybody thinks that they own it. And so when you as an organiza-
> tion go to give a tour . . . who speaks for these streets? People have vested
> interests, and it gets confusing.

The importance of these connections, and the complex and at times contra-
dictory interests at work within them, cannot be overstated.[11]

While several guides mentioned so far may illustrate these issues adequately (e.g., the food-tour guides who contact the cheese shops and delis
of the Lower East Side so participants can sample different foods, to the
theater troupe that makes agreements with local bars for the pub crawl),
it is perhaps best to begin with the guide at the center of this chapter, Eric
Washington. Seemingly socially isolated on the street corner, the Sightseeing Guide License around his neck and his sponsorship by the MAS are clues
to the wide-ranging network of relationships he holds. Eric exemplifies an
autonomous player who nurtures these associations and integrates himself

into several social spheres. He shows us how these relations shape a tour as well. He carefully traces out hidden borders, old neighborhoods, and Jewish demarcations on the sidewalk; his working life also traces the potential connections a guide can hold. These ties are as evident as the partially buried Manhattanville train tracks connect to distant historical and geographical events. Eric is licensed by the DCA and became a member of GANYC. He was mentored by Justin Ferate, who introduced him to the programming director of the MAS. A personal connection with Reverend Koopercamp provided access to the church as well as a short speech injected into the tour content. At the same time, a request to curate the library exhibit came from City College's chief librarian, Dean Pamela Gillespie (who had been given Eric's Manhattanville book from retired chief archivist and local resident Barbara Dunlap, whom Eric met a few years prior). He then asked Ethan Cohen, the head of the City College Architectural Center, to collaborate with students on the exhibit, bringing together previously unconnected entities within the university. In a later interview, sitting in a swanky new Italian restaurant in his neighborhood, he told me, "Without these groups there wouldn't have been a tour at all. I'd just be a guy in the street with a few really great stories to tell." Without the connections of "supporting cast members" like Koopercamp and Dunlap—even the Orthodox Jew who passed by and knew Eric's name—the tour would not have been as dynamic an experience. These groups are all tied together through Eric and his tour.

Institutions share in this embrace. A BID tourism director told me she doesn't even bother advertising their tours anymore because they are "overpopular." Someone who books guides for his cultural organization described them as a great way to provide a "public face for our institutions," saying that "tours are—and I think that every organization does this, including BIDs—a way to introduce your organization, your area, your mission to a public."[12] Robin Lynn sees tours as vitally important for the MAS because they are "inevitably the first step [for membership]" and can be a "highly effective . . . link between the public and the organization." As with the New Museum's Counter Culture tour, walking tours can be an enormously successful way to provide an interactive experience for an organization to integrate into, and introduce itself to, a target community.

Employing freelancers, however, is a mixed bag. On the one hand, these organizations do not provide benefits or job security, employing guides, according to one, "at a very small price point." On the other hand, a programmer for another cultural institution asked rhetorically, "These are freelancers, not members of our staff. How do you control the message?" An events coordinator for yet another organization expressed a negative impression of tour guides overall, even though he hires thirty to forty guides annually and believes they do a "fine job":

> If the first thing they say to me is that they are a Licensed New York City tour guide, I almost don't want them. The first thing I want is to know their knowledge: to know how much they studied, to know how articulate they are, to know they can articulate in depth. I don't want generic tours.

By keeping guides marginalized within their organization as freelancers, institutions understand that they lose some control over information, as they provide minimal training and required content. Many coordinators would agree with their colleague who stated that guides "work on about a thousand different levels for our organization, from outreach to creating group collegiality and are worth the tradeoff."

For guides, the "tradeoff" is not always clear because it may compromise their vision for a tour. Brendan FitzGerald was concerned about collaborating with the Municipal Art Society for his privately owned public space tours. They wanted to pair him up with urban scholar Jerold Kayden. The potential for giving up his decision-making on routes and content gave Brendan pause and, weighing the legitimacy of the MAS and an affiliation with a Harvard professor against autonomy over his content, he eventually decided to strike out on his own: "I thought our project was fun and interesting and I didn't want to hand it over to someone else. . . . I knew that they wanted to take a more legal route, which is fine and effective, it's just not what I wanted to do."

Bruce Kayton is an extreme example of how guides are wary of these associations, as he adamantly expresses his fears that any affiliation would compromise his content and compromise a key quality of his image as a radical. Contrasting with tours conducted by the Central Park Conservancy, and reinforcing most guides' own disposition against the large-scale urbanism described earlier, Bruce's tours are very critical of Gotham icon Robert Moses and the conservancy itself for being only interested in protecting real estate investments and ignoring the other parks in the city. To not "sell out," Bruce remains vigilant about keeping his social and organizational networks and, therefore, his content, free from influence. There is, however, contrary evidence to the notion of organizational pressure as well. On the five BID-sponsored tours I've taken, their backing was mentioned only once, as compared with cultural institutions that were always announced as affiliates.

Only a small minority wants to shirk all contact, however. Most try to use an assortment of affiliations to their advantage. And here we can see best how the life of this untidy career illustrated in the last chapter matches up with the world of informal contacts guides exist within. For Harry Matthews, juggling these relationships has actually provided him a modest safety net:

> If you can find someone to list you on their continuing education program, you send out enough press releases that you can get a tour listed in some place like *New York* magazine, or *Time Out*, or the Friday *Times*. . . . You then get people showing up, and also, once tour operators know your name, sometimes they will call you, too. . . . It has gotten to the point that I don't have to work *too* hard. Enough people know me. Calls come in.

Katia Howard saw her various alliances as key to her success. She started off on a "low level" and when she complained about only making $10 an hour, her mentor recommended she contact the MAS with an idea for a tour. From there, she was able to use that credential to land gigs with the 92nd Street YMCA, Times Square BID, and the Cooper Union's Adult Education Program. "I've worked," she says, "for all of them at one time or another."

At the interpersonal level the connections in Eric's story (and Mark Levy's Five Points tour for other guides to give him feedback) may reinforce the image of a tight-knit, conflict-free community, but it is not so black and white. This kind of social capital proves to be beneficial for some, and it depends on whom you speak with.[13] Independent guides, for example, have expressed feelings of isolation, a lack of legitimacy, and tension over competition and camaraderie. Some feel ambivalent about rivalry for clients and "turf." Eric himself only feigns shock at the notion of someone else encroaching on the tourism area he has worked hard at specializing in. Others admit they have a difficult time seeing anything more than jealous and petty self-interest because of the constant competition for these limited resources. One guide, for example, describes the field as "a disgusting, unethical, pathetic business [in which] most have no ethics." For another:

> Let me put this way. I have warm associations with many guides, who also have their important personal and professional networks. We exchange jobs as conditions permit, and share advice on making tours more successful. But all efforts to generalize or codify these networks in a unified professional association have failed. My personal diagnosis is that it's a nest of poisoned egos. We're all used to working on our own. Many of us doubt the competence of other members.

If, hypothetically, a guide receives a request for a tour he or she knows a friend focuses upon, the first guide is torn between referring that client and taking that tour for him- or herself. Is the money worth the extra work? Is it worth possibly offending a colleague? The closer the tie to a fellow guide, the more likely one will honor an area of specialty. There is a very loose code of ethics depending upon financial need, the closeness between individual guides, and intent. Jeopardizing long-term connections must therefore be balanced with self-interest. The social and even physical proximity that provides comfort and assistance is also the source of competition, conflicts of interest, and the petty gripes that occur in any workplace. This ambiguity can strain personal ties, but the benefits of associations are important, too.

The public resources of urban spaces and culture are free, but these opportunities for social capital are limited. We can see exclusivity at work with Big Onion. BOWT maintains what they call "programming partnerships" with the New York Historical Society, the Union Square BID, the Lincoln Center BID, the Downtown Alliance BID, and the Eldridge Street Project (which highlights the East Street Synagogue on a tour of the Lower East Side). These affiliations have many positive outcomes for Seth Kamil and BOWT. In exchange for running an organization's tour program, these connections deny other guides' affiliation. In addition, because these BIDs offer their tours gratis, freelancers are at a further competitive disadvantage. Even though there is nothing stopping independents from advertising and running tours at the exact same time, on the exact same historical theme, even on the same block, Big Onion's BID tours are often better attended because of their combined advertising muscle and low price point. And at the level of the BOWT guides themselves, their lack of prolonged investment in the field, low competition between each other, and common status as fellow Ph.D. students lends itself to a collegial community that borders on a blissful ignorance of the more cutthroat tourism field that circles around them. For Joyce Gold, BID tours like these "make it hard to run a competing business."

In regard to the tension between legitimacy and autonomy, many of the guides from this chapter accept the conditions of these ties as they navigate through these connections.[14] To illustrate this point in conclusion, we can look to the relationships guides have with a particular kind of organization: institutions of higher education. Eric Washington's relationship with the City College Architectural Center and library is one kind of tie, and BOWT guides' collegiate affiliation is another. On Big Onion's Web site the profiles of all listed guides have their collegiate affiliation prominently displayed in their biographic information, highlighting their advanced degrees and teaching experience to evoke their particular research and academic ethic. (It should be pointed out that, by hiring employees who are not seeking tourism as a career path, Seth Kamil further decreases competition, since few, if any, of his guides would strike out on their own.) Such affiliations play out on tour. BOWT guides will, for example, often mention they are working on a dissertation at Columbia University. But independent guides promote their own relations with schools, too. Mark Levy, for example, mentions working on a master's degree in history. Several well-established public history and tourism classes offered at Cooper Union and City College draw practicing guides, aspiring ones, and everyday folk. Guides feel that announcing their affiliations and bona fides upfront establishes some credibility and mitigates some challenges to their authority on tour.[15] It was interesting to hear someone within another organization, a BID tourism director, recognize how this added value of legitimacy could even be calculated into how he compensates his guides: "Guides might get paid from $100 to $200 for a tour," he said casually, "but they also use our name to market themselves." Guides' problem of a potential loss in autonomy must be levied against this key additional benefit.

The sum total of this tension between legitimacy and autonomy makes for at least two ironies. First, earlier discussions demonstrated how many independents sought out the freedom and autonomy of the guiding life only to still need affiliation of some sort, albeit on their own relative terms. Second, while those independent guides draw from the widest swath of social contacts and cultural capital, they are the least legitimated as compared to those who are more closely tied to a corporate entity like Big Onion, are less likely to want or need multiple personal and organizational connections, and are expected to leave the industry. These issues of competition may tarnish any community and informal labor markets in general.

Another, more individualized irony I found revolves around Justin Ferate himself, whose aforementioned centrality made him an important figure among guides and cultural institutions, elevating him to being not only the perfect candidate to write the new licensing exam, but also the primary focus of many guides' ire. The critical position that Justin plays underscores the theme of this chapter: at the center of these webs of relationships sits the guide, who ties a wide swath of different groups and institutions together. Tour guides are not like the manufacturing workers of old Chicago or anyone in the more formal economy. Unlike docents or bus tour guides who are strongly attached to, even dependent on, organizations like the museums or bus tour companies that dictate their working conditions, guides are similar to many informal cultural workers who have to negotiate working relationships on their own accord. Every relationship appears to change over time and is based upon associations with other individuals and institutions. The legitimating factors in one tie, as we have seen, may preclude one relationship or solidify another. For the majority of guides these connections are not hierarchically organized and not routinized. Rather, they are the results of innovation and constant supervision on the part of the guide. Substantively, it makes sense that we now, finally, turn to the construction of the walking tour itself. The irony of Justin's at-times-embattled yet central position is only one aspect to his character. As such, his background and a walking tour of Grand Central Terminal are highlighted in the following chapter, as we move from the struggles to craft a guiding career and the relationships that guides have to do their work to the work itself.

Shticks of the Trade

4

"We Change Our Environment"

I met with Justin Ferate at a diner just a few blocks from Grand Central Terminal. Over coffee, we covered just two of the forty questions I had planned to ask. Justin's background is less "New York" than I presumed: Justin was actually born in Port Orchard, Washington, a small logging town. It was while earning his bachelor's degree in education at Antioch College in Ohio that he began giving tours as a hobby, and when he moved to New York in 1978 his interest in guiding grew. He came across Gerard Wolfe's *New York: A Guide to the Metropolis*, called Wolfe to tell him how much he appreciated the book, and accepted an invitation to join a tour. Justin was hooked. Ever since, he has worked in just about every capacity within the tourism industry. In his twenty-plus years of giving tours, Justin has served as the director of adult education at Cooper Union and the director of tour services for Gray Line Bus Tours, mentored dozens of guides, given tours for the MAS and several BIDs, and was the sole author of the 2003 licensing exam. In his city hall testimony, Justin described his outlook from a prepared statement:

I believe in education and in professionalism in guiding. For years, I have demonstrated a commitment to education. My goal in writing the exam was to elevate the professionalism of the tour guiding industry. I *must* say that I am proud to have created the new Comprehensive Licensing Examination. I am passionate in my love for New York. I believe that writing this examination was one of my most important personal contributions both to New York and to the industry.

In the café he explained how his disposition affects his tour interactions:

I try to physically involve people in the tour. I will use people as part of my demonstration. Now occasionally that will backfire. . . . It's just silly. I'll do some shtick. It's pure shtick. I'll talk about the building, the shape, I make them all look at the top of the building. I'll say, "Chin up, chin up." [Then] I'll start pushing on them, how the building physically changes them, and discuss how our environment changes us, while we change our environment.

But what Justin halfheartedly devalues as "pure shtick" is, in fact, deeply tied to using interactions for education, place-making, and group cohesion. They allow tourists to discover stories, unknown tidbits, hidden urban treasures, and amusing anecdotes. These elements provide the vital, unique, almost whimsical parts of the tour. The expectations are quite different from a conventional learning exercise. "A walking tour does not necessarily have a coherent beginning, middle, and end," Eric Washington explains, "and there is overlap, and there are gaps." From stop to stop, a tour can weave together wildly different topics and historical epochs; if it was a lecture, the disconnections would cause concern, but the tour provides coherence through the walking guide's shtick and the tour experience itself.

To understand how Justin Ferate and his colleagues bring their content together and share it, this chapter examines the early stages of preparation, explores how a tour evolves into a series of *in situ* guiding strategies and exchanges, and finally discusses how experience plays a key role in the process. This discussion further develops what has been covered in previous chapters on the careers and relations guides have and how that shapes the tour, and in so doing, this chapter fleshes out yet another of the key tensions introduced earlier: There are differences between guides in how tours are put together and how they are told, some of whom are academically trained while others are autodidacts. Justin is an excellent embodiment of these processes. He is a seasoned and reflective autodidact who provides some of the best examples of shtick in the business.

A Blur of Information (Grand Central Terminal Tour, June 2003)

In the public plaza of the recently renamed Philip Morris Building on 42nd Street and Park Avenue, about forty people wait for the guide. As I find a seat on a nearby bench, I overhear accents from the American South and Germany. The Grand Central Partnership BID sponsors this free tour every Friday at 12:30. At 12:31, our guide enters through the doors and smiles at the security guard. Justin Ferate is stately, looking younger and more vital than his fifty-three years. He has a trim mustache, a thin herringbone bowtie, and a small black tote with books sticking out of the top.

To begin his tour of Grand Central Terminal, Justin says, "Gather 'round, gather 'round." Then, begging us to get nearer, "Come closer." He beckons us further, and our group finally forms a tight arc around him. He asks, "Where y'all from?" spending a few careful minutes learning about his clientele. At every third or fourth person, he asks a follow-up question: "You're from New Jersey? The *whole state*? What *part* of New Jersey are you from?" When he recognizes a little discomfort from a German, looking sheepish after self-identifying as a tourist, Justin says that no one should worry if he or she is from elsewhere. "I tell all my groups that it takes three hours to become a New Yorker"—a span that happens to match the length of the tour.

Justin then churns out a dizzying blur of information. Within fifteen minutes, he weaves together a patchwork of urban ephemera in his dandyish elocution: The station was the hub of Cornelius Vanderbilt's consolidated railroad empire; before the establishment of Standard Railway Time in 1883, a man traveling between New York and Pittsburgh had to change his pocket watch thirty-six times because of the lack of a standardized time system; pulling pictures of the dirty, smoke-stained rail yards north of the terminal from his tote, he talks about how they were covered by the soon-to-be-elite Park Avenue; he says, "Fifth Avenue is an American street—it is where we prove that some are more equal than others," and adds that Cole Porter said Park Avenue is "where bad women walk *great* dogs."

Moving us out from the air-conditioning into the hot June sun, Justin yells over the 42nd Street traffic, holding his own against the current of pedestrians on their lunch break, and continues to address the group. He turns our attention to the characteristics of the building that is the focus of the tour. First, he addresses the name— "Grand Central is a *terminal*, not a *station*" —and explains that this common misconception can be traced back to the introduction of an old radio show that declared that "Station" sounded much better on-air. Then he takes on the building's most prominent feature: *Transport*, Jules-Alexis Coutan's sculpture that sits atop the building's façade. Mimicking the artwork, Justin molds a woman's arms around to mirror Athena's pose— calling her "The Kitty Kelly of the Ancient World"—to evince the importance of columns in beaux-arts architecture ("It's spelled B-E-A-U-X-A-R-T-S"). He lines us up into two rows and has two volunteers walk between us, waving, to show how architect Whitney Warren wanted buildings with huge columns because walking through a grand colonnade makes people feel more important. Some people giggle, some move to the back of the group. "Now, why are sculptures like *Transport* placed high?" and he answers his own question: "Because when you raise your chin up your chest opens, and your lungs get more oxygen, so the body feels good." Each exercise details the architectural style but also underscores the architect's intended effects, as the spaces viscerally draw in the visitor.

We cross the street, finally, and Justin stops us again outside the terminal's narrow, unadorned main entrance doors to spend a moment poking fun of Walt Disney. "There is no evidence," he tells us, "that Disney was ever caught reading a book." He asks what color Alice's hair was in Lewis Carroll's book. When someone guesses blonde, he pulls out an illustration to show that her hair was, in fact, short and brown. Clucking his tongue, he declares, "See? He didn't even look at the pictures!" But here, at the entrance, Mr. Ferate points out how plain the entry is. Right before we go through the dull wood doors, he tells us, "Real life rabbit holes are actually quite boring." And in we go, down into another world.

Routemaking

This fieldnote evinces just how Justin positions his clients' bodies, but also how he refashions the group into a kind of community of learning via a series of storytelling devices, physical activities, and an extended set of introductions and questions. The subtle practice of explicating the key characteristics of beaux-arts design through interactions illustrates how guiding is a special enterprise, facilitating exchanges between participants and the city itself, but these actions are hardly born in the street. They are crafted over time, through a lay version of what Mitchell Duneier valorized as a "shoe-leather" method of knocking on doors and talking to everyday folk (2004), and more traditional research. They are rooted in a set of practices, described below.

Selecting Themes and Neighborhoods

For activist-guide Brendan FitzGerald, "you need to have a perspective on the city." He explains his angle: "I look at it and I see zoning laws, and I really want to lend some of that to people. I'd love people to *see* this space. I'd love people to look at it and know how a building might be zoned." In this case, his perspective provided the first germ of an idea for privately owned public space tours and (evident in chapter 7's fieldnotes) a critical analysis of zoning patterns, searching for a place on the map. When he found the largest geographic concentration of cases in Midtown Manhattan, his theme had its match. Why offer a tour of the Jewish history of Midtown, for another example, when the Lower East Side has so many knish shops, delis, and old synagogues? Other guides may begin with a neighborhood and then pick a specific theme as a way to edit down all the possible content into a manageable set of ideas and locations. Conversely, well-trodden areas like Greenwich Village and Times Square might be attractive, but they are crowded with other guides and might be *too* well known. In those situations, a guide might have to distinguish him- or herself with either a unique twist on a familiar theme (e.g., instead of "Harlem" focusing on "hidden" Manhattanville, or performing out a historical character), or provide unique access (e.g., an "inside look" at the theaters). Furthermore, one's politics also require some conciliation. Bill Brown's and Brendan's political perspectives, for example, trump their interest in profit to the point of offering their tours—on surveillance cameras and privately owned public spaces, respectively—for free.

The guide is not merely debating these choices in a marketplace of ideas: The majority of guides need to make these decisions to attract clientele in order to make money. Independent guide Joyce Gold stated that no matter how passionate she is about a particular topic or area, or how great the idea may be, "if you don't take it on the first time, and nobody else does, I'll never give it again." Having more financial and organizational security, a cultural institution has greater latitude when it comes to these choices. MAS director Robin Lynn told me, "I don't want to just take Central Park. I don't want to do the East River. I don't want to just do the Upper East Side. Everyone thinks tours are a [pure] profit center. . . . It's simply not the case when you are offering [tours of the marginalized, impoverished neighborhood of] East New York." She continued: "Art deco, Midtown tours are always a sure thing. Anything with light and sound usually gets an audience. [Brooklyn] tours of the conversion of vacant buildings to sustained buildings? . . . That is a money-loser right off the bat." The balance is, therefore, crucial. On the one hand, a counterintuitive idea may differentiate the tour and attract participants, but on the other, it could just as easily be too strange to gain interest. Such choices are also mutable: Speaking with Robin a few years later, she told me that Brooklyn tours are "hot."

Kinds of Research

No guide I've interviewed said that he or she has given a tour without needing to do research beforehand, and company guides have several large advantages going for them in this regard. The academically trained Big Onion guides, for example, are free from the demands of business and planning aspects of the trade. Seth Kamil provides 20–25 single-spaced pages of data—enough for eight hours of content—for his tour guides to work from. Seth feels that his guides "don't learn *routes*, they learn *neighborhoods*," and they adapt or alter their tours as they see fit. One told me that the information they're given is helpful at the start, but there are more practical considerations as well: "it is always useful to get an idea of where to stop, and a rough idea of a path." And, as aspiring scholars, their other work helps. According to Jeffrey Trask, "If I learned something new from my own research, it goes in."

Autodidactic guides collect information in a different fashion. Their "jack-of-all-trades" and "aggressive generalist" tendencies lead to a panoply of research techniques: In addition to more traditional historical and archival research, they are more likely to amble through a neighborhood talking to locals in the street. Because of this, some material comes from heresy and casual interactions. Mark Shulman explained with embarrassment how a particular bit of information made its way into a tour:

> I saw a picture in a newspaper, a free city newspaper, of the space south of Madison Square Park, next to the Flatiron Building, and there was a second Flatiron Building that somebody had superimposed on it. And they said that, "Prior to a fire in one of the Flatiron Buildings." And there was a pair of them, and now there is an ugly apartment building on the site. Somebody with twenty minutes of Photoshop made me into an *idiot* for a year and a half repeating a completely inaccurate comment.

Similarly, Eric Washington talked about using information he heard from a friend, but that he would use it depending upon "how credible it sounds [laughs] and the person who tells it." Overall, however, Eric privileges primary sources, and likes to say, "I am a lay historian, but that doesn't mean that I'm an easy lay historian."

If a guide shares Eric's passion for primary sources, there are plenty of cultural repositories for guides to choose from (e.g., Brooklyn Historical Society, the New York Public Library, the Municipal Archives, the Museum of the City of New York). When I ask which books they use for their content, both academic and autodidact guides list Irving Howe's *The World of Our Fathers*, Luc Sante's *Low Life*, Herbert Asbury's *The Gangs of New York*, George Chauncey's *Gay New York*, Christine Stansell's *American Moderns*, Burrow and Wallace's hefty *Gotham*, *The American Institute of Architects' Guide to New York City*, and the *WPA Guide to New York City* most frequently. Autodidacts will also cite tour-oriented books like the Pressentin Wright's *Blue Guide New York*, and three books penned by walking guides: Wolfe's *New York: 15 Walking Tours* and *New York: A Guide to the Metropolis* and Joyce Gold's *From Trout Streams to Bohemia*.

Autodidact Katia Howard describes how she hits the streets more than the books: "I like to start on a very narrow focus, on food, and then open the neighborhood up based on seeing who the merchants are, seeing the various emporia that have to do with food. And so, food is the departure point." After she knows her topic—which resonated with her passion as a foodie—she starts walking. She shared one particular development of a tour with me:

> I chose Ninth Ave. I walked up and down from 40th Street to 57th and ate at a number—many, many, many—restaurants. Chit-chatted with the proprietors, bought a lot of olives, bought a lot of bread. And isolated the merchants that I wanted to deal with, based on quality of merchandise, personalities, and their willingness, and also the ethnic diversity. So that is one layer. And then I needed to know more about the history so I went to a bookshop in Rockefeller Center, I asked their advice, bought the books. I reference it. I went to the community board, went to the school board, I went to a church to find out the history of the religious institutions, and I let it fly!

Similarly, when I asked two guides who run a "Literary Walking Tour and Pub Crawl" about how they research their tour content, they tell me they "get information from history books, but mostly from interviewing the bar owners themselves." Brendan FitzGerald exhibits an almost guerrilla-style approach to his research. He described for me one of his first tours, with only two women participating, wherein one of them was offered and accepted a free makeover in a space he wanted to know more about. It allowed him the opportunity to conduct a seemingly innocuous interview posing as a curious boyfriend.

Such street-level investigations are much less common among more academic and historical guides, but it has less to do with BOWT guides being inherently more scholarly and more to do with their corporatized structure, focus on history, and overarching career paths. Autodidacts, on the other hand, have a more diverse palette of topics and methods, and are more inclined to knock on doors and "sniff things out," as one described it.

Plotting the Tour

In her quirky travelogue of the places and history of murdered U.S. presidents and their assassins, essayist Sarah Vowell writes that "every pilgrimage needs a destination" (2005, 15), but they need their proper beginnings and intermediate stops, too. Seth Kamil has a clear rule of thumb where his Big Onion tours should begin. He told me, "I think that the biggest mistake that my competitors make—they don't start at subways. I'm sorry, but people have to be able to *get to you*." Access, however, is not every guide's concern. Autodidact Alfred Pommer describes his way of thinking through a specific theme to identify a starting point for one of his tours. Back in the mid-1990s he was commissioned for a gargoyle tour, to be a part of a promotional prize vacation for a television cartoon about superhero gargoyles. The theme was given to him but the neighborhood and the structure of the tour were not. With the entire city to choose from, it took a while for him to settle on the New York Life Insurance Company Building as the beginning:

> It has 60 gargoyles on it, and is a site of New York City folklore. [It's] where the second Madison Square Garden was built. It's the one that Stanford White built, and he had his house there, he was shot and killed by a jealous husband. Of course, I have a picture of Stanford, and [his mistress] Evelyn Nesbitt, the world's most beautiful woman, and do the whole spiel.

It was a good balance: "Great gargoyles, but it has that great story so that's a perfect place to start."

From there, Alfred had to find his way. He hit the pavement with the *AIA Guide to New York City* in hand. "I walked around," he told me, "and that book usually leads me from one spot to another." Similarly, another guide reports:

You walk around the neighborhood; you get a feel for what's going on. You get a feel for what could be historically significant buildings. You plot on a map those buildings, your parks, your landmark plaques. You plot the buildings that you want to get more information on. You outline the landmark district. Once you start plotting that, you start to also simultaneously do reading about the history of the neighborhood.

Joyce Gold begins planning her tours by leafing through a library of materials she has built for over twenty-five years. "I spend lots of hours every weekend, just getting these files in case I ever needed them." To start an idea for a tour, she says, "I'll go through my files and books, and run it through me, what stands out, what would I like to see, what I would like to see more of."

Guides craft a kind of "through line," so narrative becomes crucial. As one guide said, "My tours evolve like a plot novel, rather than a character novel. They are governed by the [streets]." Harry Matthews, who gives tours of an upper-class neighborhood in Brooklyn, explains how geography and history provide his storyline:

I like to start at the north end of [Brooklyn] Heights—the oldest part—to give some historical background, and also to show the least spectacular sights, and you can actually show people buildings later on. . . . It is a good place to set a certain amount of historical perspective, you know, how the neighborhood grew up, the relationship to the waterfront, which has now been cut off.

Jeffrey Trask's "Before Stonewall" Big Onion tour is plotted deliberately, and it is something that he explains to the tour group. From my fieldnotes:

After our fourth stop, on MacDougal Street, Jeffrey tells the group, "I want to let you know that the geography of this tour mirrors the chronology of how gay culture in New York moved through the Village—from its early beginnings at Bleeker, up MacDougal—where bohemians settled at the turn of the century holding and challenging new categories of sexual identity—to here on Eighth Street, which would become the gay and lesbian drag, to Christopher Street and the conclusion of our tour at Stonewall." The group emits an audible "Oh" sound of appreciation for the tip. There are nods, and the man next to me says "Wow, that's great," to his wife as we all walk up MacDougal.

Once a guide has the dominant theme fleshed out and has a good sense of the narrative, he or she may then bring in a little variety. According to Harry Matthews: "You try to get a mix, I mean, there are some sites that are architecturally interesting [but also offer] lots of anecdotes. 'This is the house where Marilyn Monroe and Arthur Miller lived when they were married.'" After participating in a tour on the Jewish history of the East Village, I asked the guide to talk about why she mentioned a methadone clinic on Avenue A—something tangential to her overarching theme. She told me it was a way to talk about the drug culture of the neighborhood today, but it was also located on an otherwise less-exciting stretch between two main points on her tour: Katz's Deli on Houston Street (mentioned as the location of the famous faux-orgasm scene in *When Harry Met Sally*) and Tompkins Square Park (mentioned as the location of a brutal riot between the police and the homeless in 1988). She added, "it's good to mix it up." After a tour of Greenwich Village, I asked another guide about her process:

> You figure, "Well, I'll go across Eighth Street, and take them to Christopher to Eighth Street, and then I've got to get from Eighth Street to Fifth Avenue to go down." All of the sudden you go, "Well, Eighth Street, what's there?" You then have the Electric Lady recording studio where Jimi Hendrix recorded, and the first Whitney Museum. You fill in the blanks.

Those "blanks" are of interest. The physicality of the tour shapes the content not just by what can be included, but also by what is *not* proximate. Even in a place as historically rich as New York, pertinent information will rarely be found in contiguous spaces and, unlike those dark decades in history books that get skipped over to arrive at the next event, there are blocks that serve as something of a potentially dead narrative space, obliging guides to discover and redefine their main points of interest. "You try to look for interesting sites that are in geographic proximity so that you don't have to do a lot of walking." This is where broader content may come in, such as when guides offer the history of Harlem or gentrification in SoHo, the explication of Brooklyn Heights' fruit themed street names, like Pineapple Street and Orange Street (a pre–Civil War family feud where the result was that only the Middagh family name remains on the area's signs), or to describe the origins of Manhattan's orthogonal street grid. When I asked an academic guide about such considerations, he shared his own emphasis:

> That's where you have nonspecific historic information that you do research on and develop. Migration of Polish immigrants to America, how, why, why

here? Okay, we're getting closer to the waterfront. I need filler. Okay, let's start talking about the history of the waterfront and building of iron-clads. So in-between you combine site-specific history and neighborhood history that is not site-specific. And you weave them together, so that you are never walking a block or two blocks without stopping.

The physicality of the neighborhood itself also demonstrates what may be edited out of the story because it might be a few blocks out of the way. The potential weakness of the walking tour experience—the determinants of space and time—can be transformed through the insertion of tangential information into content that reinforces a secondary tour theme, presents a larger frame of meaning, or provides variety.

Feeling Out the Space (Grand Central Terminal Tour, May 2003)

Inside Grand Central, Justin is in his element. "Beaux-arts was always about more than the practical." After going through the entrance and down an incline, Justin stops us to talk about how the architecture is designed to affect how the traveler feels. "Don't you feel your heart racing?" He tells us there used to be two consecutive sets of doors placed only ten feet apart right here, laid out in this fashion for two different reasons—temperature control and regulating bodily movement—as a kind of "experiential pacing." Visitors, he told us, would be distracted with having to negotiate the doors but then be surprised at the majesty of the room once they reached the other side. To simulate the lost effect, Justin shuffles in before us, sticks out his arms, and makes us bump through one by one. The group giggles, as he yells out: "The doors are the wrapping for the Christmas present of the interior!"

Making our way into the grand space of the terminal, Justin stops again and says, "Come on in." Sticking his chin out, he demonstrates how the ramp arches our backs so that we can easily see the famous Zodiac ceiling mural. He talks about how the pattern of stars are oddly reversed from how we would see them gazing up at the sky. He ventures to guess that it was either a terrible mistake, or that it was designed so that the viewer could experience them "from a God's-eye view."

He then races off into the crowd, hopping between couples and commuters and circling back to us to demonstrate the careful mass-ballet that occurs every minute. We head over to an overpass, where we look down on commuters rushing off to their trains. Justin invites us to wave. A few rather sheepishly wave until someone enthusiastically returns the gesture. "See? You've made someone's day, and they've made yours. Grand Central is calculated to be all about social interaction."

We head downstairs to the concourse level, with its shops, food kiosks, waiting chairs, schedules, and ramps to the train platforms. Justin walks down to an empty platform and asks us why it was designed with a ramp rather than stairs. As a prod, Justin says, "It's not because they had rolling suitcases or the Americans with Disabilities Act." When no one guesses, he performs a slow-motion run up the ramp to show how it prevents commuters from bolting onto the concourse, thus controlling the speed of foot traffic as they enter the larger space.

Checking his watch, he brings us to a favorite stop: the Junior's Restaurant dessert case in the food court. Huddled up against the Plexiglas, he teaches us two important lessons. The first is how to pick out good cheesecake. We're told that a real one has no graham cracker crust, nor "that schmutz," gesturing toward a lesser variety with strawberries on top of it. For the second lesson, he turns serious: "If you are going to be a New Yorker, you have to learn the second official language of New York City. Anyone? Yiddish."

Last, we head over to the famous "whispering gallery." Located directly below the railing where we waved at people, the alcove's ceramic ceiling is designed upon the structural principles of an egg, and is without steel reinforcement. Justin gets four volunteers and sends them into the corners, telling them that, due to its geometry, if you put your nose up to the tiles, your whisper carries over your head, along the vaulted arch ceiling, and to the person thirty feet behind you. A former girlfriend once showed me this place and told me Charles Mingus brought his girlfriend here and whispered quietly, "Will you marry me?" I stand aside to let everyone have a chance, but Justin tells me, "I know you've done it a million times, Jonathan, but you have to play with everybody else," and escorts me to the corner by my elbow.

Eight Storytelling Tricks

The research, plotting, and preparation are all designed to present content to a tour group, and while there are a few guides who are not as adept at this, or desirous of interactions (e.g., as one told his group, "We're going to have to curb the questions, since there are too many of you"), it is at the junction of exposition and communication where walking tours truly take form, breathing life into inert historical and cultural information with social interaction. Guides often contemplate how effective their storytelling tricks are, how one is a favorite, or how they have honed, stolen, or augmented a trick.

Urban ethnographies have often highlighted the particular strategies their subjects use to interact with their clients or audiences. Howard Becker, for example, examines the jazz musician's relationship with the crowd (1951), and Fred Davis details the strategies by which cab drivers cull tips from their patrons (1959, 161–62). Guides use strategies as well, depending on the context, the group, and even their own moods. Earlier, Justin was quoted using the term *shtick*—albeit with a little disparagement—but such phrasing is common. The term, of course, is Yiddish—Justin's "second language of New York"—and holds two relevant definitions: often translated as a sort of whimsical trick, it also implies the strategic usage of "pieces" of speech. This second component is analogous with the "bits" comedians use as various components of a stage act. To say "tricks" is not to be pejorative in the context of this book either. It is analogous to Becker's use of the term, as they are "ways of interfering with the comfortable thought routines . . . ways to turn things around, to see things differently, in order to create new problems" (1998, 6-7).[1] With these connotations we can examine the particular *narrative tools* (as compared with career strategies) used by guides. The following are eight such tricks—gleaned from observation, elaborated upon in interviews, and inspired by Becker's book on the tricks of academic research—deployed for a variety of reasons: to evoke emotions, pique curiosity, foster group solidarity, to "break frame" in a Goffmanian sense, establish one's own authority, ground historical content in personal experiences and places, and to elicit discussion. Put plainly, a guide told me, "It's the shtick that draws them into a world." Justin demonstrates a few of the particular tactics guides use to engage with people in public spaces, and they should be catalogued in greater detail here.

Trick 1: The "Perfect Tour Guiding Moment"

Particular stories can define a culture, a city, and therefore, a tour. These moments are ideal in simplicity yet speak beyond the particulars. Guides relish tales that illustrate multiple layers, perhaps of architecture, history, political action, cultural change, or ethnic diversity. On a tour of Lower Manhattan, our Big Onion guide Jennifer Fronc brought us around to the unadorned, plain back wall of City Hall, near the old Tweed Courthouse. From my fieldnotes:

She explains that the northern wall was faced with brownstone rather than marble when it was dedicated, "either because of a failure on the parts of the architects to forecast the city's growth further north, or as a way to cut costs

due to a labor dispute." Because the building was completed in the same year
as the establishment of the grid street system, Jennifer tells the group, "you
have to wonder what the reasoning was."

She uses this single wall—without knowing the exact historical reasons behind the unusual choices in siding the building—to talk about labor history,
the processes of sprawl, and population migration. When I asked Jennifer's
colleague, Erik Goldner, about these tricks, he nodded in appreciation. He
called it a "perfect tour guiding moment" and instantly volunteered his own,
from a tour of Washington Square I had observed a few weeks earlier. At 85
West Third Street, he talked about how New York University razed the house
where Poe wrote "The Fall of the House of Usher" as a way to elaborate on
the heavy-handed real estate aspirations of the university and its tussles with
neighborhood activists. He went on to discuss how NYU nearly tore down
another Poe residence in order to build its new student center, joking that
these events must be manifestations of the school's feelings on nineteenth-
century antitranscendentalism. Erik stands on the element that serves as an
overarching metaphor for another of his tours:

> I have my own little story that I can tell them with an overarching metanar-
> rative, which is just my own thing. Other people could do something totally
> different. But a story for me is [that] when the Brooklyn Bridge was being
> built there were two cities. Brooklyn had a certain urban vision. Brooklyn
> was founded on an urban vision called "the American City": trees, parks,
> wide streets, and churches. American, Protestant, prosperous middle class,
> right? And they looked across the river and they saw New York: Tammany,
> immigrants, corruption. And the bridge as going to connect these two very,
> very different cities and ultimately form this cosmopolitan—both American
> and somehow not American—city.

Touching on broad themes while simultaneously being dramatic and heuristic, these stories provide resonant meaning and ground the guides' vision of
the social order. A walking tour will often include several elements that are
difficult to wrangle into one coherent narrative, and these elements offer a
kind of synecdoche: guides will offer some part of tour—an urban form or
anecdote—that works as an overarching theme for the whole experience.
Through this trick the audience is given something to grasp onto, as the
guide marries an idea with an image.

Trick 2: The Twist

When I asked about his use of Disney's misrepresentation of Lewis Carroll's Alice and the curious reversal of the Zodiac, Justin said it is one of his best strategies to prod curiosity: "I try to twist people." He sees turning a tourist's perspective as central to his work, saying, "I believe in taking an idea and turning it at a right angle into something totally different. And I do this based on what people know. I start with the familiar and then get into the weirdness, leading to unfamiliarity." On the Grand Central tour, for example, Justin nudges the audience with his stories, feeding off startled looks and puzzled expressions, quickly asking them what they think. By starting with the common conceptions of their participants, guides are able to elicit discussion from the group. "Why," Justin will ask, "does that strike you as odd?"

Andy Sydor uses this tactic, too, explaining on tour about how his research has led him to believe that the story about Dylan Thomas having eighteen straight whiskies at the White Horse Tavern is possibly fiction and that Hell's Kitchen derived its name from Davy Crockett. Joyce Gold uses the tag line of "There are 20,000 people buried in Washington Square Park" on her brochure. Similarly Martin Scorsese's *Gangs of New York* is an enticing foil. Mark Levy uses it without much critique, but it was soundly debunked on Seth Kamil's walking tour wherein he talks about how the two riots in the beginning of the movie were only four years apart "but that didn't work for the plot," that the Chinese were victims of gross stereotyping, and even that the cutlery in the film was historically inaccurate. Such expositions are used to tweak the familiar into something a little more strange, or to demythologize and debunk commonly held beliefs in an effort to make participants feel clued in, as well as to elevate the guides' own stature. The twist fits well with guides' overarching desire to flip expectations, privilege unconventional phenomena, and offer counterintuitive perspectives.

Trick 3: Evocation

From EPCOT to Colonial Williamsburg to western ghost towns, touristic experiences are often seen as fabricated schlock, where venues are more like stages and where actors play out scripts, but "reenactment"-style simulations in walking tourism (e.g., dressing up as Lincoln, or in Mark Levy's case, Bill O'Toole) are less common.[2] When asked about more touristic experiences, Justin cites a truly Chuck Connors–level ruse:

I know a tour broker who arranged to have a bus held up. This just played right into everyone's fears. I don't know the end result, but I was flabbergasted. This woman, this high-end [tour broker said], "Yeah, and we're going to have this person pull them off on the expressway . . ." and I say, "You're going to do what? What are you thinking?" Totally crazed.

Beyond the pale for most guides, this elaborate event contrasts with more common and subtler approaches to evocation. As evidenced in his tour, Justin physically involves people, molding them into columns and weaving them through pedestrians in a conga-line. Other guides oscillate in and out of character as Mark Levy does, and the two actors who give the Literary Walking Tour and Pub Crawls. From a fieldnote:

Our guides brought us to Chumley's. We squeeze between the diners and rowdy revelers of the dark woodpaneled bar. One guide tells us about how the term "86"—restaurant lingo for an item that is not available, but also meaning to kick someone out—originated here. "During Prohibition the bartender would have a clear view to the courtyard—as he points from the bar to the doorway—and when he would see the police come in, he would yell out, '86 Everybody!' and people would file out the side door, which was over there, and out to 86 Bedford Street."

Continuing on, we learn how, during Prohibition, you could order "Kentucky" or "Irish tea" to get your favorite bourbon or whiskey in a teacup. He then calls our attention to the ribbon of old dust jackets circumscribing the space. Mead, Ginsberg, Kerouac, Fitzgerald, Miller, Mailer, Dreiser, Faulkner, Nin, Steinbeck. Tough to pick only one of those who alit these barstools, they chose Steinbeck, perhaps because the guides' phenotypes lend themselves to *Of Mice and Men*.

Our guides stand on a raised platform, clear their throats, and with a bow of their heads they indicate a scene is to begin. They launch into the part wherein George discovers that his fellow farmhand, Lennie, is carrying a dead mouse in his pocket as a pet:

"What'd you take outta that pocket?"

"Ain't a thing in my pocket," says the bigger, more dim of the two.

"I know there ain't. You got it in your hand. What you got in your hand— hidin' it?" The smaller one takes a step closer.

"I ain't got nothin', George. Honest." He turns away from the group.

As the guide-actors run though their lines, a slightly amused busboy nudges between the two with orders of cheeseburgers and fries. 'Lennie' tries not to break character, but 'George' smiles mid-line. Once the scene is completed the whole room claps—patrons and tour participants alike—and someone yells out from the back, "Can you do *Who's Afraid of Virginia Woolf*?"

Few scholastic guides would use this level of theatrics but those like Justin and Mark Levy would agree that there is a pedagogical purpose in balancing make-believe and real life to educate and entertain through physical experience. Evocation is an effort to bring added sensation, a crafting of a scene in order to better "place" the information and stories guides provide to their audiences. It is also to "create a scene" in the sense of providing a spectacle to better draw attention to the tour. Just as the Levy family passed around flyers to the people who were drawn to the Becky the Hot Corn Girl stunt on their Five Points tour, the Pub Crawl guides were, in fact, happy to advertise their theater, and their tours, to the people who approached them after their evocation of Steinbeck.

Trick 4: The Joke

A few guides claim to be adamantly uninterested in being funny, and are successful at it, but most have standard jokes they feel are essential components of their work (e.g., "Yes. Historic neighborhood, historic jokes"). On a tour of the foliage of Central Park, Wildman Steve Brill seems to have a pun for every genus; after picking up a sprig of sheep's sorrel, he chews it and says, "It's not baaaaad." "The trick is in keeping it fresh," says one guide, although repeating a joke can even make for a good gag too. On Darryl Reilly's Times Square theater tour there were plenty of jokes:

Outside the Walter Kerr Theater, Darryl fleshes out the character and style of the playwright and critic the building is named after. "For a review of *Star-Spangled Girl*, Kerr wrote, 'Neil Simon didn't have a good idea for a play this season, but he wrote one anyway.'" He then leans into the person next to him and repeats it for effect: "He wrote one anyway." He then begins talking about all the famous plays that have been at the theater.

After the tour Darryl spoke about how being both an aspiring actor and a student of vaudevillian banter shapes his craft: He uses jokes as a strategy for directing his shtick onto the next topic, just as the miscellany of a vaudeville

show would require humorous transitions from bit to otherwise disconnected bit.

Like other tricks, the joke serves to make transitions in the narrative, but
also to shape the tone of the tour. Take Jane Marx, for example. She describes herself as "theatrical by nature" and puffed up in faux-indignation
when asked about jokes. Dramatically accentuating her rebuke with a hand
to her chest, she said: "Have you ever heard of Dorothy Parker? Oscar Wilde?
Did they tell *jokes*? No, darling, they had *wit*. A joke can be anything. Wit has
context. It has *intellect*. Don't call it a joke—it demeans my humor. Put that
as a footnote." Spoken with obvious flair, her words reveal how she sees her
work as creative and purposeful, not mechanical: Stock lines are about not
interaction, whereas "wit" is. This was on display in a Harlem tour, as she
worked her group of African American high school kids from Tuscaloosa,
Alabama:

There are a few blocks without too much to see, and when Jane recognizes
lethargy among the kids, she spins around like a top for a little improvisation. She asks the students to describe how they feel about their own homes,
and how they think New Yorkers might live differently.

"We have more space."

"Yeah, these look like they have real small rooms."

"We're spread out."

"They're stacked on top of each other here."

She then asks them about the issues of public and private space: "What is
your plot of land look like in Alabama?" The students get more nervous, and
give halted, one-word answers:

"Big."

"Grass."

Listening carefully, Jane gets the group to compare the two experiences
and draws out their perspectives on the large-scale housing projects that
we've seen on the trip to talk about modernization and housing policy. She
then points to the 10×10 patch of green-brown between the sidewalk and the
brownstone in front of us. "What's this?" The students look back at her, quiet
but smiling. "Now, you being from Alabama, you know what a yard is, right?
This here is the best lawn most New Yorkers can ever dream of. It's not much,
I know. But," she pauses to wink, "all over New York, the only grass we own is
in little plastic bags kept in the freezer. *All right*. Next!" And she quickly turns
to lead us to the next stop.

For guides a good joke is rarely simple. In this case, her allusion to marijuana gets a laugh, but it also serves as the symbolic end of a topic. As autodidactic guide Andy Sydor uses it, the joke layers in additional meaning, too:

> You are sugarcoating people's education. . . . You try to make them informative jokes. You know? I mean, it's like this line that I do about Ladies' Mile: it was the only place in the old days where a woman could walk unescorted. Now, I could go into an explanation of what that meant, in that usually, when a woman went around unescorted, she was a prostitute. But I just throw in a line "Well, there were places where a woman could walk unescorted, down by the docks, but that doesn't matter." So, that's a joke, it gets a laugh, but also it explains to them what it meant to walk unescorted. . . . You're working with less time, so you kinda come up with a way to hit it quicker. . . . It puts the idea in their head, snuck under the radar.

Andy explains that a joke can certainly entertain, but that it can also provide a double meaning to a story without forcing the guide to take valuable time to explain the complexity.

Jokes in this context are similar to anthropologist Mary Douglas's formulation (1975): they are not irrational or emotional, but are expressions of the social structure of a particular culture and practices that reinforce group cohesion. Jokes assist in moving the walking tour's interactions from one set of topics to another, bring more than one kind of information for the group, and provide a strong interactional purpose. Additionally, Darryl's repeat of a joke, for example, fills in the dead air that can sometimes occur in a tour when a laugh *doesn't* happen, smoothing over an uncomfortable situation. In the instance of Jane's joke, a laugh line provides closure of one topic and a segue into another. And the physical space and stories of a tour might be geographically proximate but relatively disconnected from each other, prompting a common joke: the familiar Monty Python line, "and now for something completely different."

Trick 5: Juxtaposition

Evidence of disparate urban elements can also have a pedagogical purpose. Tours often have moments where a guide stops to identify contrary forces, trends, or images in a single vista. Curiously contrasting urban forms are an opportunity for questions and conversation. On a tour of Greenwich Village, for example, BOWT guide Jeffrey Trask took our group to small, crooked Gay Street and settled us across from three small buildings. He pointed out the Flemish bond bricklaying on one and the different lintels above the doorways to contrast their architectural styles, and the decades of disrepair.

Autodidacts use this trick. From a fieldnote of a Brooklyn Heights tour, Harry Matthews uses the same shtick in order to spark a dialogue with the group:

At the corner of Pierrepont and Henry Streets, Harry points out a single building to evince the stages the neighborhood has gone through. He traces different colorations of the bricks—lines indicating stages of expansion—as if reading rings on a recently felled tree. "The building was once a mansion, was turned into a motel, which was then a brothel, then a convent, and are now being converted into luxury condos." A few blocks later, we stop at the Our Lady of Lebanon Maronite Cathedral (once the Church of the Pilgrims, founded in 1844).

"What do you notice about the name of this church?"

"Is there a big Lebanese population here?" someone asks.

"Right! No! Good. You probably wouldn't expect a strong Lebanese Catholic population in this gentrified neighborhood, and you'd be correct. The congregation commutes." He sharpens our attentions. "Above the entry we see two cedar trees, the national symbol of Lebanon, but what's odd about the images on these bronze doors?"

"There's a kinda Old World cottage," says one participant.

"Right. There aren't any of those around here. What else?"

Someone else adds, "Well, there's a freaking cruise ship," and points to another puzzling image on the doorway.

"Right! Weird, yes? These are decorative images that might not strike you as traditional Lebanese imagery. Why?" The group is certainly quiet and unsure. The disconnection is the opportunity for our guide to tell us that, when the Church of the Pilgrims vacated the building, they took the doors and Tiffany stained-glass windows with them, leaving the Lebanese church with too much of an open door policy. "Luckily, for them at least, around that time the S.S. *Normandie* burned down to the waterline at Manhattan's Pier 90 as it was being converted from a cruise liner into a World War II troop transport ship, and its salvageable parts were sold off—including these doors."

Churches are frequent foci for juxtapositions because their longevity allows for the explication of neighborhood succession, as was the case on a Chinatown tour with another guide who gets a tour member to point out that there are masses in three different languages (Cantonese, Mandarin, and English) to then explain the neighborhood's ethnic change.[3] Guides feel that drawing these associations out of curious disconnections gets participants to focus in on the world around them, giving them the impression that New York is an overlay of images and histories stacked upon each other, a confusing yet "readable" text that can be decoded together, provoking a Socratic interaction.

Trick 6: The Break

Jane Marx provides another trick on her Harlem tour. She took a break to encourage her group of high school students to explore a place on their own. From my fieldnotes:

As we weave back south down Malcolm X Boulevard, we come to the Shabazz Vendors Market. Jane looks at one of her watches and tells the group she'll return in twenty minutes, and disappears. The group spreads out to examine the carvings, necklaces, music, clothing, and paintings. I quietly pass by the closed shops and empty clothes racks, and smile meekly at the sellers who are there. Signs read: "Authentic," "Kente," and "30% off." I lag behind the packs of kids as they dart in and out of the kiosks, pointing and whispering to each other. A woman asks a solitary boy where he's from, and he answers so inaudibly that she asks again. She picks up a small carving of a wooden man to show him, and he gets a little nervous, shuffles his Nikes, and leaves. I smile as warmly as I can to make up for it, and head back to our rendezvous.

Most of the kids return early and empty-handed. Two bought matching pink and red Yankees hats. One girl didn't bother visiting the market at all, displaying a Dunkin' Donuts bag from across the street. When Jane returns, the group stood closer to her than before, acting more attentive and engaged.

As was the case in Jane's tour, periods of time and space between sites are common, and these are moments wherein the guide allows for informal interactions. As this ethnographic vignette indicates, these pauses have their purposes, and the break in the Shabbaz Market (in her words, a "fear breaker") gave Jane time think of what to do next and also reinforced the importance of the guide to the group: the kids were visibly relieved at her return.

On the Literary Tour and Pub Crawl, for another example, we stopped at several bars and paused to taste their wares. The guides spoke for a bit, but then offered plenty of time for mingling. At Chumley's I had the following encounter while ordering a beer:

I wedge myself up to the front, next to a thick and well-planted patron and order the house's own spicy Pumpkin Ale. As I wait, I jot down a few notes in my notebook, which catches his attention.

"Are you in the tour group?"

"Yeah," I say.

"Well then, welcome to New York," he says, returning to his drink.

"I live in Brooklyn, actually." I nod a thank you to the bartender.

"No shit," he says, turning back to me. "Well then, let me give you something for you to write down in your little book. Do you know why you are supposed to clink your glasses together before drinking?"

"I have absolutely no idea."

"The bartender told me this. Back when people were worried about being poisoned, they would tip their drinks to spill a little into each other's mugs. That way, you could trust that the other guy didn't poison your drink."

"So," raising my glass, "I guess we should go ahead then."

"Agreed!" And we clink our pints together. I don't know if any of my ale reached the inside of his glass, but I did notice I got some on his hand.

In these moments, I experienced dozens of interactions, from curiosity over my notetaking ("What are you doing, a book report?") to being asked out on a date. Those interactions are seen by guides to be just as much a part of the tour experience as their storytelling. Justin finds the success of these breaks to be humorous, at times, recalling that him *not talking* was just as enjoyable as when he was:

I try to do things where people feel obliged to talk. . . . My motivation is that I am *not* talking while we are in motion so that they can talk to each other. People take tours for many reasons, not all of which are my reasons. [Once] a women approached me and said, "I love your tours." I said, "Oh, thanks." She says, "Your tours are so wonderful!" I say, "Well, thank you, that's very sweet." "I met my last three boyfriends on your tours." What am I, a yenta?

There are several purposes here. Midway through Bruce Kayton's four-hour tour on radical history we took a half-hour break and separated into smaller groups to chat about the tour and rest our feet, and Brendan FitzGerald told me he uses the break because, after an hour or two, "it's nice to sit and have a coffee or to use the bathrooms." It is a practice reminiscent of Gregory Bateson's description of Balinese storytelling, wherein narrators will periodically halt their tales so listeners can ask questions, tension and interest can be heightened, and the group can engage in "irrelevant interaction" (1949, 41). By the spatial nature of the walking tour, breaks serve similar purposes: they afford participants time for contemplation, to ask the guide for details, to chat with each another, or to interact with neighborhood residents. While juxtaposition works to create more back-and-forth between the guide and the group, this trick allows for interaction among the group and the scene around them.

Trick 7: Show, Don't Tell

For guides *showing* is about performing the physical aspects of a point or concept, or grounding historical and cultural information tangibly, rather than merely stating it. The centrality of this trick exploits the experiential nature of walking tours, but it also creates an interaction "bit." Justin offers a microlevel exposition, creating an interactive experience:

In the Lincoln Building, across the street from Grand Central, Justin brings us to one of the five sculptures Daniel Chester French made to sketch out the Lincoln Memorial. He points out the copyright mark at the base. He explicates further, asking, "How would you describe his eyes?"

"Sad?" a man suggests.

"What else?"

Someone else offers, "Downward?"

Enthused, Justin continues, "Yes! This model—which is at eye level rather than towering over you as the final statue is—doesn't have the same feel that everyone attributes to the real thing." He bends down to look at it as if he were eye-level to the monument in Washington, D.C. "We perhaps mistake that Abe's eyes look out into the future, but that they are war wary, and downtrodden." The group nods. "Okay. What is he sitting on?"

"A throne? Or wait . . . I don't know," someone else suggests.

"It's just a block, not even a chair, really."

"Right. We think that it is a throne, but is it? It doesn't really look much like one, and French didn't want it to. This wasn't England. Now," he says, moving to the back, "look at the way a flag is draped on one side and a coat on the other." He turns to ask, "What do you think that means?"

This time, no one is sure. "Well, does it look like a fancy coat?" A few people shake their heads. "No. It's ordinary. It's the kind of coat you might leave in the trunk of your car. Look. The flag is hung the same way as the plain coat, to indicate that the state and the everyman are equal!" We nod and talk among ourselves, and a few bend down as Justin did.

Justin could have easily explained the symbolism but used the statue instead to tease out conversation.

In another example, the Lower East Side Tenement Museum uses a tenement building at 97 Orchard Street—built in 1863, it housed approximately 7,000 people from twenty countries in the seventy-two years it was occupied—as a kind of classroom to teach tourists about what it was like to live and work in that particular neighborhood in the late 1800s. They train their guides to use the spaces themselves as a part of the experience. From my fieldnotes of a tour:

Only a few seconds after entering the building, the guide encourages us to touch the newel post and banister of the stair. "It's pretty cool to think about all the residents who touched this. It is over 140 years old. One of the people whose hand passed by this rail was a young girl . . .

In SoHo, for a last example, Joyce Gold uses the physicality of the neighborhood's famous cast-iron facades to make her point and "make it resonate more with the group." Rather than merely talking, she brings a magnet to affix to a column, as she talks about the rise of prefabricated iron buildings, the era of light manufacturing, and the neighborhood's transformation into first an artist enclave and then today's boutique shopping district. Strategically deploying information as such connects the group, guide, and city in a visceral fashion.

Trick 8: Defuse

With most of these tricks guides attempt to spur interaction on the sidewalks. But guiding also has its share adversarial conditions as well, and guides must keep interactional tools to defuse both in-group and out-group confrontations at the ready. Despite the charm associated with walking amid the bustle of the city, the proximity of the city's crowds can create a measure of tension. Groups with a number of out-of-towners will often clog a sidewalk when they've stopped at a site, leading to confrontations. Guides can, in fact, be ticketed for blocking the sidewalk. On a two-hour tour with ten stops, I counted nine entreaties for a group to gather closer (e.g., "The more you cluster, the less I have to shout," "Get cozy," "Let's move in so people can get by"). At times, a passerby will disparage the group, sarcastically muttering, "Welcome to New York," as he or she pushes through the pack. I witnessed this sort of thing on a BOWT tour:

On the southeast corner of Washington Square Park, a bicyclist passing a tour of Greenwich Village shouts to the group: "He's lying! Don't listen to a word that he says!" It is a classic New York moment, and as such, does nothing to faze the academic guide, Jeffery Trask, who just waves to the bicyclist as he rides by. It was not too much of an affront, as it's obvious the cyclist-heckler did not hear a word of the tour. But at the same spot, only a few moments later, a large man and his wife walk directly through the group on their way along the sidewalk. Jeffery stops mid-sentence and smiles pleasantly as the couple weaves through the twenty-odd people. Once they are out of earshot, he deadpans, "I love New York." The group laughs and follows the guide as he walks further down the block. People turn to each other to smile at the interaction, and a few start to chat with one another about "New Yorkers."

Jeffery's quick and disarming quip is often deployed at such circumstances, but it is not the only way to defuse a tense moment as the tour and the pedestrian jockey for their conflicting claims on the city's physical space. These are not altogether negative experiences. The example of Jeffrey's tour demonstrates how confrontations can be defused but can also create a sense of community among participants. Adversity can, in fact, become an opportunity. On one occasion, Justin was confronted on the street and invited his critic into the discussion: "I said, 'Obviously you disagree with me. You've got a stage here, tell them why you think I'm wrong.' . . . They become part of the group, too. It allows for fallibility, and I don't pretend to be infallible." The resulting banter allowed for a different view and offered a guide like Justin the chance to brandish his expertise as well as a kind of "conversational disarmament."

Jennifer finds some participants particularly exasperating because she believes that they "try to run roughshod" over her. To combat these participants, she makes several attempts to bolster her credentials, through the legitimating frame of her institutional affiliations and career as a tour guide, with varying degrees of success: "Being a Columbia Ph.D. student is not enough, and having given tours for three years is not enough. Lying and saying that I am a native New Yorker helps a little bit." Joyce Gold describes how problematic this can be, not just because they challenge her authority, but because they interrupt her flow of the tour. Even if a participant has the best of intentions and has something positive to contribute, she is still annoyed: "It's upsetting, frankly, if people tell me stories, or give me data. For one thing, I'm never going to remember it, and for another, I'm trying to think of what I'm going to do next."

"Walking Is about Your Senses. . . . It's about Experiencing"

Collectively the use of these tricks underscores the interactive and experiential quality of the walking tour. Rising up from these examples, the physicality of being in front of these buildings and among the crowds demonstrates touring as a different kind of learning. The importance is not lost on guides or organizations that use walking tours. It is a disposition that is reminiscent of Jane Jacobs's commentary on how sidewalk interactions serve as the primary social site for creating "lively and interesting" cities; architect Francesco Careri's privileging of *experience* over brick and mortar to describe walking as "a transformation of the place and its meanings"; and William H. Whyte's love of the "hustle and bustle" of the city.[4] I think of these writers when I hear Justin explain his difficulty communicating the experience of a walking tour when planning for a New Jersey group's visit. When setting up the tour, he recognized a contrast between his perspective and the group's leader:

> People who are used to driving, people who are "suburbanly" oriented are destination oriented. . . . Their whole trick in the "how many minutes can you shave off, from point A to point B" it is not "Oh look, here's this building, and the façade, and my favorite little whatever-it-is." It's not about the experience of travel, it is about the experience once-you-get-where-you-are. . . . For me it relates to sentence structure: all he wants are the hit words of the sentence as opposed to the glue of the sentence. There's no fabric, *there's no fiber that brings it all together*. It really brought home that we were talking two very different languages using the same words. Because in his mind, if we didn't promise seven major hits, the tour was a flop, as opposed to what I do, which is, "Well, look at this building, let's talk about who lived here, let's talk about the origins, how does it relate to the neighborhood, how does it relate to the history, have you noticed this kind of detail before?"

For geographers like Yi-Fu Tuan, the "fiber" that Justin mentions is similar to how "transient feelings and thoughts gain permanence and objectivity" through things and spaces.[5] Through a railing, through a cast-iron column, the ability to touch and feel the city gives these tours their vitality. Experiential moments of the walking tour are what give it its character. Furthermore, this experiential quality is not just a mental state, but a social one. When Justin speaks of Grand Central as being "all about interaction," he could be talking about the city itself: he emphasizes that walking is a part of quotidian New York life, and this kind of engagement is an integral part of the daily lives of New Yorkers.[6] (As one guide proudly told me in an interview, the failure of a Metropolitan Transit Authority strike was due to the fact that New Yorkers are comfortable with walking.) But in another sense, Justin could have been talking about the walking tour as being "all about social interaction" as well. Tourism scholar Brian Moeran finds that Japanese tourists want to "participate with their own skins" rather than "see" the sights (1983, 95), and the experiential aspect of these tours, this kind of locomotion, is a major facet of what makes guides' intellectual labors unique.[7] With each stop, with each interaction, with each bit, the tour binds the participants to the city in their own skins—to its movements, habits, interactions, and spaces.

Inspired by William H. Whyte's examinations of public space, either comparing pedestrian movement on New York's Lexington Avenue and Tokyo's Shinjuku Station (2000) or his famous study of small urban plazas (1980), I wanted to closely map out how guides position themselves and their tour groups in public space. In Jeffrey Trask's Before Stonewall tour of Washington Square Park and Greenwich Village I found an ideal example wherein the guide carefully positioned the group of participants (twenty-three initially, and two more who joined at the third stop) into five common configurations clearly in dialogue with the physical surroundings and the pedestrian movements of the city. These patterns evince how guides use urban public space and illustrate how they contribute to what Whyte called "Living Street," where flow and density are key concerns (see fig. 5a–e).

Jeffrey Trask's narrative places information in these settings, as the guide fuses past and present in these spaces. And if, as Richard Sennett (1990) says, spaces are like good stories, then walking guides might be their best storytellers. This is distinctive and it brings together the particular components of the walking tour discussed here. Being *in media res* is what makes guides like Jeffrey effective educators who "story" a city in the way they piece together their talks, the way they give them, and in their placement in public space.[8] As another guide told me, "We are academics for public history. This

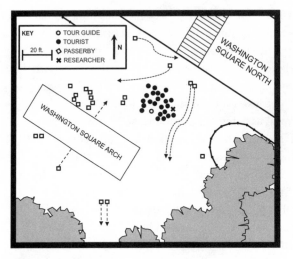

Figure 5a *The Rare Open Space.*
The tour group is positioned
between the crosswalk and the
Washington Square Arch,
and there is enough space for
pedestrians to pass by on all sides.
The group makes a four-fifths circle
around the guide, as he provides
introductory remarks about gay
culture and the neighborhood's
importance in that history. There
is zero interaction with others; no
one stops to listen in, although one
couple does veer toward the group
to listen without breaking their
stride.

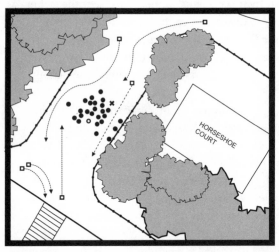

Figure 5b *In a Funnel.* This instance is slightly more confined
because it is in an area where
people are moving from the park
to busy West Fourth Street/Wash-
ington Square South and NYU's
Bobst Library. Here the guide
brings the group near a barrier of
fencing and benches at the main
avenue to the southern edge of
the park. Three participants sit;
a narrow, four-foot path remains
open between the sitters and the
rest of the group.

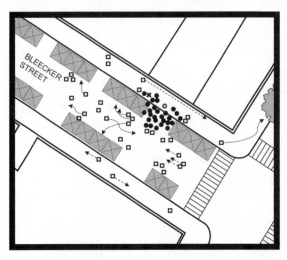

Figure 5c *The Use of the Street.*
A street fair on Bleeker Street
creates a dense setting, but it also
allows the guide to position the
group between two tents as he
speaks about the building behind
him (the onetime location of a
late-1800s gay club, The Slide).
Passersby move behind him, and
seven pause for a few of the ten
minutes we are there, congre-
gating at the edges so as to not
block the view of the storefront.
I have also seen this done with
participants wedging themselves
between cars.

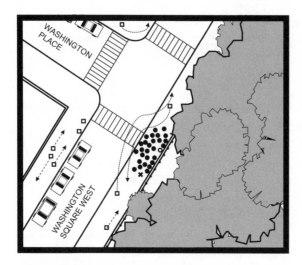

Figure 5d *The Pinched Sidewalk.* This organization, suboptimal but very common, allows the guide to lean on a railing. Washington Square West had light pedestrian traffic as compared to other streets nearby. Participants at the edges of the group noticeably strained to hear the guide because of a jazz trio playing in the park. Passersby would often grumble, as they had to walk in the street to pass the group.

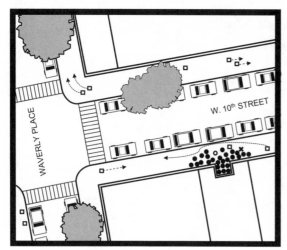

Figure 5e *The Storefront.* Here the guide uses a vacant commercial space to allow pedestrian flow behind him and to direct the group's attention to a famous bar called Julius' across the street. The guide abandoned this spot for a less desirable location around the corner because of a nearly violent screaming match between a bike messenger and a cabbie on West 10th Street.

is public history at its best: on the streets." For another: "Walking is about your senses . . . it's about experience." When I asked Mark Shulman about how this differentiates a bus tour from a walking tour, he told me:

> The more passive the tourist is, the more docile and infantilized he is. . . . A walking tour is hands on, you're walking—literally moving. You're in motion in a number of ways, and it's facilitating interaction, among people and the guide, and among people and each other. It's more of a social experience. . . . You now realize that you are making friends with people who are walking your speed, as opposed to the person who sat in the seat next to you.

Because what happens on a bus, if I might digress, is that there is a sense that whatever seat you randomly sat in is your assigned seat. People on a tour bus have just about surrendered everything and are one step away from sitting at home and watching the video.

It is not just experience unto itself that is of value to guides, but that it is tied explicitly to a set of stories and a particular kind of storytelling in place. To pick out aspects illustrated here: guides use a balustrade to talk about immigration, or a park to talk about gangs and ethnic groups, or a column to talk about labor history and neighborhood change. This proximity and the interactions with folks on tour affect not only the tour content but also the guide's own conception of him- or herself, as we will see next.

Entertaining Identities

5

Working with an Audience

We have seen how this group of New Yorkers came into the trade, conduct their work, and piece together a working life. Some give tours for fun although most do it for money, some to find meaning in guiding as a second career while others do it on their way to another path. Missing from this picture is how their interactions with audiences shape their tour content and how those interactions affect how they see themselves. This viewpoint provides a peek into how, as Charles Horton Cooley would describe it, conceptions of self are developed "from the outside inwards" (1902, 320). Guides are often adrift in a nearly limitless sea of historical and cultural information with little more than their own personal skills and capacities at their service when faced with their audiences.

Tracing the connections and tensions between professional and personal lives—of flight attendants, wait staff, and others in the service and health care industries—has a long history in ethnographies of work.[1] Howard Becker, for example, opens up his study on professional dance musicians by illustrating how the "direct and personal contact with the ultimate consumer of the product of his work" results in a "pressure to please the audience" while musicians still struggle to maintain their own 'artistic standards' to avoid becoming a 'commercial musician' (1951, 136, 141). Guides, like musicians, are wrapped up in their own negotiations between the need to entertain clients and their own desires, expectations, and self-image. A closer look shows that it is a conciliatory process, one that results in an adaptation of identity, and a balance between the guide's role of being both an "educator" and an "entertainer," offering a fusion—what some have called "edutainment."[2]

Guides might alter their sidewalk interactions just as musicians might change their set lists and banter, and the pressures of audience expectations can shape the tour and the tour guide in ways that would not be apparent to the casual observer. Like the jazz musician who fears having to pander too much to a crowd, guides struggle with eschewing a particular historical topic in favor of a more contemporary pop culture reference despite their own inclinations. This may mean downplaying "more serious" content for "more humorous" in order to present a slightly different version of a tour experience. It may also mean a more involved construction of the guide's self, or an evolution of an identity through the interactions on the sidewalk. There are a variety of ways to illustrate how the working conditions can give rise to this kind of "working personality." This chapter will tackle the way that guides' own perceptions and construction of tourist types affects their sense of self, as well as how they create a sort of "symbolic armor" to their presentation of self in order to buffer themselves from the everyday challenges they face on the sidewalk.

Anyone who has done public speaking will know how talking in front of a group of strangers can be a stressful experience. It is hard to, as Jennifer Fronc said it, "put yourself out there" day in and day out, particularly when there are such varied levels of audience enthusiasm for the work that is invested in it. A guide's presentation of material is closely linked to the feedback he or she gets. All guides have seen a battery of hard historical facts go unappreciated by a tour group, and all have seen "fluff" and thinly witty repartee effectively keep a group rapt. Concurrently, many operate on the maxim that answering a question correctly is good, but *not* answering a question in a humorous fashion might, at times, be better if the audience wants to be entertained. It depends what the group wants, but also what one's disposition is as a guide. Take, for example, Big Onion guide Erik Goldner, who responded to my questions about this by saying, "I usually just think that I have to *engage* them, and that's enough." He describes himself as a "minimalist," particularly with younger age groups. "They're not going to remember what you said an hour later," he continues, "but they will remember the experience of going on tour and that history can be meaningful or interesting—whether they got any raw data out of it." Some guides are entertainers and are deeply historical and some academics can be fun and engaging.

Big Onion's scholars-in-training are perhaps the most obvious of examples to elucidate the balance guides make between their clients' more "mass touristic" expectations and their personal, more scholarly inclinations. Jennifer Fronc was reflexive about these issues and, having led over 250 Big Onion tours on the weekends to help pay for graduate school at Columbia University, she is a great candidate to highlight these issues. Tagging along on three of her tours, we spent hours talking about her methods and her feelings on the trade. The following ethnographic fieldnote is of her "Immigrant New York Labor" tour. One of her favorites, it is included here because it was also located on the Lower East Side, a neighborhood revered as an "ethnic homeland" for American Jews and Italians, and because of that interest scholars write about the increasing commodification of its culture (Mele 2000, Zukin 2003). The perception of the Lower East Side is often idealized and that view shapes how tourists see guides' tours and the guides themselves. Negotiating the content of such a tour is a relatively tricky thing for Big Onion, as this tour attracts both locals and visitors. A non–New Yorker might find the focus too narrow, as it offers only a little general information and a more constrained cartography, while a local might already know a fair amount of the subject matter. She describes what she does as "framing" and gives the example of what she tells groups on these tours. "I say, 'This is not a history of organized labor. Yes, we'll talk about important moments in union history, but I'm more interested in the world of the worker: their social, cultural, and religious settings, surroundings, and institutions.'" She says that kind of caveat "works for the group, and for my sensibilities." Still, Jennifer voices concern in our interviews over the way that the tourism business exploits cultures and traipses into neighborhoods, but on tour she gives every appearance that she is in her element. She does not betray a hint of the vulnerability and concern she feels while out on the sidewalk, interacting with dozens of folks a day.

To Look and Feel the Part (Immigrant Labor and Lower East Side Tour, May 2004)

As Jennifer Fronc checks in the prepaid customers on her list, the underside of her clipboard, with stickers that say, "ANTI-WORKER = ANTI-UNION" and "UNION BUSTING IS DISGUSTING," is clearly visible. Beneath the Washington Square Arch and a cloudy sky, people mingle and chat. There are thirty-two participants: a mixture of foreigners, locals, students, and activists here to learn about labor history. They're excited, curious, and chatty.

"Welcome to the immigrant labor history of the Lower East Side tour," the guide says to get everyone's attention. "We'll be entering into the world of the worker, appropriately enough, on Labor Day." She tells us about the first Labor Day March, in 1882, and its trajectory from City Hall to 42nd Street, and how Congress made the day a national holiday in 1894.

We stroll around the corner to a building with a small brown plaque on it. "Some of you might take a chemistry class here, since it is an NYU science building, but it is also the site of the worst industrial accident of the last century: The Triangle Shirtwaist fire of 1911. Women who worked there were locked into the high-rise factory to either keep them from taking breaks or keep union organizers from coming in." She talks about the few laws and policies designed to protect workers and passes around a laminated photocopy of the *New York Times* article reporting on the incident. With her passion for fighting class-based inequality coming closer to the surface, Jennifer becomes spunky and engaging. At the next stop around the corner she describes the 1849 Astor Place riot in which a "super worked-up" working-class mob threw fruit and theater seats at an Englishman playing Macbeth in a "fancy-pants opera house," taking offense to the actor's upscale airs. The square was nicknamed "Disaster Place" afterwards. Continuing in a populist vein, a few stops later she refers to Little Italy (located a little further downtown) as the "EPCOT Center of immigrant communities" to deride its overt consumerism and homogenization. All this, and we've only covered a tight three blocks.

At the corner of East Sixth Street and Bowery, Jennifer talks to us about the life of working-class women. "This neighborhood," she says, "was known for being a place where women could socialize with 'drunks' in saloons." Emphasizing the public outcry as a middle-class elitist concern, the resultant "Raines Law" was passed in 1896, requiring that only hotels and restaurants could serve liquor. "This did not affect more upscale establishments," Jennifer says, "but it dramatically changed the world of the woman."

"You see," she continues, "one of the options that a woman had to make money was through selling her body for money, a dangerous profession. But bars, to stay in accordance with the new law, began to serve food as well as set up an area in the back with cots and a curtain." The group is completely silent, curious to know how this ties in, and she tells them, "Working women then moved their business from the street to the safer confines of a bar where bar owners were happy to take a percentage and generate money on an otherwise useless and profitless area they had to legally provide."

As Jennifer tells the story, two things occur. First, it starts to rain, and every single member of the group calmly takes out an umbrella and continues to listen intently. But also, two police officers pull up in an unmarked car behind the group. Without knowing this, she continues: "The law ended up protecting women in a way that was unintended: it protected them from cops and other thugs on the street." The police officer, window down, had been taking long pensive drags on his cigar while she was speaking, but he almost chokes on smoke in reaction to Jennifer's characterization of police officers. He laughs when he notices the group looking at him, and the car slowly pulls away.

Interacting with Common Tourist Types

As mentioned in the fieldnote above, a mixture of locals and visitors attend BOWT tours, but freelancers often get more locals. The common misperception of who takes tours was on display in Cobble Hill, Brooklyn, with Justin Ferate. On a quiet side street, a homeless man began to shadow the group—a class enrolled in Cooper Union's Continuing Education Program—and kept asking, "Where y'all from? Where y'all from?" No bunch of country rubes, the man with a slight limp was handled with what Goffman called civil inattention (1967) until, finally, a woman responded: "We're all from New York, if you can believe it!" Participants chuckled.

The comment halted the man's pursuit, but his mistake was understandable enough, as there is a wider range of relationships in walking tourism that transcends the visitor-local antinomy mentioned in chapter 1. Eric Washington, for example, describes his participants as locals who are "fairly urbane in their sensibilities and tend to come with a little bit of information already." "They are not an incurious traveler, for the most part," he continues after a pause, "I say 'for the most part' because you do get people who are invariably green. But it is also part of their vanity that says, 'Oh, here is something I've never heard of . . .'" Bruce Kayton gets locals, too, but also describes his appreciation for nonlocals, who may be even more familiar with his content than his native clients:

> Foreigners are much more knowledgeable about radical history: "Wow, John Reed," and all this. And the Americans, especially the younger kids are going, "Who's John Reed and Emma Goldman?" "Who's Margaret Sanger?" . . . The idea is that you can walk through the Village a hundred times and have no idea about John Reed or Emma Goldman or Leon Trotsky living in the

East Village. And you need a tour guide to tell you. Even though they walk
through, or [live] in the neighborhood, they still want to know more, and
they like the walk. It's good exercise and it's good information.

Although it may only be for an hour or two, guides are careful to nurture the
group dynamic, are interested in the kinds of interactions they have with
participants and, to minimize the emotional investment in understanding
the constant turnover of clients, many develop categories that transcend
that initial distinction between "visitor" and "local." This echoes findings
in earlier ethnographies on service industry workers, like taxi drivers, for
example, who create a typology of fares, from "the stiff" to "the blowhard,"
to establish an element of predictability and control in their occupational activities (e.g., their expectations for tips, the tenor of their conversations, and
so on).[3] The following are a few types offered to me by the guides themselves,
for purposes similar to those of the cabdriver. Guides pay special attention
to how these types generate particular interactions on the tour, but they also
inform the guides' own sense of self as, potentially, a more academic or entertaining tour leader, depending on the presence of kinds of tourists. It is
through these constructed types that guides come to understand their own
work and their own dispositions for their interactions on the walking tour.
Some tourist types draw out particular personality qualities in the guide
while others may elicit content that a guide is loathe to talk about but includes just to make the tour as conflict-free as possible. In understanding
each we are provided with a window through which we can understand how
the guide, in a way, sees him or herself.

The Groupie

On a Big Onion tour of Greenwich Village I saw a familiar figure from other
tours:

As we walk between stops the guide, Jennifer Fronc, singles out a participant
to me. He is tall, in his sixties, and wears a suit and trench coat. I have noticed already that he is carrying a plastic bag that emits a low hum of static,
presumably from a transistor radio. He circles outside the group, often in the
street, even on the other side of the parked cars, rather than on the sidewalk.
Everyone ignores him. Jennifer tells me, "He is a regular, a groupie. Every
[guide] knows him. We call him 'Lurch' or 'Radio Man.'"

On three separate occasions Big Onion guides have described the same man as an example of a "groupie." Jennifer told me he was not the only one. "Oh, yeah," she sighed, "there are Big Onion groupies who come once or twice a month." Regulars are not all so conspicuous. As she tells me, "Some have their favorite guides, but some just are tour junkies." When I asked the man who had commented on Jennifer being a very good guide, he told me, "I go four or five times a year. I wish I knew which guides are leading which tours, but I have taken enough to know they're all pretty good. I like her. I was happy to see her today." And when I asked him about seeing the same faces on other tours he told me, "Oh yeah, I actually went on a tour of the Lower East Side last weekend, too, and it turns out he [pointing to another participant] was on that tour, too." It appears that BOWT's diversity of tours and array of guides attracts groupies—and Big Onion offers a "Frequent Walker Card" where cardholders can get the sixth tour for free in an attempt to attract more of them—but independents get them as well. It seems freelancers' colloquial, informal style draws them, too. "Foodie Tour" specialist Katia Howard tells me that these clients "have their favorite guides," and that most are "life-long learners [who] are on the community board or the school board; they want to be a part of a larger community, to stay current; many are older." She says that one of her groupies is in her late eighties and still loves to eat her way across town.

Guides feel this kind of participant returns for a variety of reasons. Some just love to learn about the city. Some see tours as a mental, physical, even social activity. Many groupies are elderly and find tours attractive because they have a little disposable income, plenty of time, and a desire for interaction outdoors. I almost always see someone over the age of sixty on tour, and guides usually appreciate them, partly due to their loyalty.

The Buff

Arising from the interactions displayed at the end of the last chapter is a particular type that gets guides really talking. Repeat and enthusiastic customers are appreciated in almost any business, but participants who are passionately interested in a particular topic or theme garner a tepid reaction from guides. There are certainly times when a guide is overly exuberant about a particular architectural detail or the radicalism of Joseph Papp, and most are appreciative when a member adds a good personal anecdote or tidbit to the conversation because it enlivens what would otherwise be a two-hour monologue. We have already seen, however, that repetitive and sustained interruptions can be a problem. The line between a good-natured inquirer and the buff, for guides, is that the latter is disruptive; he will ask minute details about a topic and continually knock guides off track. Or worse, his intentions might be more self-aggrandizing—playing a game that Seth Kamil calls "Stump the Tour Guide."[4] And the frequent use of the pronoun "his" is apt here. Jennifer says she has a "buff" about once every three tours and "they are," she tells me with a sigh, "*all* men." She elaborates:

> I don't like history buffs. I'm generalizing, but the people who stand out were men, anywhere in their mid-thirties to their sixties, who have read popular history books. . . . They clearly have issues with me as an authority figure, so they have to tell me things. They can't just sit back and enjoy the tour. They are combative, and I feel it's like pornography to them. I just don't like the way they treat me.

Sometimes she ignores them, and sometimes she attempts to engage with them:

> I've had hecklers, and I deal with them as abruptly and cuttingly as I can, but these history buffs are a different breed. . . . Once I had a man, who had something to say at every single stop. He had to correct me, add something. And at one point I stopped. The whole group was like facing me and he said something. And I said, "Where are you getting this from?" and he pulls out this book called *The Armchair Traveler's Guide to New York* and he's like, "This guidebook." I'm like, "If you're an armchair traveler why are you on a walking tour?"

Seth Kamil explains that tours can attract a particular clientele: "I like to say that we get [some participants] who know just enough to sound intelligent but are really dangerous." This, however, is just a minority of participants and the hazard is relative. A guide might appreciate a good-natured caveat, but no matter how much a particular story or idea might be of use for future tours I've never witnessed a guide pull out a pad of paper and take down a new date or fact. Buffs can be characterized by their distracting questions and imperviousness to attempts to neutralize their additional commentary.

The Kid

One of the most difficult challenges is dealing with children—either as family members or a school group—and they can radically alter the character of the group and derail any discussion without attention. Teaching children can be an affirming experience, but a petulant child can be a real problem. One option is to completely ignore them and risk their lack of interest metastasizing into a full-blown distraction. There are some savvy guides who use children as accomplices, just as Justin did on our Grand Central tour:

On the Grand Concourse, Justin asks a ten-year-old boy to lock arm in arm and walk with him for a few paces. Without mentioning it, he lines up along the edge of a block of the flooring, and both take three quick paces in unison. "Do you see?" Justin asks the boy. The boy shrugs, and Justin turns the pair 90 degrees and takes two more relaxed paces, looking down at his feet. This time, the boy looks down as well and gets it, saying, "We are walking the distance of the lines in the floor!" "That's right," Justin says, thanking his assistant and turning to the group to explain how the floor blocks of Tennessee marble are designed to be the width of a single walking pace, and the length of a fast one.

Later, Justin bends down to another child's height in order to ask a silly question, as if his humor is physically at a lower register. Such efforts draw the youngster in, a gesture that appears to be most appreciated by the parents.

If there's an entire school group, a guide adapts further. One tells me:

The fact of the matter is that when you are out there with a bunch of eighth-graders, you're a busboy. You're serving something up, and if they don't like it, take it back and try something else. . . . Two hours with third-graders, with complicated material? It sucks. . . . What I've learned is that you can't yell at squirrelly third-graders . . . you have to be squirrelly with them.

Ethnographic and interview data indicate that the content can change because of the presence of kids, but sometimes the guide's business changes based on the guide's ability to work with school groups. One guide told me how she came to the realization that she was just not well suited for student tours:

I think a lot of guides are looser, and give better student tours than I do. . . . I'm very data oriented. If you get high school kids, they want to know about stuff, but it's not the kind of "tell me everything about this kind of brick" kind of thing, which I will know—the history of the brick. So why should

I be doing a tour when I can [subcontract] someone who can do great on a student tour, and know plenty and make it memorable?

Jane Marx, on the other hand, has a quick wit very much in tune with the group of high schoolers visiting from Tuscaloosa, Alabama, I tagged along with. After that tour, I asked her how she adapts her content to get children more engaged. She told me, "I'll tell them they can never know what's going to come of my mouth. Hell, I'm just as curious to know what I'm going to say next." She tells me that the minute she feels youngsters' attention is waning, she'll lean over and say something off-color just to shock them.

The Seeker

Tourism has been of particular interest because it is alternately seen as an avenue to finding "authentic" culture for the general public and, in the eyes of scholars, it can potentially undermine the very existence of that authenticity (Gotham 2007; Grazian 2003; Kelner 2010). Lower East Side guides, for example, have told me of Jewish and Italian groups attempting to return to the "homeland" through touring, looking to purchase Judaic trinkets or sip Italian espressos to enrich their experiences. A fieldnote of the "Immigrant Foods of the Lower East Side" walking tour with an independent guide provides evidence of this during a break in the tour:

Still noshing on knishes from Yonah Shimmel's famous bakery we walk up to Russ and Daughters. The guide tells our group of ten out-of-towners that "this establishment has been in the family for four generations, starting as a pushcart back in 1914. It is now in the National Register for Historical Places and the Smithsonian deemed it an official piece of New York culture." We all file into the deli to pick out something to put on a bagel. As we get our tickets from a red dispenser, the fishmonger tells us that they specialize in eight kinds of salmon, from lox, "which is cured in brine, not smoked," to "Kippered," "which is what people know as baked salmon." I get my favorite, sable (which is also called "Black Cod" and is filleted and cured in salt and brine) on a poppyseed bagel, which sparks a conversation with a middle-aged tourist from Connecticut, in town for the day with her daughter:

"A good Jewish order!" she says.

"Oh, thanks. I'm not Jewish, though."

"Have you been on this tour before?" she asks.

"No, no. I just love this," I say but, realizing she is looking for some locus of expertise, I add, "I live here." I ask, "Why did you come on this tour?"

"I wanted my daughter to know what my grandfather's life was like here in the Lower East Side. We get to taste exactly the same food that he would've eaten." When her number is called she breaks off the conversation by saying, "I want the same thing," and orders sable and cream cheese on a bagel. She tells me the tour is the educational part of their trip, a deal brokered with her teenager who "just came for the shopping."

Spilling back out on Houston, people's hands are full with coffees, bagels, and knishes. A husband-and-wife team keeps rotating the delicacies between them. We walk another block and stop outside Katz's Delicatessen. "A famous New York landmark too crowded to pop in for a taste." There's a groan from the group that rises above the street noise, even though few have even made dents in the snacks that are already in their hands.

"This place is authentic, no doubt—it has been around since 1888—but it has been overrun with tourists ever since that scene in *When Harry Met Sally . . .* , and it'll just take too long to get something from here." Still attempting to assuage the group, she continues: "If you want to go and wait in line for a pastrami sandwich, that's great, but we're going to head over to the Essex Market." She does, however, take a minute to explain a sign that reads, "Send a salami to your boy in the Army," which has hung in the window since World War II.

Erik Goldner explained his experience with these kinds of folks:

[They] come from all over the country and want to come to the Lower
East Side to learn about the Jewish history of the Lower East Side, when
the current Jewish population on the Lower East Side today is about one-
fiftieth of what it was, and it's disappearing fast. Well, some of the old places
are being rejuvenated, but anyway. So a lot of people do come to hear
about an "authentic" Jewish community. A lot of people are searching for
that.

Walking guides feel the pressure of this newfound interest, bristling when they feel a participant expects a more "touristy tour," and "real" New York experiences, when guides would like to focus on the stories they feel are most important rather than address what they perceive as the tourist's imagined cultural history.

Negotiating Edutainment

From interactions with this mixture of tour participants, the guide usually adapts his or her tour content. In an interview after the tour highlighted in the above fieldnote, Jennifer tells me how she includes the "Disaster Place" story because "it is a bit of a crowd pleaser more than anything," and she wants to make sure that tourists happy, even at the expense of her own intellectual leanings. Because she was writing her dissertation on how social activists investigated the seedier problems of brothels and gang activity in New York City, Jennifer draws from deep wells of New York scandals, but still hopes to walk the line by also sharing the more sober, social conditions of working-class folk. The topic of "Lower East Side Immigrant Labor" brings in clientele more inclined to the latter emphasis, but when taking other groups around the neighboring areas of Little Italy and Chinatown Jennifer describes feeling, "almost immoral" about telling salacious stories of Irish and Chinese gangs, and the mafia. She says it is difficult to avoid being too sensational on these "more touristic" tours and if she sees attentions wane she tends to offer up stories about the Raines Law, or how Jewish prostitutes would have to walk the other side of the street from the Italian prostitutes, or that a "stand-up" cost 75 cents. When I asked for an example of when she felt this pressure most pointedly, she described an event on one Chinatown tour:

> I had this group; I think they were ninth or tenth graders, just a couple of months ago. This kid said to me, "Don't you think that the people who are living in these tenement apartment buildings feel upset that you stop in front of their house and talk about what a crappy building it is?" And I really didn't know how to answer that. I stammered something out about how it is a historic neighborhood, and I'm talking about how the city doesn't care about working people, but I've been really plagued by that question ever since.

To moderate her self-image as a historian with the expectations of her clients, she has tried to develop a concluding frame for these reluctantly told stories about gangs and crime in the neighborhood to make herself feel better about it:

> I've just recently started wrapping it all up in something like: "It's interesting to think that—particularly among the Chinese and the Italians and less so with the Irish—these were men who were here without their families, they didn't have the sort of intimate personal relationships. So what does the gang mean for the political history of the city, with patronage, blah blah

blah." So, I try to say that it's not really about these craven, horrible immigrants killing each other, it's a different meaning. But I don't feel good about that either.

Such a balancing act is the nature of the business. Buff- and Seeker-type participants crave details and more educational tales, while Kids want to be entertained. The perspectives of two prominent guides provide two ends on this particular balance, and how they approach each other in the in-between: Seth Kamil and Jane Marx. Over breakfast at Dizzy's Diner in Brooklyn, Jennifer's boss, Seth, portrays Big Onion as giving "lecture tours." He explains, "There are people out there that sing on their tours, there are people who do a song and dance, there are people who do costumes. We don't do any of that." "Whether you are fifty years old and have lived here all your life, or you are an eighth-grader, you are going to learn. *That*," he emphasizes, "is entertainment enough." One of Seth's guides, Erik Goldner, explains how these two concepts of education and entertainment are academically, but not necessarily practically distinct, and that his tours must be founded in the historical data:

> If you are giving history, it's usually fascinating enough that you don't have to embellish that much. I mean, sure you are free to capture your own opinion about a situation, but my own personal opinion is that you owe your public, in as much as it is in your power to give them the facts as you know them. When you don't know, tell them that you don't know.

Obviously, guides with more of an academic background can still be entertaining. While Jennifer describes her labor tour as "more educational," she conducts other tours, on Wall Street and Five Points, for example, which she pejoratively refers to as "pure tourism."

At the other end of the spectrum stands Jane Marx, the silver-tongued guide who makes every attempt to create an entertaining tour, although she is quick to insist that she doesn't do "pure fluff." As we sat at an Upper East Side diner, she jokingly claimed that one of the reasons she's a guide is because she has "Adult Attention Deficit Disorder" and that her quirkiness is a draw rather than a detriment. She insists clients come back for *her* as much as for the content. As she breaks a blueberry muffin apart with her hands for us to share, she tells me, "They won't remember a goddamned thing from the tour. But they'll remember that they had a *great* time, and that they love New York. My persona is what clients come back for." I saw the aspiring actress in her come alive on tour, reminding me that jazz is not the only cultural world where idiosyncrasy is rewarded. I press her with questions that would get at how such an entertaining, charisma-based disposition actually develops on tour; she recalls that, when giving one of her first tours, a child told her that anyone who wears a hat is fun, and she has worn a hat for every tour since. She tells me she wears four watches for the same effect. "All I have to do is look," pulling her wrist up a few inches from her face, "and people get that I am a wacky person." "It's *all* presentation, dah-ling, only 25 percent of it is facts." "It's vaudevillian. Charisma, however, is god-given. People see right through someone if they are faking it." She tells me, on stage and on the streets, that she "can wake up a stone." Jane represents the sector of nonacademic, autodidactic, more performative guides that includes aspiring or out-of-work actors, like Mark Levy, Darryl Reilly, and Stan O'Connor. Arthur Marks, who is a "singing tour guide," says that while he never made it to the stage he "still gets to perform, and gets paid for it [and is] more of a personality than a tour operator" (Kilgannon 1999). Willing to get a group interested by focusing on the more humorous and engaging aspects of a topic in a similar spirit, autodidactic guide Mark Shulman explains it is all "about liking people, wanting to make the tour an enjoyable experience, and realizing that the balance between education and entertainment should skew toward entertainment." Harmonizing the career trajectories discussed in chapter 2 are, after all, just part of what attracts aspiring actors. It allows those who are inclined to present a more theatrical identity to get the emotional fulfillment of successfully "working the crowd," particularly those that are populated by the Kids and Groupies who love the shtick.

Coming from different ends, guides still hope to situate their work somewhere in the in-between. A few describe themselves as "pure" historians who divulge facts and tell precise stories, vehemently opposing the idea of being an entertainer, but most negotiate these distinctions, offering what has been called "infotainment" or "edutainment." Autodidactic Brendan FitzGerald speaks of how he balances this tension:

> One of the important things is to have a good time. . . . To provide people with some kind of thing to do, rather than go to a movie. . . . Not only is this a form of protest, and consciousness-raising, 'cause that's really important, but also to have a good time. I do think that's huge. The main reason I do this is because I like doing it. It's really fun for me, and it's useful. If you can be fun and useful at the same time, you're pretty lucky.

Such issues over edutainment are not particularly new. As a prime mover of Disneyfication, the tourism industry writ large is often seen as staging "pseudo-events" and "invented traditions" to leave a subgroup of tourists seeking canned experiences for at least fifty years.[5] Research on the topic portrays tourists who have a fully developed "symbolic complex" or "set" of expectations—existing before arriving at any touristic destination, like the Lower East Side or Harlem—that determines the success of their thematized visits.[6] As the evidence of Seekers and an earlier fieldnote of an "Immigrant Foods" tour (in chapter 3) indicates, these touristic desires are tangible and can be a source of great anxiety for guides, particularly for those who disliked the more "mass touristic" aspects of bus tourism and those who come from academia.[7] Even still, guides spoke with empathy when talking about the expectations of participants, particularly Seeker types. Erik Goldner told me:

> I wrestle with presenting [these touristic aspects]. Personally, I don't want to say it's crap. I tell them that Hasia Diner writes about how a group from Iowa will come to the East Side and buy a loaf of rye bread from a kosher bakery, and by the time they get back to Iowa, it's stale. And basically, it's the same as the rye bread that you can get from the kosher bakery in your hometown. But to them, that bread, that's from the Lower East Side. That means something. And that's a very human impulse, I'm not against it.

To grapple with these impulses another BOWT guide, Annie Polland, described her strategy of flipping the mass-market expectations into a history lesson that she is more comfortable with when faced with a challenging group from a "spoiled suburban school" by reorienting their pervasive interest in shopping to talk about how their grandparents (particularly if they are Jewish) were at the very beginnings of the fashion industry in New York and on the Lower East Side, as both producers and consumers. She says, "All they can refer to is shopping [and ask] 'Where is H&M?' 'Where is Niketown?' and they are completely divorced from that historical perspective. As an academic I feel comfortable dealing with it my way." Both Erik's and Annie's comments pivot upon sensitivity to a group's perspective, but also their own feelings of who they are as aspiring academics and how they believe they should present their material.

"They Expect You as the Product as Well"

A guide's identity is very much a part of the tour package and is intertwined with the expectations, interactions, and content of the tour. The industry itself is diverse in part because tourism enables folks to capitalize on their ethnic, racial, cultural, religious, sexual, or gendered background in addition to their knowledge of a specific set of information. Most feel their clients want a "Real New Yorker" to lead a New York City tour; a gay, lesbian, or transgendered person to conduct a tour of Greenwich Village; or a Jew to give a Lower East Side tour. Others give tours only in Russian or Chinese. "Racially coded" areas and topics, like the "Harlem Renaissance" or the "History of Hip Hop in South Bronx," open up niches for African American guides, and Black History Month has the added benefit of attracting tours at a time of the year that is, otherwise, a barren tourism season. Personal facts and details will routinely seep into tour content as well: to foster their local identity, for example, some trumpet their "New York Like a Native" or "Real New York" tours by announcing "I've lived here all my life" and, with a slight qualification, "I've lived here all my adult life" before a single story is told. An independent guide even cited the fact that she took her first breath at the NYU Medical Center, as if it were a line on a résumé.

Andy Sydor explains that his clients "want a personal touch." One of the most common questions he gets is "Are you from here?" "Technically, I am born in Manhattan but I grew up in New Jersey," he admits, "and that satisfies them, though they have a problem with my lack of an accent." When I probed further to find how such statements add to the tour, beyond the added perception of native vérité, Andy described how his personal biography provides a frame to his tours. He will mention that his parents lived in a Greenwich Village loft, which he says is "a personal story that [unfolds into an account] about how it was illegal to live in a loft, which is kinda a dry real estate fact made personal."

As members of an ethnic or racial group, other guides feel that such beliefs are further pressure to confine themselves to giving certain kinds of tours in particular neighborhoods. After a tour of Manhattanville, Eric laughs when talking about being African American and feeling the expectations of his tour groups, telling me, "I can assume it's an issue to some degree; I know I've been asked to do tours because it is assumed as an African American I can do Harlem tours. I've been African American long enough to know how that works." And similarly, those who identify as gay, lesbian, or transgendered may offer a "Gay New York" tour or specialty tours during Gay Pride Week, feeling mixed about avoiding their sexuality as a central component for some tours and flaunting it for others. After Big Onion's "Before Stonewall" tour of Greenwich Village, Jeffrey Trask shared with me his feelings on being gay, and giving a tour on gay culture in New York as an issue that he feels is less important to him than to his tourists. "I don't think [identity] should impact a historian's ability to understand, and explain, the experiences of people in the past," he tells me, citing that he also discusses the experiences of Italian immigrants, African American women, and women who could "pass" on his tours as well. "On the other hand," he adds, "it may matter very much to the people who took the tour whether they perceived me to be a gay man." Jeffrey tells me that these interactions and "perceptions about the group" change the way he "presents certain ideas or work through arguments." Another guide described for me situations wherein his identity has clashed with participants' expectations: being a white guide giving a tour of Harlem, for example, made participants question whether or not he should be offering a tour at all.

To get a better sense of how these more personal issues are connected with walking tours, Jennifer Fronc was particularly reflexive on how her personality has been shaped by the tour interactions she's had over the years. Even on tours that are not particularly coded as "ethnic" or "religious," Jennifer describes "almost blacking out" when her groups are disengaged or antagonistic, and wonders aloud if it is a defense mechanism. But dull groups aren't the worst of it. Participants have inappropriately touched her, older male clients have interrupted or contradicted her stories, and people whistle at her on the street (which occurs in the following fieldnote). In a list of discomforts, however, she jokes that being asked when she will finish her dissertation is an affront on par with asking about her weight—a jest we both laughed at, but one that highlights the sensitivity surrounding the deeply personal nature of intellectual labor. As Jennifer tells me, "It is such a weird thing. I mean, you're giving them a product, the product is the tour. But they expect you as the product as well." The guide is part of the commodity, lashed up with the content itself.

Through our interviews, Jennifer's struggles with how she constructs her own sense of self and how others see her came up repeatedly. After a tour I met with her at Phoebe's, a café in Williamsburg, Brooklyn, and we talked about this at length. She told me the story of leading a synagogue group from upstate New York on a tour of the experiences of immigrants on Ellis Island and the Lower East Side. At Ellis Island she talked about how officials would stand on the balcony and assess the flood of people passing below to explain that a "kind of pre–racial profiling" occurred early on in our nation's history. She emits a sense of pride over her minute, almost semiotic, analysis of the great many commonalities between nineteenth-century women from southern Italy and orthodox Jewish women; how their similar skin color, hair, and clothing led to misidentification. She tells me this bit is a "perfect tour-guiding moment" on ethnicity, history, and religion that informs the rest of the tour. Later, as the children ran around outside, the group's rabbi sidled up to her and said, "Oh, I'm glad that Jewish and Italian women are no longer mistaken for each other." Sensing a teaching moment, Jennifer told the rabbi that she is, in fact, of Italian, not Jewish, heritage. Stunned, and a little hurt because she felt that Jennifer had misrepresented herself by leading a tour on Jewish and immigrant history, the rabbi spent the rest of the day testing her on Jewish history and tradition in front of the group. Walking through the Lower East Side a few hours later, the rabbi asked her to read Hebrew signage repeatedly, but would then say, "Oh, that's right, you're not Jewish." In between sips of coffee, Jennifer still blushes at the retelling of it.

In a later interview, I asked Erik Goldner similar questions on identity and the pressures of guiding, and the first thing he asked was if I had heard Jennifer's rabbi story yet. The tale had made the rounds at Big Onion. He then offered his own experience:

> At first I was very conscious about doing the Lower East Side walking tour, because I'm not Jewish. I hadn't been in a single synagogue, except for one bar mitzvah eighteen years ago. Now I take people into synagogues, and I don't know what goes on in there. . . . It's like a white person giving a tour of Harlem. Can you speak for this community? I think you can. But there are people walking on the street giving a tour, you will get heckled. If you are a black person on the street giving a tour you will get heckled. You will get even *more* heckled. I've gotten that a lot: "Are you from around here?"

Erik echoed Jennifer's feelings that expectations and misperceptions of identity are often at issue with his tour groups. While Jeffrey mentions "passing" as a part of his content, Erik explains that guides also know a little something about passing personally. "My last name is Goldner, so they mostly assume I'm Jewish," he tells me, "until about fifteen minutes into the tour, and they look at me—I don't know why, maybe it's the way I speak—some go, 'You're not Jewish are you?' and [I say], 'No.' And that's where it ends." He told me he's received positive feedback, many commending him for knowing so much about Jewish history. This is a common-enough occurrence that guides who are mistaken for a different social group have learned to leave participants to labor under their own misperceptions. And like the historical tale of immigration officials "reading" character traits, this is a story of constructing and shaping identities.

Nearly every guide I've spoken with has described positively and negatively charged moments like these. In light of David Grazian's work, which found white blues musicians to have a relatively complicated understanding of the relationship between their ethnic identities and their cultural labors,

Erik's and Jennifer's tales are, perhaps, unsurprising.[8] Here we see these concerns shape the content, take their emotional toll, and affect how guides present key personal qualities. Attending to these small manipulations is the subject of this chapter's final section, following a fieldnote on the continuation of Jennifer's tour.

Robert Moses and the Need to Tell a Controversial Tale (Immigrant Labor and the Lower East Side Tour, May 2004)

On the corner of Rivington and Eldridge the group gets to see the 1886 University Settlement House, the nation's first center for providing social services for urban poor and immigrants. The house was only for men, but there was also a growth of college-educated, unemployed women. The result was a lot of women providing food, shelter, basic health care, and education at the Settlement House. Jennifer mentions how Section 7A of the 1933 National Industrial Recovery Act sets the minimum wage and maximum hours, but how it took until 1935's Wagner Act to allow the government to oversee the implementation of those laws. On the front stoop of a bodega across the street, three men begin whistling and catcalling. Jennifer barrels through the discussion but looks over at them to roll her eyes.

Every time she talks, Jennifer's face gets red; she has been shouting over the traffic for the last hour. She's shouted about Emma Goldman's belief in free love and Margaret Sanger's fight for women's rights. She's shouted about the Wobblies, and how the Women's Trade Union Brigade struggled for equal rights against their employers and against the prejudices of working-class men who wanted a family wage.

On our way south, down to Second Avenue to Houston Street, with the group trailing a bit behind us, Jennifer tells me, "I've got this whole Bob Moses thing that I love, when we get to the Sara Delano Roosevelt Park." When we get to the park across the street, she talks about the public feud between Moses and Eleanor Roosevelt. "While they waged a particularly brutal battle over Moses' attempt to extend Fifth Avenue through Washington Square Park, they battled over slum clearance on this spot, too." "This park was created by the decades-old, two-faced tactic that privately wanted 'slum clearance,'" she continues, "effectively uprooting hundreds of families and irrevocably altering the neighborhood, and publicly stating that he wanted parks for the public good." Roosevelt fought Moses' housing practices but had always wanted a park in the area. Moses outmaneuvered her by doing both: using her desires to have a park on the Lower East Side as an excuse to clear out the housing on the site. "To rub it in, Moses used his authority as New York's Parks Commissioner," and she pauses for dramatic effect while pointing to the big green sign behind her, "to name the park after Eleanor's mother-in-law, who, it was well known, Eleanor disliked." The audience chuckles.

Our final stop on this tour about working people is the *Jewish Daily Forward* building at 175 East Broadway. The *Daily Forward* newspaper, founded in 1897, was the first Yiddish daily newspaper in the world. In its heyday, she tells us, the paper would print on Jewish unions and strikes, help with boycotts, and cover African American struggles, as well as the Triangle Shirtwaist fire—the very first topic of our tour. While currently shrouded in scaffolding, we can see engravings of four men's profiles and Jennifer tells us that there is a good deal of debate about who those men are but, assuredly, two of them are Karl Marx and Friedrich Engels. She talks about how the building was bought by a Chinese religious group, who had a billboard on the side about the work of Jesus, yet had a sweatshop on the top floor. She shares some gossip about the property being converted into condominiums, and Jennifer muses aloud that she has a little fantasy about the ghost of Karl Marx roaming through the hallways of upper-class condos there. With a last thought, we turn to the left, to the Wing Shoon Seafood Restaurant, the site of the Garden Cafeteria, where many of those mentioned in the tour—Emma Goldman, John Reed, Leon Trotsky, and Fidel Castro—broke bread at one time or another. We end the tour on a rumor: that Trotsky's assassination plot was hatched at the table in the back. She tells the group that it is one of the more controversial and possibly inaccurate New York stories.

Situational Identities and Symbolic Armor

Teaching different types of tourists while navigating through the tension between education and entertainment can provide significant concern for the guide. Few cultural practices depend upon this balance of information, entertainment, performance, and affect as this one does. At the same time guides can be compared with other culture workers whose economic and labor situation mandates what Goffman (1959) called "impression management" as an industry standard. This interactional process, in this context, moderates guides' reactions to participants' expectations by a developing a "front." In a way, these social forces and historical tales reach through decades and centuries to shape the presentations of self guides create on the sidewalk. As such, the pressures of edutainment and expectations of personal attributes (including but not exclusively having to do with race), may compel some to augment, embellish, even fabricate, a particular version of their identity to a group, ranging from slight adjustments to the more elaborate. Rather than a particular trick of storytelling, these are common adaptations in "performing self." Bruce Kayton, for example, silently reinforces his New York "cred" by sometimes wearing a Mets cap despite a dislike for baseball, and another guide explains how embellishments on his own "New Yorkness" can create a kind of authority, or even elicit sympathy from his clients. As one told me, "I'd be talking and suddenly I'm [breaking into a Brooklyn accent] y'know, I'm sayin' it like dis.'" He tells me that his clients felt he "had overcome some childhood limitation." This guide describes the added benefit of creating a character: "I liked being from Sheepshead Bay. Because I always liked the name, and nobody was ever from there, or knew it." In Goffmanian terms, using hats as "props" and accents as linguistic "footings" (in addition to guides' announcement of credentials and affiliations) creates the "symbolic armor" of being a native.[9] Illustrating these adjustments in self presentation are another way to understand the way these occupational conditions shape the guides' sense of identity.

Seth Kamil feels his guides' academic credentials should provide sufficient footing for any perceived lack of other attributes. He says, "Most are not native New Yorkers, I'm not a native New Yorker. You don't need to be from here to know the city," His guides need to "be a good academic to be able to do what we do," discounting the notion that any particular personality trait could disqualify a guide in the eyes of his or her clients. But when I asked Jennifer how negative experiences like the interaction with the rabbi have affected her tours, she provided a vivid reminder that even academics succumb to embellishing identities. As she explains it:

It seems that people *want* me to be Jewish. And they react very badly when they find out I'm not. They act as if I've tricked them somehow. I have light eyes and dark curly hair—that's not a trick. It's very offensive to me the way they react. They react as if I just sold them the Brooklyn Bridge. It's really unbelievable. Um, so I've started lying. It's easier to lie and create this persona that makes everybody happy and it stops some of the questions and the more offensive stuff. . . . So, my persona is that my mother is Italian and my father is a Polish Jew. (He's Polish, but Catholic.) And that I was raised totally secular, nonobservant. That I was born in Brooklyn, but raised in Chicago. That I'm thirty. Sometimes, I've been in New York seven years. It depends. It's been five years for a *very* long time. It's now officially six, for real. I also adapt my dissertation topic, when they ask. People who aren't writing dissertations don't really understand, so sometimes I'll gloss over it. Sometimes I tell them that I'm writing about prostitution and crime in the immigrant neighborhoods. Because that's really titillating and sexy, and they get all excited that I'm going to tell them about scintillating stories, sometimes I do, sometimes I don't.

Given that so much of a guide's authority can dwell in ethnicity, gender, race, neighborhood affiliation, and even baseball team allegiance some, like Jennifer, have developed a repertoire of affective tactics and personae. These attempts to create legitimacy are efforts to create a kind of protective coating. Even when a guide is fully equipped with the academic and institutional legitimacy that comes with being a Ph.D. student and a member of Big Onion, guides construct a *situational identity*.[10] When I asked Mark Shulman about how his new personae was developed through giving walking tours he explained "that it is *very* important to create a persona for tours—whenever necessary, whenever possible—[because it] creates a kind of protective shield." He went on to tell me that it "works on multiple levels" because such constructions allow him to "amplify and enhance [his] legitimacy." He then explains how guides' motives and dispositions are fused together in the content, which dictates if and how a guide's identity is augmented:

> It comes back to [the question]: what's your source as a professor or as a teacher? What legitimacy do you have? Interestingly, with the Jewish population, you could be a secular Jew versus a Ph.D. in religious studies who's Catholic. And the secular Jew, somehow, is going to somehow come out on top. . . . Your basic Knicks fan is somehow going to have greater legitimacy because he's able to pronounce Yiddish words he's heard all his life in a way that someone who hasn't been around that, but knows deep, deep amounts of information [cannot].

On the one hand, a guide's identity can be a source of humor and provide a touchstone for tackling broader themes. On the other hand these personal takes on a neighborhood are something guides feel makes their tours eminently unique. As Eric Washington explains, "The anchors may be the same [but] the personality factor will create a dynamic that shapes how information is disseminated." Eric is not alone in feeling this way. When reading fieldnotes of Mark Levy, Brendan FitzGerald, and others, we can see how guides' distaste for the more formal workplaces they left behind seeps into their commentaries but—sticking with this chapter's tour guide—we can readily find evidence of Jennifer's display of an antiestablishment disposition on our tour. She had participated in a citywide graduate student unionization movement in 2003–4; this wrinkle unfolds when our tour group passed NYU. From a fieldnote:

At the edge of Washington Square Park, across from the original New York University building, Jennifer describes how the university was originally designed to be a school for the regular working-class folk of New York. "But they violated these principles very early on," she tells us, by hiring prison labor from Sing Sing to cut the stones for this building in 1834. This sparked what's been called the "Stonecutter's Union Riot," and the 27th Infantry had to be called in. She continued with, "I have to say, NYU isn't much better today," to talk about the recent difficulties of graduate student unionization.

Of course, such a disposition might expand to the point of being a tour's primary focus or draw. Politically themed tours, for example, are often attended because clients *expect* to hear about New York through a particular worldview, not an objective, historical one. In these instances, guides feel less pressure to layer their tours with lighter content. For example, Bruce Kayton's radical left politics so strongly affect his shtick that he could sit at the foot of the Empire State Building's soaring art deco façade and ignore it for a story about how the B. Altman Department Store across the street housed a school for worker's children and provided health care for its employees, and Bill Brown—the guide from the following chapter's fieldnotes—will ignore the famous Chelsea Market to talk about what he suspects to be a secret government building across the street.

But it is not just that these guides show a different side of themselves on tour; it is that they have developed a self in response to their interactions with participants. Jennifer, for example, describes feeling vulnerable on tour and, having paused her story about the rabbi to refill our cups of coffee, continues by explaining how experiences like that one have led her to strategically present a different version of herself, as "Tour Guide Jennifer," who differs from "Regular Jennifer":

So I guess, yeah, I've sort of begun giving these people what they want and what they expect. I guess, in no small part as a way of sort of, keeping—it sounds so cheesy—But, like, keeping myself, back behind this defensive sort of persona. So it's not . . . it was hard in the beginning when I was being myself giving tours because when things didn't go well, it was hard not to take it personally. It's hard not to take this kind of stuff personally. And I mean, a lot. . . . I guess it's kind of like . . . I mean, I've never been an actor, but I guess it is kind of like *being* an *actor*. You feed off of your audience, and if you have a bad audience, you give a bad tour. Yeah, so I guess it's like: "Here's the character, I hope you like it." It has nothing to do with who I am when I get back on the subway.

I asked her, "So, it's not just for them, it is also about self-survival?"

It's really—it is really draining to do this. I mean, it's not draining like digging ditches, but I mean, I'm trying to say that I am some kind of exploited, underpaid worker. It's weird. It's—I don't know.

Through actions like these, the guide's innate or constructed attributes can become as much a part of a tour as any specific anecdote or building, shaping the historical tales being told while the historical tales shape them. With this understanding of the walking tour as a kind of performance filtered through a particular individual—to a greater extent than any specific personal or organizational relationship—as well as the more structural issues of urban culture that affect guides' emotional work and the products they create, we can see how the labor of these individuals is at once a locus of strain and at the same time a potential source for effective strategies of the presentation of self.[11] We have also seen how the guide's working personality develops—resulting in some of them creating a kind of symbolic armor—through their construction of tourist typologies, through the tensions they feel exist between their more educational and entertaining instincts, and the microlevel adjustments they make to their presentation of self. It is from here we can say that the tour, in a fashion, shapes the guide from the outside in.

Re-Keying the City

6

Neighborhood Narratives and Urban Cultures

So proud of his 1893 Columbian Exposition in Chicago, chief designer and architect Daniel Burnham personally led dignitaries on walking tours of its exhibits and buildings. The fair was to be a global metanarrative at fifty cents a ticket. The square-mile world-within-a-city held more than 200 buildings and was a patchwork quilt of global cultures. Even with such a large canvas at his command, Burnham still conducted these personal strolls for high-profile guests so they could see the fair "the way he believed it should be seen, the buildings presented from a certain perspective, in a particular order."[1] This historical moment not only offers a glimpse into one of the major spectacles that undoubtedly whetted twentieth-century America's appetite for the themed, commodified extravaganzas of Disneyfication, it also shows that even the most engineered landscape still requires smaller-scale narratives.

Wrangling together varied perspectives for their groups, urban walking guides encapsulate the fusillade of overlapping meanings, histories, symbols, interactions, and practices as well. They are peddlers of ideas. A world's fair may make an attempt to summarize the global community, but city guides offer interpretations

of their neighborhoods and urban cultures with their very modest set of resources. New York's locals and visitors are confronted with an overwhelming
array of cultural wares (Central Park alone is 30% larger than Burnham's
fair) wherein walking guides make their humble offer: for your time, and
likely some money, I will weave together some of these stories into a coherent narrative for your education and enjoyment. Cold data on a neighborhood can be found in a library or on the Internet, and no one needs a
ticket to walk down a sidewalk. As Mark Shulman described it, "I'll give you
one little slice of the Big Apple. Others have their own, I have mine." After
all, guides depend less upon a storehouse of facts and figures than on their
abilities to manipulate these elements into a story. Their representations
collectively add to city life, entering in what Hannerz called the "traffic of
meanings" (1980, 11). These *in situ* stories offer the rare "connections that
make sense of forms" that urbanists like Michael Sorkin feel are absent in
contemporary cities (1992, xii). Now that we have seen how cultural conditions and interactions have shaped guides and their tours, these thoughts
bring us to the stories themselves—the cultural content guides contribute
to the urban sphere—for a better understanding of the guide's place in the
world of ideas and public culture.

New York City, like many metropolitan areas, has a near-infinite set of
stories that can be exploited by a guide. How these tales are the products of
interactions between guides or across their social world—from the trans-
mission of stories from one guide to another to the subtle adjustments they
make to avoid encroaching on a colleague's cultural terrain—and what it
is that these stories actually convey, are the concerns of this chapter. The
overall picture, however, is to show that the cultural material of a city and of
a walking tour may have wide possibilities but still hold commonalities with
other activities across the tourism field. To understand how people make
meaning out of the cacophony of social life, Erving Goffman borrowed a mu-
sical term, "keying," to explain the selection and interpretation of information and, if that content runs counter to a dominant or accepted narrative,
he called it "rekeying."[2] For Goffman, all keyings are representations of a
sort. Like a musician placing a song in a particular key, guides bring together
a variety of urban content into what they see as a harmonious storyline. They
draw some tales into the frame of the tour, while others are omitted. There
are many guides, and through this process there are many different versions
of New York. And we will see that it is often in their best interest to offer
countering, unconventional, or contrarian narratives to differentiate themselves. The importance, then, is not to focus on the variation, but on examining the commonalities across their "rekeys" to the city.

One of the guides who wades dramatically through the traffic of meanings, bringing together a specific kind of tour content into his own unique narrative, is Bill Brown, who offers free tours on the issue he is most passionate about: how surveillance technologies creep into the public realm. He is a forty-four-year-old legal proofreader by day who lives in Brooklyn. He earned his doctorate in American literature, worked in academia for a while, was a newspaper writer, "zine" publisher, and punk musician before focusing on being a performance artist and activist. He founded a group called the Surveillance Camera Players in 1996, which performs skits in front of security cameras, like Orwell's *1984* in Washington Square Park, *Animal Farm* in Times Square, and Poe's "The Raven" and Beckett's *Waiting for Godot* in the 14th Street and Seventh Avenue Subway Station. He started reading about the Situationists and their social movement–alchemy blend of the aimless stroll of the flâneur plus the inquisitiveness of the detective. One of their favorite activities was to send gangs of artists and everyday folk for a "walk with a purpose," called a *dérive*. When Bill read about how the founder of Situationism, Constant, led tours of Brussels, he realized this could be an effective form of activism. He gave his first tour on Thanksgiving 2000; they have since eclipsed the plays in their importance to him. "I find them more rewarding," he told me. Bill's walks are a sort of performance, "but with more explicit information." He says he often feels he's "really on to something"—citing the interest of journalists, NYU film students, activists, and the occasional Ph.D. student. The tours themselves are experiential, educational, and contrary enough to mainstream culture be considered a "rekeying" of the city.

Cameras Obscura (Surveillance Cameras in Chelsea Tour, October 2004)

On a blue-chill day in Chelsea at the corner of Eighth Avenue and 14th Street, I come up to a group waiting for a free tour on surveillance cameras. Uneasily bundled together, we make small talk about our reasons for coming along. It is a mix of local artists, activists, and students. Our guide, Bill Brown, walks up and talks for a half an hour about different types of cameras, audio surveillance systems, and police tactics. A few pedestrians who had just been walking by and were hooked in join us out of curiosity, including a homeless man who ends up coming along for an hour. The rest of the group is white. A few, like me, have notebooks in hand. Two have with nice manual cameras at the ready. It is a talkative group of twenty-three today. The participants seem

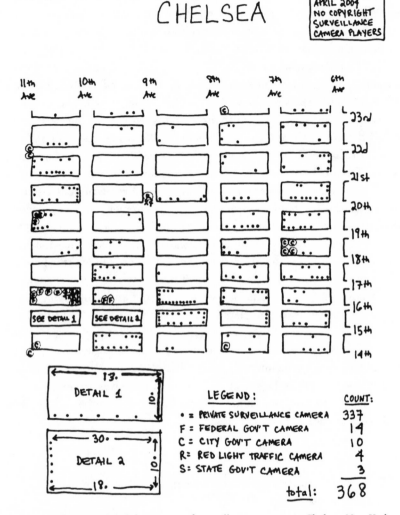

Figure 6: Bill Brown's hand-drawn map of surveillance cameras in Chelsea, New York
Source: Not Bored! (2008).

to be checking each other out, trying to gauge just what others are thinking of it all.

Bill has a two-day old beard, black stocking cap, and a puffy nondescript coat. When he points up to the cameras, he exposes a hole in the armpit emitting puffs of down. He seems to have the nervous energy of a pigeon with a few too many pedestrians walking nearby. Whenever I chat with him, on the street or in a café, he looks around continually, and today he's the same—either preoccupied with the cops standing behind us or looking for more participants to arrive.

He talks about what he sees as aspects of urban living that are slowly being eaten away: "One of the greatest things about New York is that people can come here to not know anyone." From the anonymity of the street, Bill tells us that, thanks to technology, police can now violate our Fourth Amendment rights by performing "search and seizures" of our race, our class, even our "antigovernment feelings." He describes the differences between "first-generation cameras" and their black domed kin. These newer cameras are harder to spot and are often located at traffic intersections and in parks. "One has been watching us all along," he says, and points to a dark orb hovering fifteen feet above our heads, a steel and glass gargoyle. He passes out photocopies of his own map of the neighborhood—one of the dozen or so versions documenting cameras in Manhattan (see fig. 6).

At the intersection of Ninth Avenue and West 20th Street—in the heart of Chelsea, an important center for New York's art industry and gay community—Bill focuses on three traffic cameras hanging over the street. He tells us the unit was sold to the city for $60,000 and that Lockheed Martin advertised it as paying for itself in a year with tickets at $120 a person. He develops the point into a discussion of the conflict of interest a city has, when there is a financial motive for slightly altering the timing on a yellow light. I find myself nodding along. He talks about a San Francisco court case that threw out hundreds of traffic tickets because of just such a modification.

What Bill perceives as ineffectiveness doesn't seem to hinder the proliferation of these technologies. He mentions that the New York Police Department tried to use surveillance cameras in Times Square twenty-five years ago, but couldn't make it cost efficient. Manpower is the real problem. According to Bill, a viewer's vigilance will drop after twenty minutes regardless of what he or she is watching. He returns to the more sordid side of "Big Brother": given that these watchers are undoubtedly male, they are prone to amusing themselves using the scanning and zooming functions of cameras to gawk at women.

"I Don't Own the Neighborhood . . ."

This tour, like all of Bill Brown's outings, is dutifully documented on his Web site, which includes maps, links, information, and his press coverage. Similar to Bruce Kayton, who gives away his bibliography and says he is "just happy to get the information out there," and another who says "the idea is to get all that dusty history out," Bill is eager to share. This is an important instinct. The perspectives of guides like Bill and Bruce further the idea that many in this field understand that they are actively culling the free everyday molecules of cities to create new, interesting cultural compounds in their own fashion. But guides must balance the reality of using the nearly boundless resources of urban history and public space with their feelings of ownership over a neighborhood and a sense of propriety over the personal touch they believe makes their tours unique. This is yet another key tension in the field, between public goods of urban space and culture and the private feelings of ownership that a tour guide may hold over the content of his or her tours.

Just as in fields like journalism and academia, concerns over the exchange of information affects the sometimes-contentious, sometimes-cooperative community of walking guides and illustrates the way that cultural content is freely available yet somewhat "owned." Unsurprisingly, these issues arose at the June 16 city council meeting, when Marvin Gelfand (who happens to also be legally blind) said of his colleague's work, ". . . and Joyce Gold, we've all stolen from her with both hands. As Picasso said, 'We all steal; the only crime is in copying yourself,'" which garnered a good chuckle from the crowd.[3] Not everyone, however, is as open to sharing as Bill and Bruce, or thinks of it as a laughing matter. Guides get very suspicious when a participant takes lots of notes. A scene from a Greenwich Village tour provides an example:[4]

There is a tourist who looks pretty familiar. I'm sure that I've seen him on another BOWT tour, but can't tell for sure. I think he recognizes me too, since we are both carrying notebooks. He's frantically scribbling, until he notices that I am watching him. He acts more guarded, more self-conscious. The guide doesn't seem to notice, but I'm lagging behind the group with Jennifer Fronc (who is coming along because Seth Kamil requires his guides to take a few tours with another guide before leading his or her own new tour). She has noticed him too. I ask her about it, and she tells me it happens at the start of every tour season.

When she sees people taking notes, she tells me she'll saunter up to them, and ask: "Are you a reporter?" then, "Are you a student?" and finally, in a mockingly coy voice: "Are you a tour guide? That's not very cool. You can't do that any more." While he encourages his guides to share information amongst each other, Seth has a strict policy prohibiting videotaping. Jennifer and I both discuss it and are pretty certain that he is a rival guide but she decides to let him off just to avoid any confrontation.

When I asked Seth about copying tours, he became quite animated. "I think," he told me, "that these guides who talk about the proprietary nature of what they do are full of shit." "They want to go on any tour, write down anything, and use material any way they see fit," he continues, "but don't feel anybody should take from them."

Surrounded by her own expansive library, and over 35 years of detailed notes and files, Joyce Gold talked about her feelings on the matter. On the one hand, she knows what it feels like to be taken advantage of. She recalls a guide who came on a series of tours, taking extensive notes and, at times, audio recording her. After the ninth tour Joyce confronted the woman and was dumbstruck at her lack of appreciation. She had to ask the notetaker not to come back, a request that was returned with indignation: "But," this woman told her as a defense, "I won't give *your* tours." In another example, Joyce recalled a Greenwich Village tour and kept seeing the same guide with another tour group at every stop, just a little ahead of her. "I realized," she said, "that he had copied my tour from my book *From Trout Streams to Bohemia* stop for stop, story for story!" Wanting to know more about these struggles over the public culture and her investments in her own interpretations of it, I asked her to tell me a bit about how this relates to the larger tourism industry. She told me that she unknowingly "helped train plenty of guides," but that she wouldn't take other people's tours because, "aside from the time, I don't think it's ethical for me to take somebody's tour if I think that I will ever be giving a tour of that route." But at the same time, Joyce describes it as "tricky" because she emphasizes new guides need to start somewhere (even stating "I guess I took people's tours early on, and that's how I started") and that she also just thinks that guides might be inclined to learn from a colleague (admitting that she has been yelled at for notetaking on a Big Onion tour, even when she tried to explain that she was just there to get access to the historical site to take a few pictures for her lectures).

For the most part, guides express feelings of resignation. Bruce, for example, understands where Joyce is coming from:

> In a sense I don't want them to steal what I've done. But I can't say: 'The Bread and Roses Strike of 1912, that's *my* strike, and only *I* can talk about it.' Even though they found it in a book. I mean, once I put [my own] book out, I knew that everybody was going to st— I read other people's books as well.

At this moment in the interview Bruce stops himself from saying 'steal,' and opts to emphasize that he draws from other people's work as well. It is a telling moment of ambiguity. Eric Washington told me he relies on a simple maxim: no one holds the rights to an area or set of facts. He said, laughing, "I say that, even though I may open up the paper [to find that] somebody's giving a Manhattanville tour [and say] 'Who would *dare?*'" He continued: "Listen, I think that all guides steal from each other, [but] it's a *neighborhood*. I don't own [Manhattanville]. I didn't discover the neighborhood." Reinforcing the public nature of the craft and content, Eric expresses pride in excavating 'his' corner of the physical and intellectual world, a feeling that any academic could empathize with, but he also realizes that anyone could essentially 'take' his content. It is out there, freely available for anyone to incorporate into their own tours.

Such resignation cannot be helped in an industry that is also a kind of knowledge community, an invisible college of guides and participants. On the one hand there are guides like the Levys from Chapter One, who offer tours for fellow GANYC guides, and many autodidacts take each other's tours for their own enjoyment and education, as a kind of 'busman's holiday.' On the other hand there are guides who are suspicious of others, and feel ownership over their content. Joyce Gold, for example, is in a good position to think reflexively on this issue. She can't really do much about a guide copying a tour from one of her books because, as she says, "the information is out there," but she is careful to point out that there is "something different" about copying her more personal take on an area. "There's so much work goes into the telling of the story on a walking tour," she explained to me, "it's like designing a dance." Eric Wakin, a senior member of Big Onion, mulled over this issue, so much so that after our interview he sent an email on how the personal crafting of a tour is difficult to duplicate, and sits at the center the guiding experience:

> We all have our own styles and delivery and it's hard for someone to mimic those aspects. As for the knowledge, I think it is good that people listen to other tours, read, and learn. I say it is good because I am not in the business of running a tour business. If I were, I would be very upset if those outside of my business took my ideas and the way I have arranged my research, which is copyrightable, one might imagine, and then sold or used it. That's why I discourage note taking, filming on my tours and encourage other guides to do so. The tour is 'public,' but it is a public performance of an arrangement of material that is private in some sense.

It is clear that guides cannot claim ownership of a date or fact, but they do feel that it is within their rights to feel pride and propriety over their narratives and the particular shtick they use. Joyce told me that her decision to exile the rival notetaking guide was as much a decision about the number of tours she took as it was "that she was copying my entire arrangement of the tour; brazen enough to pull me aside after to make sure she had my joke word for word!"

As we chatted, Joyce reminded me that the personal take is what makes this such a vibrant field. She encapsulated this polyvocality in a single recollection. While waiting for a group at Washington Square, she looked around to find "three or four expert guides talking about the same spot: one was a very curmudgeon[y] viewpoint, and Arthur Marks was doing a singing tour, and it was fascinating that they weren't alike at all." Beyond establishing one's niche, she summarized, "guides give different kinds of tours because they are sifting through for what is interesting to them." By participating in multiple tours by the same guide, and multiple tours of the same site conducted by different guides, the diversity of 'arrangements' or 'rekeyings' can be shown here. Take, for example, fieldnotes from two tours of two guides. Their different deconstructions of the same façade demonstrates the multiplicity of stories that can be told on the same location. The first is Evan T. Pritchard, a Micmac Indian, who has written several books on the topic, is the founder of the Center for Algonquin Culture, and has used his research to garner positions as an adjunct professor of Native American History at a number of colleges in the Hudson Valley:

Evan begins his tour at the Smithsonian's National Museum of the American Indian's home base: the wedding cake-like U.S. Customs House. He asks my 76 person group to use our imaginations, bellowing with grandeur: "Here is the Customs House, built in 1907, but look past that—to Fort Amsterdam!" At the base of its Beaux-Arts pedestal, he tells us the walls of the fort, built by Angolan slaves in 1626, were in the same position as the walls here, and that the architect, Cass Gilbert, represents how over 80 Native Americans were tortured and beheaded here by placing an American Indian bust on each wall. He describes the location of the fort in a different geography. He points up Broadway, to what is now Route 9 past Albany and Montreal, to where the Algonquin people believe that fire was brought to Earth. This, Evan says, is the 5 to 7,000 year old Mohican trail. He talks about the Sapohannikan Unami Indians who lived in what is now the West Village, and the Canarsie who lived at what is now the East Village up to 14th Street, and also in Brooklyn.

The second is Big Onion guide, Jeffrey Trask, who specializes in nineteenth and 20th century U.S. History:

At the U.S. Customs House, Jeffrey Trask, shows us a laminated map of the southern tip of Manhattan, talks about nearby City Hall, the reasons why Manhattan became a good port, how this building was the residence for George Washington but that he never lived here, and then deconstructs the sculptures. There are four Daniel Chester French statues that dominate the façade, but Jeffrey jumps to the second tier of 12 smaller sculptures on the cornice, which, he tells us, indicates the great seafaring nations of the day. Teasing out the historical significance of a detail, he asks: "Now, you may not be able to read them, but 'Belgium' is on one of the shields. Why would that be?" After a long pause, tells us about post-WWI anti-German sentiment and large-scale xenophobia, lead to Germany's name being replaced.

Focusing on different tiers of statues, the first, autodidactic guide is seen to be speaking from his own ethnic and cultural perspective, while the second, academic guide bases his talk on symbolic references and connects them to geopolitical and historical change. Clearly, a façade can have multiple 'rekeyings.'

Another set of examples offers two versions of a single room in Grand Central Terminal. The first guide, Francis Morrone, is a more architecturally-oriented guide who works for the Municipal Art Society and is the author of several books on the architecture of the city:

In the ornate and cavernous Vanderbilt Hall, Francis gathers us around a wall to ask us about what it is made of. The group looks intently, but no one offers their analysis. "Marble?" someone finally guesses. Our guide walks up and itemizes the materials from the floor upwards. "The walls might look like it, but it is not French Limestone, not Limestone, and not even stone, but gypsum plaster molded to simulate French Limestone." He describes this as a bit of architectural trickery: a 'curtain wall' that gives the illusion of being a load-bearing wall. The bottom rim of stone that comes to eye-level is Botticino Marble, and the flooring is Marble from Tennessee. He says the latter is sturdy material, faring well, considering "one million feet, give or take a few" walk on it daily. He invites us to touch the different materials.

This can be compared with Justin Ferate, who gave his tour under the auspices of the Grand Central Partnership Business Improvement District:

Justin describes women's travel experiences in the 1920s, when this served as the main entry point to the city. "Once," he explains "this was called the 'Waiting Room.'" He describes how wooden benches filled this now empty space. He points to where the elaborate powder rooms and resting areas were. He talks of how travelers would arrive, grab their luggage, walk through this hall and out a few blocks to a hotel, and be reclining in bed within minutes. With a rhetorical furl, he asks, "Now, where were you ten minutes after arriving at JFK? In a cab on the BQE? Still waiting for your luggage?"

While these two guides are socially quite close, their inclinations frame these two tour moments differently: the first emphasizing the architectural, the second takes a cultural approach.

The permutations on display with guides reminds me of Italo Calvino's playful *Invisible Cities*, wherein Kublai Khan commands Marco Polo to tell him tales of all the places he has traveled. Polo describes wondrous tales of 'thin cities,' 'trading cities,' and 'continuous cities,' and as these passages layer upon one another the reader slowly begins to suspect that Polo is offering exaggerations of the same place, his home of Venice.[5] Calvino joins E. B. White, Colson Whitehead, and other writers who dramatize how the same city can be many things to many people, each reinforcing Goffman's contribution. Every point on the map is not just *a* place in history as Adrienne Rich says (1986), but *multiple* points. It is, however, not enough to make a claim that different guides do things differently. Rising up from the variation there are commonalities, a set of tour emphases that connects diverse guides like Evan and Jeffrey, Justin and Bill Brown. These shared traits, and how they coalesce into a different kind of tourism will be summarized in the next section.

Eyes on the Street (Surveillance Cameras in Chelsea Tour, October 2004)

Bill tells us how he joined up with an activist group to count surveillance cameras throughout Manhattan, finding 2,397 of them. Five years later, he followed up in selected areas to estimate a 300 percent increase. By extrapolation, he puts the current count over 7,000. On the corner of 17th Street and Eighth Avenue the tour group is counting twenty video cameras as Bill describes their effects on city life. He describes what he sees as a growing police state. He talks about a $10-million spy helicopter given to the city by the Department of Justice, and the twenty-four satellites with state-of-the-art cameras that orbit above our heads.

He then gets more grounded, pointing out how a particular building's security camera isn't trained on that property at all, but rather on a children's playground across the street. He wonders aloud, "What exactly is it these cameras are viewing?" and indicates his deep mistrust not just of those who could potentially abuse power, but also the male gaze. For another example, he cites how security guards in Tuscaloosa were caught checking out young collegiate women's breasts with traffic cameras. Due to a lack of oversight the men wouldn't have been found out if the images were not also broadcast live on cable television so that drivers could make commuting decisions from home. After the close-up images made it to hundreds of suburban homes, the security guards were fired.

For our next stop, we come to the dim and wet West 16th Street, alongside the famous Chelsea Market. On a tour with another guide a few weeks ago, I heard about how this building is where the Oreo cookie was invented and how there is a new plan to transform the abandoned elevated rail line at the end of the block into a public park. Instead, Bill tells us there are sixty-four cameras on the entire block, thirty cameras on this side alone, and over 200 more inside the market. Mid-block we stop in front of a blank façade across the street, and Bill claims that the building is the secret New York headquarters for the Federal Organized Crime Task Force. He bases this claim on an experience wherein a plainclothes officer forcibly dissuaded him from taking pictures. Like many of his projects, the tours have received their fair share of attention from the media but also from the authorities and he is sure to regale this group with stories of his interactions with police and federal agents. Rather than a source of embarrassment, they are a badge of honor; only further proof of how right he is about the "control society."

The experience of walking, for Bill, is an effective kind of "slow media," but it is something that can be interpreted as subversive. He tells us walking slowly and stopping periodically can trigger warnings on the latest counterterrorism surveillance software.[6] He begins to wrap up the tour by telling the group, "Public space is owned by using it, and not by holding a deed." Public space, he says, "is for the public to use as they see fit."

Back on Seventh Avenue, Bill ends by fondly talking about "how to be a New Yorker." He develops the riffs on Big Brother into broader themes of urban living. "I hope," he implores, "you all explore your own neighborhoods." The undercurrent of voyeurism and the urban gaze, however, is still present when he tells the group to investigate their own social landscapes: "New Yorkers rarely look above people's chests. We don't look people in the eye, and we want to watch where we are stepping. Only tourists look up." He ends with a general call for New Yorkers to slow down and pay attention.

A Different Kind of Tourism: "Teaching the Stuff That People Don't Even Know They Want to Know"

Bill's tour was unique in many ways, but one way it stands out is that there were so many notetakers. College students take notes in lecture halls but few, if any, tourists come with pen and pad in hand. This made me wonder what it is exactly that guides share if not raw information. I started to ask guides questions about what it was they wanted participants to get out of the tours, paying less attention to the details and more mind to the common ways guides try to shape their tour content and reorient the tour participant's perspective. Guides feel that New Yorkers seek out alternative stories like Bill's. They "love to be tricked," as Eric Washington told me, "and I love teaching the stuff that tourists don't even know that they want to know." This phenomenon reminds me of Jay McInerney's *Bright Lights, Big City*, wherein the jaded protagonist narrates that he only begins to love New York City after he convinces himself that he should see it through the eyes of a tourist. The urban dweller takes this position on a walking tour: learning a fresh take on an old city.

By pulling back from the specifics, my fieldnotes reveal three emphases to explain how guides present the city anew: a kind of local particularism, a contrarian disposition, and a "do it yourself" (DIY) approach to urban life. In the world of tour guides, it is important to point out that the three emphases highlighted here contrast with the popular laments of urban life as increasingly homogenized, commodified, and banalized. In this light we can return to the metaphor introduced earlier, to say that walking guides provide a different kind of tourism—by "rekeying" the urban scene for their participants—which challenges the tourist to think about the city in a new way while at the same time differentiating the tour itself. As a result, the participant, whether a local or a visitor, is invited to see the city in a new fashion. The tour is a chance to reorient the everyday, to make the city strange.

The first and perhaps most apparent commonality among guides is that they relish the distinctive character of a neighborhood. They often talk about "how great New York is," but more important, "how great *this particular neighborhood* is," as one announced to her group. This is based in no small part on the clear economic necessity of becoming specialized (e.g., becoming "Mr. Manhattanville," or offering a "Peter Stuyvesant's Bowery" tour) and in expanding their repertoire beyond common tourism spaces (e.g., Times Square, the Statue of Liberty) to bring folks to smaller, less-traveled—and therefore less-known—neighborhoods.[7] But the content and interactions on tour reinforce this perspective as well. Take autodidactic Harry Matthews, for example, who encourages his participants to see beyond what he calls the "creeping sameness of city life," even trying to nurture a distaste for the way mass culture obliterates local nuance. My fieldnotes of his tour evince this emphasis, common among many guides:

On Cranberry Street we stop across from three houses, built at the same time but altered over the years. Harry talks about the different housing styles. "You probably see these all over New York and don't think about them at all." He points out that the stoop on one of the brownstones has been dismantled. He explains that stoops used to cover the service entrances—since there were no alleyways that might have provided rear entry cooks and maids all used the ground floor—and allowed the second floor to become the "main floor." He points out the mansard roof on the corner building, explaining how this style apes French roofs made around the 1890s as a way to circumvent laws taxing space above the roof by simply sloping the roof at a steep enough angle as to envelope one or more floors. He talks about the film *Moonstruck*: how Cher was supposed to live here but the bakery where Nicholas Cage worked was six miles away in Bensonhurst. Harry laments that Hollywood is too quick to make the disparate neighborhoods of New York appear to be the same one, stating, "Historical and geographic accuracy are to be valued."

Evidence of guides positioning their tour content against mass culture and the more formal tourism industry is extensive. *Moonstruck* is just one example of a foil. The *Gangs of New York* film was used in a similar way for a BOWT tour, wherein the guide began by saying, "We'll be covering the book, the movie, *and reality*." In interviews and on tour, guides told me they felt parts of New York were becoming like any other downtown. The directors of organizations like the MAS and the Conference Board further reinforce this emphasis via their patronage of guides and selection of tour topics. Collectively, this "local particularism" reinforces an antihomogenization rekeying of the city.[8]

The second and third emphases are perhaps less obvious but no less important to understanding guides' tour content as a rekeying of urban culture. Also lost in the diversity of content is the overall antiestablishment, contrarian dispositions of guides, and Bill's tour is only one example of this second emphasis. Take, for example, the M27 Coalition's tours of "war profiteers headquarters," which coincided with the 2004 Republican National Convention. From my fieldnotes:

After offering a thumbnail sketch of what war profiteering is, and passing around materials (resource lists, and a map of war-related conglomerates), our group sets out to visit six corporate headquarters. The free tour was deemed a political protest by the NYPD, so a cordon of ten officers accompanies us (one for every two participants). There are "Got War?" picket signs that mimic the milk advertisements and some carry "Buy a Hummer! Buy oil! Buy our war!" signs. After stops at the Carlyle Group, Chevron, GM, and Lockheed Martin, the officers loosen up a bit. I approach two who were joking with one another and ask about the tour. The burlier of the two expressed appreciation, "Hey, it's a nice day, y'all are being good in a peaceful demo, and I'm learning something!"

Chapter 2's Bruce Kayton is another example, as he gives a "Non–Jerry Seinfeld Upper West Side" tour that includes stories about Noam Chomsky, FBI arrests, 1940s resident Fidel Castro, ACT UP, and the destruction of a Puerto Rican neighborhood to build Lincoln Center. And by teaching how to eat flora in public parks, Wildman Steve Brill intends for his tours to be a protest against the Parks Commission, quite proudly speaking of his confrontations with police as a way to signify and embrace his alternative vision:

On a stop just near the lake, while we were filling up Ziploc bags with our freshly dug burdock (which, he tells us, tastes like artichoke hearts when cooked), Steve told the group the story of his 1986 arrest—by undercover police who were taking his tour—for eating park vegetation. They'd been after him for a while for bringing people to the city's parks and teaching them what plants were good to eat. Apparently, he created such a stink, appearing on national talk shows and evening newscasts, and brought the police such bad press that charges were dropped and he hasn't received any trouble since. Quick to pun, Steve told the group that the media "ate up the story." The local reporters picked up the good "man-bites-dogweed" tale.

Brendan FitzGerald, whose tours comprise the next chapter's fieldnotes, describes his tours as "an educational process [and] a protest, in a sense." When I asked him about this potentially antagonistic relationship between his tours and the private businesses that poorly manage the public spaces he critiques, Brendan reflected back on feeling uncomfortable when other antiwar activists would yell at police, and strives for a better tone. He gave an example of being confronted at a high-end boutique called Henri Bendel's, a regular stop on his Midtown tours which often include video and photographic documentation, as an example of how he prefers to be contrarian but respectful:

> I want to show people that just because somebody's wearing a jacket doesn't mean that you have to back down from them. If you know your rights, and know what you are talking about, they're going to leave you alone. [On one tour] they came up and asked, "What are you doing in here?" They said that I needed to see marketing, and I said, "As I understand it, this is a public space and so, I don't really need to see marketing." And they said "Yeah, it is a public space, but you need to call marketing." Finally they said, "Can you just not photograph our merchandise?"

He cautions his groups against being disrespectful to security guards who, he reminds everyone, are often working for an hourly wage and have little say in regards to the public space violations they are there to learn and protest about. Academic guides turn a similarly critical eye on established institutions. Jennifer Fronc's "whole Bob Moses thing" (as she calls it) evinces this quality, and when I asked her about it she describes why she uses a particular story:

> I think that it helps non–New Yorkers be more anchored in what they are going to see, what they are going to experience. . . . The Sara Delano Roosevelt Park story is another one that I tell all the time, because it is about Bob Moses, who I hate, and I want everybody else to hate him and imagine that the city might have been different without him. And it is funny: every-

body loves a story about mean mothers-in-law. It doesn't work with kids, they're like, "What the hell are you talking about?" but middle-aged New Yorkers are like: "Wah ha ha! That's hilarious!"

Rather than what blues musicians describe as a "set list from hell," in which they must play the same songs night after night because their audiences expect to hear them, these contrarian inclinations demonstrate how these guides are eager to spin away from touristic expectations and mass cultural consumption. One guide, who prefers to focus on architectural details and cultural oddities rather than what he calls a more "packaged, digestible" tour, echoes what Grazian (2003, 410) and Becker (1963, 89–90) found in their studies of urban cultural consumption. This antiestablishment vision is true to the spirit of the aforementioned founder of the modern walking tour, Henry Hope Reed, who used tours to make his antimodernist, anticommercial architecture, and "contrarian opinions well known" (Gray 1999).

Autodidactic guides like Bill and Brendan also evince a third common emphasis of this alterative form of tourism: they espouse a clear DIY ethic that clearly contrasts with the more polished, cultural profiteering of urban culture exhibited by the business improvement districts and "tourist bubbles" they work within and through.[9] Hardly the passive consumption of Disney-like activities, there is a strong strain of engagement in walking tourism. A stop on Brendan's tour offers an explicit example of how DIY information is shared, and the hidden rules of the city are illuminated:

At a passage running directly through the city block between 53rd and 54th streets, Brendan explains these public spaces were designed to relieve some of the foot traffic on the heavily used sidewalks of the major avenues. Brendan shows us what he sees as the conquest of these spaces: "This is what I call 'café creep,' or 'extending the architecture.'" Here, a restaurant has placed its outdoor seating into a walkway that is designated public space. Pulling out a handy tape measure, he gets a volunteer to help him measure how much the café takes over the walkway. The result: including the large planters differentiating the spaces, the dining area takes up 60 percent of the public space, leaving the rest to foot traffic.

While Brendan tells his groups how touring can be an alternative to watching television or going to a movie, Bill Brown talks about using his own passionate struggles as the orienting concept, his own map for when he visits other cities. On tour, Bill conveys that "rather than the museums and tourist traps," walking with one's own agenda is a better way to explore a city. Just like the M27 Coalition, Brendan, and Bruce Kayton, Bill Brown embodies a "be your own tour guide" mentality. Autodidact guides like these are likely to be comparatively evangelistic about their form of knowledge acquisition to their participants.

Adding guides' need to distinguish their individual talents from their peers' areas of expertise with their own personal dispositions as critical thinkers, DIY historians and activists, and even as expatriates of the formal labor market, these emphases separate walking guides from the larger tourism industry and the mass-commodified culture swirling around them. (It is this framework that makes these emphases "rekeyings" rather than "keyings.") With taglines like Joyce Gold's "There are 20,000 people buried underneath Washington Square Park" on their brochures, we can see how guides pull away façades, pique curiosity, challenge "blandness" in order to re-enchant, or de-banalize the urban everyday world in similar ways. These rekeyings make guides curious urban investigators as they map hidden zoning laws or the cameras in public spaces, protest war profiteers, or educate about which particular urban flora are edible. This chapter concludes with a discussion on the particular role guides play in this process of an emergent urban culture.

"Learning 'the Connect' ": Tours and Street Intellectualism

In describing what he believes is the major attraction for his clients, one guide told me, "participants think tours are edifying"; another said being a guide is "almost like being a school teacher"; and yet another, when complaining about a disinterested tourist, said to me, "Well, you understand. You're in a related field." Summing up his work, one asked me, "I get to work outside, in the street, teaching. . . . What could be better?" Many see the walking tour as a kind of mobile classroom. It is a fair comparison in a way: after all, some of them are aspiring teachers, and all are attempting to share history and culture in some capacity. But at the same time guides know they are not doing academic or intellectual work in any traditional sense. Some are just finding a second career that is more akin to an out-of-reach aspiration of being a teacher, while others are on their way to being professors. The large majority of the people in this book are more like perpetual students of history, of culture, of public spaces, existing in a kind of interstitial social space. As Justin described it to me, "A lot of guides are former teachers—people who've retired but still want to be engaged and believe that they have something to share." Guides are unconventional intellectuals, and the role they take on stands somewhere in the in between.

Eric Washington is emblematic of how guides see this position. When I asked him about his personal goals, he talked about wanting to be a public historian, a well-rounded community figure somewhere between an academic lecturer and an avid history buff. By taking steps to teach in a continuing education course and curating the Manhattanville exhibit at City College, he moves closer to that goal, even if he cannot imagine juggling graduate coursework to earn an advanced degree. Bruce Kayton's story echoes Eric's: only when he was middle-aged did Bruce realize that he should have been a teacher, but he sees little chance for becoming a traditional educator now. He tells me, "I know I don't have the money and the years to get a Ph.D. [but guiding] is kinda like teaching, because you're doing a lot of reading and research, but you're sharing it with people." Without guiding, he says it is like he's "reading a great book with no one else to discuss it with." Then, at the other end of the spectrum, we see those who use guiding on their way to an academic career rather than as a way to live a kind of teaching life. Big Onion guides emphasize the comparable aspects of touring and academic teaching. Jennifer, for example, sees little difference between the academic history in Columbia University classrooms and her sidewalk public history, save for the fact that "one group hasn't done the reading." She says both "put minds to work." Academics and autodidacts both may want to move perceptions of tourism closer to the academic: BOWT guides want to lend academic heft to work that could be seen as mere popular culture, while autodidacts want to emphasize that they are more like public historians.[10]

Academics and autodidacts both value the nonacademic aspects of guiding as well, particularly the experiential quality of walking tourism absent in most conventional academic education. As Eric Washington explains it:

> One of the fun things about doing walking tours, and I think beneficial
> things, is that you are really *experiencing* by being on the street what you
> don't get to experience when you are looking through the window on a bus
> or sitting in a school. . . . You're learning something but there are trees in
> the room and cars going by. What an odd classroom!

In listening to guides talk about teaching, and working with public histories and cultures, our conversations often shift to these intangible qualities of walking while teaching. They will invariably resort to classroom or museum imagery as a way to differentiate what they do from more traditional educational enterprises just as they juxtapose it with the mass culture of bus tourism. For example, Mark Shulman describes living in New York as living in "a museum with an ever-changing series of exhibits [whereby] some people go through without reading the map, and other people go through having done the homework." And when I asked about this kind of street education, Jennifer Fronc talked about her own Socratic back and forth with participants and used Big Onion's analogy of layers to explain how this plays out as an educational process:

> [Another guide] worked mostly with synagogue groups, these Jewish teenagers from Nashville, or whatever. . . . She's taking them through the Jewish East Side and Chinatown and they are so unfamiliar with *cities* in general, not just New York City. That they don't know to *read* what they are seeing. They don't know how to read the neighborhood: is it dirty or is it clean? Is it safe? . . . And that is why it is better to give the tour to New Yorkers than the tourists. [Visitors] don't know what they are seeing. They don't know. They just see the dirt, the garbage. They are not attuned to the minor architectural differences between the dumbbell tenements and—

When I responded, "Flemish bond . . ." she said, "Yeah, exactly. . . . I teach them how to read is [by] using this Big Onion analogy of *layers.*"

For guides, the city is a shifting and wondrous place, a repository turned inside out, a place for all. Eric insists that anyone can mine public spaces and histories for their own purposes:

> Everybody has a history. . . . So, I think walking tours are really fascinating because people do what they do all the time. They get up off the couch, they get dressed, they go out, and they walk. So they are maybe walking in an area they don't generally walk in, and they are seeing things that perhaps have been there the whole time that they've been there, that they have not taken notice of before. And then they go back to their neighborhoods and they see that their neighborhood, their block, has history, too. Their building has history, and I think that is so valuable. That's so exciting. Which is why I think that there is plenty of room for nonacademic historians to do this kind of stuff and they should be encouraged. [Think about] all the school kids who are not going to have this information in their schoolbooks, who feel disenfranchised by the history that they are being dosed, and can now discover [history themselves].

I asked him if he was saying that his participants felt disenfranchised from history, but also from the process of learning, he agreed, saying that they need to "learn 'the connect.'"

This notion of a disenfranchisement from the processes of education is an interesting one in relation to Bill's, Eric's, and Bruce's perceived position as academic outsiders. Their DIY style indicates a willingness to be on both ends of the process, as learners and teachers.[11]

Most of these folks are not academic experts or specialists,[12] but they are not the average urban dweller either. They are more like what Alfred Schutz called the 'informed citizen.' As compared to the *expert* (who is preoccupied with a field of expertise) and the *man on the street* (who is concerned with his or her own problems) stands an erudite "third" person with no real desire for specialist- or "academic"-level knowledge yet "does not acquiesce in the fundamental vagueness" of quotidian passions and sentiments (1970, 240).[13] Someone in this in-between role

> finds himself placed in a domain which belongs to an infinite number of possible frames of reference. There are no pregiven ready-made ends, no fixed borderlines within which he can look for shelter. He has to choose the frame of reference by choosing his interest; he has to investigate the zones of relevances adhering to it; and he has to gather as much knowledge as possible of the origin and sources of the relevances actually or potentially imposed upon him. (242)

Of course, the sort of well-informed citizen that a walking guide embodies is quite literally a man on the street, but the importance of this concept comes from guides' relative in-between position—even if it is in "becoming" some other role (e.g., the BOWT guide being in the process of becoming an expert, or a guide trying to become an actor). Guides feel compelled to publicly share through their experiential learning and their predilection for what Schutz called the 'infinite frames of reference.' They offer egalitarianism and a democratization of meaning-making itself. When Eric, for example, says he teaches participants by getting them to learn through doing "what they do all the time," he is speaking of the transforming tourists into informed citizens.

Most would agree with one of their own who concluded our interview by stating, "It is in our abilities as provocative and engaging people—rather than stodgy academics—that allow us to be successful at what we do." As compared those in the ivory tower, walking guides are "street intellectuals"—a term used by Mitchell Duneier to describe how people on the street are valuable members of urban environment (1999, 3)—who speak to a wide audience without the various trappings of academia. Bill Brown was a good guide for illuminating this position, as he often expressed being interested in "getting people to interact with one another." He provided an example of this when I asked him about how his perspective plays out on tour. He reminded me of the homeless man who shadowed our group, describing it as a "great experience" for showing participants how everyone can and should be concerned about what he sees as the oppressive police state of the post-Giuliani New York City. A walking tour like this is a binding ceremony wherein participants' values and cultural meanings are communicated in an interaction ritual, the foundation of which is this kind of relearning of the city.[14]

Through their tours, guides contribute to city culture but in a very distinct fashion. The strong emphasis urban theorists and commentators have placed upon large-scale works of architects and planners, government policies and commercialized Disney-style corporatism, or upon the Schutzian man on the street (as is the case with MacCannell's tourist) evades urbanites who exist within these dichotomies and the ways urban culture is continually up for negotiation and reinterpretation by those at the street level. Guides work through their own sets of personal interpretations and negotiations of content—at the level of understanding the cultural world of New York City, but also the social world of the guiding field—for a common, countering version of city culture. The emphasis in studies on urban culture, then, has been on the "keyings" rather than the "rekeyings" that have been on display here, and on the intellectual instead of the street intellectual.

Urban Alchemists

7

The Transmutation of the City

The modern metropolis has been conceptualized as the epitome and symbol of rationality, anathema to the enchantments of traditional societies. It is a theme that runs through Max Weber to Robert Park to Richard Sennett.[1] Sennett used a lecture in Karlsruhe, Germany, to voice his fears about contemporary urban life. The endless strings of Gaps, Starbucks, and Niketowns, he told the audience, denies urban walkers the chance to discover "the strange, the unexpected, the arousing" and, correspondingly, "shared history" and "collective memory" were slowly being forgotten, then concluding by wondering what might be done to create complexity in the public sphere and nurture mutual attachment among city dwellers (2005). But creative folks are everywhere, and every sort of person can engage in cultural work to shape the city. Only some do, and even fewer get noticed in the academic and sociological literature. There is, in fact, a long history of characters who have labored against such trends of homogenization, commodification, and banalization—from the flâneur's poetic exploration of the commodified palace of the arcade to the Situationist's excavation of the psychological barriers and pathways of the city (Sadler 1998). If commercialized, Disneyfied cities stand at one end of the continuum, the picture at the other end should now be in focus. There we find characters who nurture attachments, re-enchant neighborhoods, and embrace uncertainty. Guides use public spaces and resources to lend themselves an endeavor, a goal, a value, for some a career, and give something back to the city while doing so. When Justin Ferate told a *New York Times* reporter that "The city is so magical. It never runs out of stories" (Hedges 2003), he contrasts the work of guides with the Disneyfication meme and urban commentators like Sennett and Sharon Zukin.

Alkemie, as a term, has its root in Old French, and possibly Arabic, to mean "the art of transformation." Across the languages and between the worlds of science and magic, alchemists labored under a primary dictum: *solve et coagula*, "to separate and to join together." Via a metallurgical process, alchemists sought to convert objects, usually from inexpensive metals, into gold or silver, and this allusion works for characters like walking guides, who infuse the city's fabric with curious stories, re-enchant neighborhoods, and offer a sort of magical urbanism to their clients.[2] They detach the elementary molecules of the quotidian world, or rescue pieces of landscape from obscurity and incoherence and place them in temporary cultural compounds. The richness of interaction is what makes urban living attractive, even necessary for its inhabitants. Because cities are so full of these free resources (e.g., public spaces, cultural history, opportunities for social action), there are many others who create marketable goods out of these raw materials. Some alchemists, mentioned earlier, are lower on the scale of interaction: Gregory Snyder's ethnographic account details how New York graffiti writers gain respect and create public art with little more than an abandoned wall and some cans of paint (2009) and Teresa Gowan examines how San Francisco's homeless recyclers and how they construct their identities through their practices (2000). There are others who organize in groups, such as "radical nonconsumerist" urban "dumpster divers" or "freegans" (Essig 2002). Then there are those who are much more explicitly engaged with their audiences: in addition to tour guides, Mitchell Duneier adds his account of how New York's "unhoused" reinvigorate sidewalks and, through scavenging the city's refuse emerge as public figures (1999) and street thespians and sidewalk buskers who set up shop to reinvigorate the sidewalk with prose and song (Flusty 2000; Bywater 2007). Some offer fleeting moments of alchemy, like "flash mobbers" with their impromptu "cultural situations" (Wasik 2006, 56). Then there are more resilient installations of these alchemic practices, such as the Lower East Side's "Green Guerrillas" who develop a sense of community and pride of place by creating public gardens in abandoned lots, or Sabato Rodia's found object-monument, Watts Towers (Becker 1984), or Pittsburgh's Howling Mob Society, which posts its own landmark plaques to unearth neglected historical tales like "The Great Railroad Strike of 1877."[3] Irrespective of scales of intensity of interaction or permanence, the sense of urban transformation courses throughout each of these realms: the street musician enchants the corner with a familiar Dexter Gordon riff and the "found art" artist takes pieces of urban flotsam and configures them into an art object, the inert wall becomes a mural and the derelict lot becomes a community garden, one person's garbage transmutes into someone else's subway reading the same way a mute façade is given meaning through storytelling.

For their part, guides offer an intensified, more social interaction—what Goffman called a "focused gathering" (1963, 89)—through three kinds of transmutation by using a mixture of falsity, myth, and curious revelations to uproot standard and banal visions of the city; aiming to incorporate serendipity into their practices; and attempting to transform their participants through the experience of the walking tour. By showing these alchemic processes we can see how guides and others like them create something transcendent, something beyond their own lives or to any particular organization they might work for, to provide something invaluable. Guides' dispositions match up with their tour interactions and urban culture at large—a perspective urbanists like Lyn Lofland and William H. Whyte advocated for.

A few years ago, Brendan FitzGerald was constructing cell-phone sites on historical landmarks, a job he describes as a front-row seat to flagrant code violations and building practices and, paired with the 2002 antiwar protests, he became energized over the use of public spaces. As he told me, "In a lot of ways I feel the issue of private and public space is not unrelated to issues of the war protests. It seems like there is a constant challenge from certain groups to take public space away from citizens." His interest in activism and photography mesh with the survey work of his day job to come together in guiding:

> I've always liked talking. I like walking. I used to be an outdoor education guy at one point, where my job was leading groups on adventures. I knew it was the most practical, easiest way to get this across to people. People got fired up and wanted to go to see these spaces. That struck me as odd, because these are the spaces, these plazas that you walk by every day.

Energized, he started giving tours every other weekend, first with friends and later through listings in local weeklies. Brendan, occasionally joined by his brother Patrick, regularly documents his groups, building violations, and the changes over time, and publishes those findings on a Web site. In one of our interviews he told me how an important piece of his work is to not just take the walks, but provide the data he collects to municipal authorities:

> I've read a lot of Jane Jacobs, who is a great example of how you go up that ladder, and how you get to the top. And I think city council members are an excellent way to do that. Also, I go straight to the Department of Buildings. The one thing that I do have going for me is that there is a whole organization that is supposed to be monitoring this that doesn't have the resources [and I] just go and say: "Here are some photographs, here's a petition, here's the reports, can you get a guy out to the building?"

It is not purely altruistic, however. He also uses the documents he collects as a guide—particularly the photographic work he does of the public spaces—to build his resume as a production designer in the entertainment industry.

Such a perspective is on display in the following fieldnote of his tour of Midtown Manhattan. The example of this tour not only demonstrates how a guide can relish in the work, transforms his city, and change himself in the process, but it also establishes our final discussions on three types of alchemy at work on the sidewalk.

Spatial Struggles (Privately Owned Public Spaces of Midtown Tour, July 2003)

A tight-knit group of twelve gathers on a Saturday in front of the Ritz Hotel. Brendan FitzGerald and his brother Patrick emphasize they aren't urban planners, real estate agents, graduate students, or professional guides. They are unshaven, in jeans and T-shirts. Patrick is a software engineer and Brendan works in film production. Brendan tells me in an interview, "I have a lot of fun with the city."

On the street Brendan admits to the crowd, none too sheepishly, "Some people go to a bar or watch baseball on their Saturdays. We give walking tours. . . . It's a hobby." For an overview, they start with how the 1961 zoning law established an incentive program for developers. "While it's different from place to place," Brendan says, "they are given seven to ten feet of rentable space outside their envelope for every square foot of public space."

1 **825 Eighth Ave.**
One World Wide Plaza

Public Space: Elliptical Arcades- 12,000 sf
Plaza- 26,806 sf
Subway Access- 3,500

Public Space Designer: SWA Group

Building Architect: Skidmore, Owings & Merrill

(Residential building) Frank Williams & Associates

Building Owner: EOP-World-wide Plaza LLC

Building Completed: 1989

Notes:

W. 50th St.

8th Ave.

W. 49th St

■ Indicates Public Space

REQUIRED AMENITIES

Elliptical Arcades: Restrooms 2

Subway Access: Elevator and escalator to subway

Plaza:
Bicycle Parking 2 Racks
Drinking Fountain: 1
Food Service: 2 Retail pavilions with eating establishments
Litter Receptacles: 8
Planting: 2,065
Trees within space: 48 of 10- to 12- inch caliper
Seating: 707 linear feet of fixed seating, 134 movable chairs
Tables: Yes
Water Feature: 450 sf fountain
Lighting: Yes
Plaque/sign: 4 entry signs, 1 information plaque
Access: Elliptical Arcades 6 am to 9 pm
Plaza, subway access areas 24 hrs

Page 1

Figure 7 Brendan FitzGerald's handout for his Privately Owned Public Spaces of Midtown walking tour.

Brendan continues to tell us how, for the 3.58 million square feet of public space that private companies provide, the city permits more than 20 million square feet of additional floor space. They plan to show a few of the good, bad, and ugly of those 509 privately owned public spaces. They pass around a worksheet that they use for their tour groups, giving the impression that this is an educational exercise (see fig. 7). But there are things the brothers are happy to admit that they don't know. Unlike guides who brandish their affiliations and credentials, Brendan and Patrick work hard to establish their naiveté. Their unpolished personae endear them to the group.

Brendan starts with the small square we're in. The Firefighters Memorial at Ritz Plaza sits across from the Engine 54, Ladder 4, Battalion 9 firehouse. "It is what planners call an 'urban plaza,'" he tells us. His sinewy frame jauntily shifts as he tells us about how, through the 1990s, developers would obscure their public spaces with hidden entrances and high hedges. While intended to keep undesirables out, these practices resulted in secluded areas ideal for drug dealing and crime. Brendan gives us a few moments to mill around—to see the surveillance cameras, smell the odors wafting from a neighboring restaurant, and hear clanking sounds of a nearby AC unit. In the center is a torqued obsidian cube with the engraved names of sixteen firemen who died on September 11, 2001. I read them: Battalion Chief Edward F. Geraghty, Captain David Wooley, Lieutenant Daniel O'Callaghan, Firefighter First Grade Jose Guadelupe. . . . Water trickles out of the top of the cube, and ripples over the gold lettering, glinting in the sunlight.

At the next stop, the One World Wide Center on Eighth Avenue and West 50th, we stand outside a Starbucks. He tells us that this is where he usually starts his tours (as indicated on his handout). In the midst of making a point about how it is a more open space than the first plaza, a participant casually offers him a drag of marijuana. Brendan declines, and refocuses on the building's violations. A little later, a professional guide who saw their tour listed in *Time Out New York* asks the brothers why they don't charge a fee. Brendan says profiting from the tour, and the spaces, would almost be hypocritical. "It would ruin the tour," he says, insisting on the value of giving away the information.

At 1350 Sixth Avenue and next to Robert Indiana's LOVE sculpture, we stand at a "plaza" that is nothing more than an empty fifty-square-foot space created by setting the building back from the sidewalk. Brendan pulls Jerold Kayden's book, *Privately Owned Public Spaces*, out of his bag and flips to a map of the Midtown area we are in. He passes around the book and continues to examine the plaza. "There are no benches," he says with a wave of his arm, "no fountains, not even a step to indicate that you are moving from public to private space, and yet, they get a massive break from the city." Here, the brothers talk about their research methods, describing how they mainly use the city's Web site, Kayden's book, and records from the New York Department of Buildings, which provides detailed information about codes, regulations, violations, and developers' agreements with the city. In addition to circulating a petition, he directs us to their Web site for maps of their tours and other information if participants want to use the information to enlighten their own city walks.

"It's a Charming Story, and I Couch It That Way": Shifting the Cultural Ground

Brendan's tours are grounded in very tangible facts and recent phenomena, but guides dip into grayer and perhaps more obscure areas of information as well. Many engage in what I call "shifting the cultural ground." This first alchemic category can actually be subdivided into three subsets of actions: fabrication, mythmaking, and revelation.

Fabrications have a rich historical precedent, as tourist information and falsity have been closely connected for millennia, and today's mainstream press has perpetuated the image as well. Historian Lionel Casson, for example, writes:

> Much of their information, of course, was useful, even essential. . . . But useful was not their only stock and trade. . . . The guides who took Herodotus around the pyramids fed him a tall story about the fabulous amounts paid out for supplying the workers with radishes, onions, and garlic; six centuries later, their descendants were telling Aristides that each pyramid extended downward into the earth the same distance it did upward (1974, 265–66).

And an antiquarian named Lucian once wrote: "Abolish all lies from Greece, and the guides there would all die of starvation, since no tourist wants to hear the truth—even for free" (Perrottet 2002, 107). Chuck Connors, introduced earlier, didn't help the image of guides, and contemporary dailies still characterize guides as hucksters (Feiden 2005). Many guides feel an ever-pervasive stigmatization of the industry. Throughout the course of this study I found most errors to be minor ones, along the lines of miscounting a few theaters on Broadway or an incorrect date. Such a lack of empirical data could obviously have to do with a Hawthorne effect (the phenomenon wherein a subject modifies his or her behaviors because of the presence of a scientific observer, in this case trailing in the back of the tour group), and I pressed guides on this issue in interviews before and after tours. Many admitted to giving false information at one time or another, often explaining any inaccuracies as part of an effort to include thought-provoking, attention-grabbing content, even at the expense of truth.[4] Mark Levy told me, "If there are two different dates, or two different facts, go with the one that is the most interesting. Never let the truth get in the way of a story!" A second guide explained: "a little bit of schmaltz never hurt anyone; in fact, it could be good because it gets them thinking." And a third told me, "in fact sometimes the wrong piece of information will encourage interest in a specific area or point." As Mark Shulman explained it to me:

> People want to know what that building is, and it's the difference between saying, "I don't know," and my saying, "That's the building where Samuel Goldwyn made gloves in 1899." And you know what? They'll forget that in fifteen minutes or less, but you've made their tour better rather than making their tour less enjoyable. Because that's what they're there for . . .

In a later conversation Mark refined this comment—only half jokingly—with a kind of rubric for different buildings: he'd say a factory was where Goldwyn made gloves before becoming a movie mogul if it was any older manufacturing building, or the ex-headquarters of Visa or American Express if it was a newer office building, where Greta Garbo lived if it was an older apartment building, and where Nelson Rockefeller died if it was a newer apartment building. Reinforcing Mark's comments, Andy Sydor explained to me that not knowing an answer undermines one's credibility and laughs when telling me of a guide who would brush off questions he didn't know with the same sort of answers: "If he didn't know the address: 70 Pine Street. If he didn't know the year it was built: 1892. Architects: Smith and Wollensky. He'd say it with complete confidence. It sounded good. That's a trade secret by the way." More broadly, however, many comments indicate a rationalization for what one called "good-natured schmaltzy stuff" as a way to construct a bond between the guide and group. As Mark Shulman was careful to point out to me, *not knowing* an answer denies participants the feeling that they have asked a good question, forecloses opportunities for discussion, and undermines the learning community.

And then there is the more careful kind of mythmaking, commonly exhibited by guides relishing in retelling an apocryphal story, explicitly citing it as an apocryphal story. Outside the White Horse Tavern, for example, one of the two guides leading our Literary Pub Crawl and Walking Tour tells the group, "professional psychics still feel the presence of Dylan Thomas," and later, at Chumley's bar, after pointing out the hatch that allowed the bartender to escape prohibition raids, "It is said that Orson Welles, while working on *Citizen Kane*, left a $1,500 bar tab—and that was at a time when beer was a nickel." Such blurred lines are to be expected, according to Jeffrey Trask, because "that's history." He tells me that "not all of it is going to be true. And the untruths tell a story too—about the context, about what stories get told, and what stories are ignored." His perspective was on display on tour, which was captured in this fieldnote:

In Bowling Green Park, near the tip of Manhattan, the guide discusses the myths of the angry mobs that supposedly congregated here around the dawn of our country's independence. "It is said that after hearing George Washington read the Declaration of Independence a mob marched down to this triangle-shaped park to pull down a statue of King George III." He points to the location of where the statue would have been.

"But these are New York rumors," and, with a shrug, "Again, whatever, it's a good story." The guide shows a laminated reproduction of a French engraving of the scene for another reason. It portrays a Parisian-looking square, curiously, with Native Americans pulling the ropes, and he notes how the buildings look nothing like the group's current surroundings.

A block later, he uses the ten-foot monument in Battery Park that portrays Peter Minuit purchasing Manhattan from Native Americans for $24 to talk about how it was a highly unlikely occurrence.

Then there are stories so thoroughly obscured by history that guides offer several possible versions out of necessity, further perpetuating these myths. A guide working for the Central Park Conservancy—the official management organization of the park—for example, offers three explanations for what happened to the sheep in the area called Sheep's Meadow: the sheep were being inbred and started to look "peculiar," and the homeless who would steal and eat them were getting sick, so the ruminants were moved out of the park; that Robert Moses was getting tired of waiting for them to cross the street on his drives through the park; and that Moses was jealous of the parties then-mayor Jimmy Walker was throwing, so he turned the sheep's fold into Tavern on the Green for his own galas. As we walked away, we were left to decide for ourselves which one to believe. And my fieldnotes of another tour, of Broadway theaters, indicates how the elucidation of myths can become a way for a guide to stimulate conversation:

As the group settled into the front rows of the empty Walter Kerr Theater, Darryl Reilly talks about the stage and how it is set up for *Take Me Out*, which won three Tonys. He talks about the set, pointing out the fake grass and the backdrop of outfield lights.

"But, does anybody notice something that doesn't belong? Something that would not be on the stage during the show?"

Without a beat, an older gentlemen yells out, "Do you mean the ghost light?" Darryl agrees, pointing to center stage, at a solitary, bare bulb.

Darryl's Socratic shtick about the ghost light and the stories behind it was thrown a little off track by a correct answer but, after a little banter, we get to hear more about it. "It is said that the light wards off the ghosts of jilted understudies—a story dating back to candles being left alit during Shakespeare's time. Another story is about a burglar who once broke into a dark theater, broke his leg by falling off the stage, and sued the owners."

"These are good stories, but," he says with a dramatic sigh, "the real reason for ghost lights is for insurance purposes. Now, does anyone else know some other theater mythology?"

"Break a leg!" someone yells out.

"Right. There are a number of stories for that one too." Darryl continues, "One is that it is just the opposite of good luck. Another is that the people would hope the audience would love the play so much the actors would 'break their legs' bowing so much during the ovation. The real reason is that 'Have a heart attack' didn't get enough votes. Okay." After a beat, "Anything else?" When no one can think of another superstition, he fills in the empty space. "Well, it is said that it is bad luck to say the name of a particular Shakespearian play."

Many nod. A man next to me asks his wife, "What? Which?"

"The one with the three witches?" she whispers, " 'Tomorrow, tomorrow, tomorrow?' No? Honey, it rhymes with 'MacDeath.' "

Now having the full group's attention, he straightens up and excitedly says, "Oh, *Macbeth*?" Everyone groans and Darryl rolls his eyes.

Eric Washington cites a popular example of a myth to describe how he rationalizes his usage of this kind of questionable content: the naming of the Dakota. This was the first major building in northern Manhattan on Central Park West and 72nd Street, built for the Singer sewing mogul in 1882, and infamous as the site of John Lennon's assassination, but it is often said that the building was so far from the rest of developed Manhattan that a common joke was "you might as well live in the Dakotas." As Eric told me:

Well that story has been told and told and told and retold. It may well be true, it may just be a story. . . . You should say: "I don't know if that story is true, it's a wonderful story and it well may be true." Because it brings you to another point: It tells you—whether or not the story is true—something about people's attitudes about moving to what was considered a rural area. Another [tale] was that its design was to look like an overgrown chateau. To psychologically foster the idea that, hey, "Living in an apartment building isn't so bad, it even looks like a house." I don't know if that's true, you know? I think it's a charming story, *and I couch it that way.*

In each of these examples, guides clearly frame their stories as myths, pivoting on phrases like "it has been said," "some people say," and "so the story goes." In this fashion, they are couching their tales.

Then there is the process of revelation, through which guides uncover the hidden aspects of the city for the group; aspects obscured by time (i.e., guides will say "This is the place where . . .," "On the same spot as . . .," and "It was where George Washington . . ." as a way to bring the past into the present) or by participants' own lack of awareness. As Brendan tells me: "I try to make them look at something they've seen, but maybe not seen the same way." Earlier fieldnotes show examples of this, including Eric Washington's exposition of the *eruv* in Harlem and the exposition of the reversed Zodiac on the ceiling of Grand Central Terminal, but of this kind of revelatory practice can be found on nearly every tour. A few examples from my fieldnotes reinforce this point:

On a BOWT tour of the tip of Manhattan, looking north up Greenwich Street, our guide points to the blocks of buildings to the west and says, "Greenwich Street is where the shoreline used to be, and all that area to the left there is just landfill . . ."

On a tour of the Cathedral of St. John the Divine in Morningside Heights, our guide starts to talk about religion and history, by pointing out the masonry: "Do you see the line where there is a different color of brick? That's called 'the Pearl Harbor Arch': a line where masons stopped working at the onset of World War II."

Outside 157 Willow Street in Brooklyn, the guide follows a circular cut in the sidewalk, about one foot in diameter. "What's this?" When no one answers he tells the group about how these were once coal chutes for the brownstones, but they have now been filled in with concrete, and then describes how homes were heated in the nineteenth century.

Across from the New York Supreme Court, our guide describes the obsidian monument standing in the traffic circle as a Mali slave boat with its long central mast reaching up to the sky. He adds, "To me, it is like a massive black fist giving the middle finger to the courthouse. I say that seriously."

After we reach the Great Lawn of Central Park, the group circles around Bruce Kayton. "Right here," he tells us, "was an African and Irish American settlement called Seneca Village, founded by freed blacks around 1825. The history books like to say that there was 'nothing' on this site before the park, but it has always been, historically, the place for people outside the mainstream of society. During the Depression there were massive groupings of homeless, called 'Hoovervilles,' located here as well."

Dutch "starchitect" Rem Koolhaas talks about how cities have become "progressively meaningless, their substance increasingly insubstantial . . . banalized, and nonspecific" (Rajchman 1994, 99), but from a curious remapping of constellations and a religious boundary to the hidden shoreline and a line in brickwork, from a crease of cement to the hidden meanings of public art and the histories obscured by time, the above examples show that guides lift a veil off of urban culture and history, debanalizing and re-enchanting the city. This process of revelation, along with the tactics of fabrication and mythmaking and revelation work to "shift the ground." This is just the first step to an understanding a guide's alchemic practices.

"Do You Want to Come In and See My House?" Spontaneity and the City

Fodor's *New York City* travel guide (2004) tells visitors that New York City has two things going for it: charm and spontaneity. We will set aside the first quality to focus upon the second, more tangible one, which also serves as the second of guides' alchemic processes. Guides told me that the greater potential for the unexpected is one of the most unique and valued things about walking tourism, and is unlike the more scripted elements of a Disneyfied urban culture. The walking guide and participant may well be in a focused interaction, but they are also engaged in what Goffman called *uncontained participation* wherein any 'contingencies' or 'fortuitousness' may interject themselves in these exchanges (1961, 1963, and 1974: 33): from the guide, group, passersby, or the city itself (e.g., a new building, or a new event).[5] Walking tours lend themselves to this kind of openness.

Guides, for all their planning, know that anything can happen. As one said, "My tours tend to evolve on their own." Accounts of serendipity are pervasive in interviews, as guides love to report stories of a local or homeless person who argued over a story, or of being invited into a church or someplace where they wouldn't normally have had access. Eric Washington sees the whimsy of other city dwellers as one of the most important parts of his experiences: "Somebody will interrupt, somebody will come up off the street and panhandle, or will see you and ask directions. There's this dynamic that just doesn't occur on [bus] tours." Justin Ferate agrees, telling me that a moment like that is "one of those blessings of New York," even "a godsend." He leans back and laughs, saying, "Crazy people are part of the magic of the city." But not all chance occurrences are from "crazies." He was once talking about a row of Flemish houses standing behind him, and a man came out to listen. After a while he asked, "Do you all want to come and see my house?" Their answer was, "Of course!" As he continues:

> He and his wife bought the house from the first owners, and they bought it with all the furnishings and when the neighborhood went into decline in the 1950s, with the coming of the highways out of New York, his wife said, "I love the house too much, I just can't leave it." So they never left. So, while the world changed around them, they still have this 1890s microcosm, in which they lived. . . . It was like stepping into this fancy land that never would have happened if I had planned it. . . . Those moments get me excited.

In a similar moment, Katia Howard describes how her investigative spirit paired with an unexpected opportunity shaped one of her tours:

> The first time I did a tour, someone asked me, "Do you know anything about that building over there?" [and points] over their shoulder—a low-rise building with a little backyard. And I really didn't know anything about it except that that it looked mid-nineteenth century. So, when I was repeating the tour, I went by the house, and I rang the doorbell, and it turned out that the daughter of the owner was there. "Yeah, my father owns the house and you can call him." So I called him. He was an Italian immigrant who owned a barbershop in the Port Authority and [the next time I gave the tour] he was having a family barbeque in the back. He invited the whole tour into his backyard, which was very serendipitous and wonderful.

She goes on, "I could have stopped the tour then, because everybody felt very satisfied. It was early on, and I knew that it was going to be the highlight, meeting this wonderful character." Joyce describes her group's reactions to such moments as a kind of fear that then turns into an "excitement over seeing something new."

Autodidacts are more likely to embrace these more quixotic moments because their tours are more politically or culturally based. Academically inclined guides share fewer of these stories, and I have noted a tinge of envy when I relate one to them. Still, Erik Goldner reminds me that academics can have these moments too because they are all doing what he calls "open-air history." He says that "something happens" almost very tour, and cites an example of his tour group being asked to come into a synagogue on the Lower East Side. Because of exigencies, Erik states with a wry smile, "No tour is like any other." Jeffrey Trask told me that his tours are "constantly changing." And another BOWT guide described that she's "much more spontaneous on tour than in class." Their boss, Seth, explained that these freedoms in changeable content are an additional benefit, even a necessity. "Imagine," he tells me, "if you taught the same thing, going to Ellis Island everyday for five days. By Friday, I'd want to kill myself." He says that he knows more than a few tours worth of material for areas like Ellis Island because he wants to "do something different to keep the material fresh so that Friday's group doesn't suffer."

Unlike the more carefully orchestrated touristic "pseudo-events" (Boorstin 1961) of theme parks, "historical sites," and museums, the walking tour's openness valorizes the unexpected aspects of urban life. Seeking out this kind of interaction is part of their disposition, since many feel that serendipity is a worthy part of the process of discovery, echoing Louis Pasteur's famous dictum: "chance favors only the prepared mind." Guides feel these sorts of interactions make participants feel they are in dialogue with each other and with the city. As Alfred Pommer described this perspective to me, "the best way to encourage it is [to] step back, because sometimes an interloper is looking to say a little speech." In the end, he feels that it's a win-win situation in that "they give their speech, the group loves it, and you know, it adds to my tour for free." Seth Kamil says he trains guides to "learn neighborhoods" rather than a particular route as a part of this "necessity of chance":

> You *have* to be flexible. You have to be able to come to an intersection and say [to yourself], "Okay, police action on this corner, we're gonna cross the street, go two blocks around, come up on the other side," and *the client will never know* because I know enough to detour without them knowing it.

There are a few guides, in fact, who do not prepare extensively, claiming they want to be open to the creativity and fluidity of the experience. Wildman

Steve Brill told me that "jazz," for him, "is a big inspiration. The improvisation of guiding gives me a sense of freedom and variation, it 'keeps it fresh.' A plant can be presented in different ways—medicinal, ecology, cooking— depending on the interactions and what else we find." Brendan told me, "I want tours to be fun and a little crazy. I never know what will happen."

"I Tell Them How to Dress": Transforming the Visitor into a Local and a Local into a Tourist

Guides will often frame the information they tell as "Stuff Every New Yorker Needs to Know," which can include anything from how to find a good cheesecake to knowing that Truman Capote wrote *In Cold Blood* at 70 Willow Street in Brooklyn Heights. New York City is a warehouse of information big enough to get lost within. Guides manage to impart information to transform participants into "knowledgeable locals." This is the third and final alchemic practice of the walking guide, and it is one that dovetails again with one of Lyn Lofland's uses of urban public spaces: they teach people to be more tolerant and aware of the multiplicity of lives, histories, and perspectives of a city's dwellers, and can transform inhabitants into savvy urbanites (1998, 232, 236–42). Tour guides assist in this endeavor.

By making the everyday places of the city "strange," guides transform locals. Joyce is fond of saying that it's her job to "make tourists out of New Yorkers, and to make New Yorkers out of tourists," and Bill Brown tells me he wants to "create a state of mind" in his participants. Brendan, for another example, describes his tours as "encouraging people to create and make their own understandings of the city," and something that can "take people who don't know about their environment . . . and let them realize what's going on around them." He finds it even more gratifying when he gets "emails from people who started giving tours themselves." In describing his goals, Brendan cites Francesco Careri's *Walkscapes* (2002): "he lays out that walking can be a political event. . . . I think that book is really great about teaching people that walking doesn't have to just be about walking." By altering the landscape with their roving sidewalk classrooms, guides like Brendan mold their clients into what they see as invested locals and engaged urban walkers.

At the same time, guides attempt to make tourists feel like knowledgeable locals. It can be their advertising pitch, like the invitation to see "New York Like a Native."[6] In fieldnotes and interview materials I found guides peppering their commentaries with their lessons on what they feel makes a New Yorker a New Yorker:

In an interview: I tell people about New York City, about how to be a New Yorker. I tell them how to dress: black. Black doesn't work on me, but New Yorkers wear black. No khakis, and white socks are for people with athlete's foot . . . and no stripes.

On tour: You have to learn the second official language of New York City. Yiddish.

In an interview: I teach them to look *up*.

On tour: Don't walk in the crosswalks; it makes you look weak.

In an interview: [A walking tour] opens up the city, it makes the city a very livable place.

On tour: We're going to do a very non–New Yorker thing and wait for the light to change.

Such sentiments create the "mutual attachment" between people, and between dwellers and the city itself that writers like Richard Sennett fear have been lost.

Mark Shulman reflects upon how an avid participant can become a potential fellow traveler. Being a member of a group might be a stigmatizing role for some, particularly if they are tagged by a sticker—as is the custom with some tour companies—which signifies their status as "tourists." He explains it from his participants' perspectives:

[I am] willing, throughout these two hours, to—even if I have to wear this orange sticker—to have the experience of learning, being the student. Then as soon as I peel that sticker off, man, I've got those facts and I'm going to turn around and impress 50, 60 people over the course of the year. . . . I peel off the sticker and I'm the guide taking my aunt with me.

Across the wide array of positions and dispositions, several guides I interviewed talked about how they hoped their practices would be replicated in some way—by engaged citizens, city boosters, or even guides themselves. Eric Washington speaks of such aspirations:

So, I think walking tours are really fascinating because people get to do what they do all the time. . . . They see things that have been there all along, but they have not noticed before. And then they go back to their neighborhoods and they see that their block has history, too. Their building has history. And I think that is so valuable, and that's so exciting. Which is why there is plenty of room for nonacademic historians do this stuff and should be encouraged. . . . They go and become stewards for their neighborhoods, their blocks. It makes us all better citizens because they have a hands-on relationship with history. They feel they are a part of it. You don't need a degree for that, and one shouldn't demand one.

Bill Brown told me he believes his tours teach New Yorkers how to be better New Yorkers by getting them to claim ownership of public space through *usage*. Like all guides, he attempts to nurture the most transcendent of all effects, by trying to alter participants' dispositions. I found Bill's interest in "teaching a *way of life*" and trying to create a "state of mind" to be explicit references to something more implicit in other tours. We've seen how Brendan, Bruce, and Bill distribute bibliographies to their groups, cite their source materials, and describe their research methods so that any one of their participants can follow suit. These guides actively want others to join in and share their own experiences, too. Guides hope to pass their passionate and specialized perspectives onto the audience members more than any particular fact or date to transform them into well-informed citizens just like they are.

Rather than the conventional perspective of the tourist as a passive, acquiescent subject who buys into the image of the McHattanized city or of the knowing and jaded local, guides like Brendan highlight a blurry alternative, wherein a visitor is made to feel like a local, a local is made to feel like a tourist, and everyone is encouraged to be a student of the city with workbooks in hand. While the larger processes of tourism have been propped up as handmaidens for Disneyfied and passive consumption practices, walking tourism can provide the countering evidence of urban alchemy. To continue with that evidence, we can return to Brendan's Midtown Manhattan tour, in which chance encounters and transformations of clients are on display.

Through Fifth Avenue Couture (Privately Owned Public Spaces of Midtown Tour, July 2003)

For the tour's second half, Brendan leads us west, stopping us at La Premiere, a residential building with a small wedge of bushes to the west of its entrance. Designated as a "residential plaza," it is small, gated, and devoid of benches. Through the gate we see a blue mattress leaning up against a broken nightstand and a pile of garbage bags. The only places to sit, if we could get in, are concrete, sloped ledges that are overrun with what Brendan calls "hostile planting": branchy shrubs that poke into the back of anyone trying to sit there. The shrubbery even manages to hide the flowerbed behind it. On the outside of the gate seating gets more precarious; in addition to the planting, there is a row of serrated metal triangles on each surface, making it impossible to sit. Brendan pulls out a digital camera and has his brother demonstrate, then has us all pose for a picture for his Web site. He quotes William Whyte's book *The Social Life of Small Urban Spaces.*

The tour wanders north, from the Midtown office buildings to Fifth Avenue's upper-class chic. We settle across the street from Henri Bendel's boutique. Brendan tells us this site troubles him most. There are no identifying signs, no indication whatsoever there is a public space inside. Thanks to a ninety-seven- or ninety-three-year old glass carving that is a part of the façade, the entry of the building is a historical landmark.

"The first time we went in, we dragged a huge group through, with two video cameras and a shotgun microphone. It was maybe too much." The commotion got them ejected. In telling the story Brendan is so enthusiastic he attracts two middle-aged out-of-town visitors. As we start to make our way across the street, the group collectively convinces them to come along. "The tour's totally free, and we're going to go in there," Brendan tells them. "It's going to be fun," another participant says. Once they are told they might be kicked out, the women join us.

After jaywalking, we enter the building chatting with our new comrades. Before stepping in I take stock of our motley group: the men are unshaven and the women aren't wearing makeup. Once inside, everyone avoids eye contact with us, does not make overtures to give us a free makeover, and, all in all, looks through us as if we were cultural pariahs.

We are confronted not with security cameras or railings or gates but with a different color of dissuasion. The entry space is filled with vendors: a glut of perfumes, hand creams, "defining whips," and heavily cosmeticated, over-smiling saleswomen. Brendan stands amid it, saying, "This is public space, and *Bendel's is renting it out for their own profit.*" The building received a violation for this misuse and had forty-five days to remedy it. With ten days left, there was no sign that Bendel's was about to change anything.

Once we are packed into the completely obscured elevator to head up to the second floor, we talk about how we are a little disappointed that we've been allowed to wander. After the doors open, we wind our way around the red and black lingerie to the windows. In his characteristically self-effacing way, Brendan tells us, "I don't know anything about glassmaking, but I would think that people should know about one of the most important glassworks in the country." We examine the closest section of the windows (that are three stories of forty-six 14×14-inch panes of glass). Awe over the etchings of braided vines and ripe poppies quiet the otherwise chatty group.

Although we leave and head over to the AT&T building's atrium and examine their different technologies of dissuasion, Bendel's is the crowning moment of the tour.

Ghosts in the Machine

During our tour of Grand Central (described in chapter 4), Justin Ferate stops us in front of a stairway, right before we head down to the train platforms. He talks about how, in the spirit of the beaux-arts tradition, the shape of the railing is based on the dimensions of a woman's wrist and how the tread and riser of a proper step use the ergonomics of the average human stride. He then gets whimsical, and says, "Great French stairs are just like great sex: they are a lot of fun but you don't really know where you are going!" This was a nice moment, but what I liked about it was that Justin might as well have been talking about the whole building, or even the city itself. While Sennett (1990) and others feel great urban spaces like these—wherein "to know too much might weaken the desire to know what will happen next . . . [they are] endowed with the possibilities of the unexpected" (195)—may be diminishing in number, the actual cultural practices of urban re-enchantment and place-making are alive if one knows to look for them, or who to look for. A few theorists gathered as much. Michel de Certeau, for example, wrote from the perspective of the World Trade Center and claimed that one cannot be a voyeur when understanding the stories of the city, and must plunge into these "dark space where crowds move back and forth." The obliteration of that totalizing and objective vista from New York's cityscape perhaps forces us to re-examine those he refers to as the "ordinary practitioners of the city . . . walkers, *Wandersmanner*" (1984, 92–93). As the interlocking bureaucracies of cities work to revitalize central cities from "above," a ragtag group of erstwhile public urbanists produce an alternate culture from the street level. If homogenized, mass-produced culture is as pervasive as many believe, walking guides exist at the other end of the spectrum.

To conclude this book on the notion of "urban alchemy" is not an attempt to embrace magic over science but to reintroduce just such a perspective to urban studies, one that includes the microsociological *practices* rather than the structural forces of a city. This view contributes the unpredictable re-enchantments and the chorus of footsteps as compared to the larger forces that attempt to rationalize and sterilize the "universal placelessness" and ersatz commodified culture of cities but also to privilege a different kind of diversity at a different scale. The work of academic historians like Natalie Zemon Davis (1983) and Carlo Ginzburg (1992) reminds us that there is always a substratum of culture that blurs the lines between the accepted ideologies and everyday mentalities of non-elite groups and that this folk culture is there in the public sphere. With their amalgams of DIY politics, a neighborhood- and city-level localism, their desires to reinvigorate the street with personal narratives and hopes for a more engaged public, urban alchemists serve as ghosts within Lloyd and Clark's "entertainment machines" (2001) and Logan and Molotch's "growth machines" (1987). Characters like guides and graffiti writers, horticulturalists and street musicians, all re-enchant. The institutional agents who worry over guides "using their name to market themselves" and even fight over the licensing exam are reminders of the alchemist's stake in shaping urban culture but also that the city's agencies and growth machines are invested as well.

But here it is the sidewalk-level practices of transforming culture that should be dwelled upon last. We have seen how guides are able to piece together experiences in order to create something precious out of the cultural equivalent of common metal. Evoking Wildman Steve Brill's feelings of a tour as a kind of jazz performance, this cultural process is not unlike the evolution of a jazz standard: it is drawn from a variety of older sources of folk, blues, or Broadway, and then reharmonized and improvised upon again, and again. Take "My Funny Valentine." This song was first a 1937 Rodgers and Hart show tune that was refashioned by Chet Baker, Miles Davis, and Bill Evans. More recently hip-hop performer and impresario Kanye West sampled Etta James's version on his 2005 album *Late Registration*. Then, on the sidewalk, it is reinterpreted, somewhere, by a street musician, maybe just as you walk by. I'm reminded of Walter Benjamin's stroll through Marseilles, as he contemplates the relationships between the mechanized and rationalized city and his own sidewalk flâneur-trance, wherein he happens to pass a jazz club and is swept into the rhythm "against his education."[7] Like the work of infamous graffiti artist Banksy, which creates a trompe-l'oeil on a wall that appears to open to a tropical oasis; like a political protester transforming an idle passerby into a more informed citizen; like an urban horticulturalist creating whimsy or instigating random interactions through unexpected flower arrangements; like an improvisational performance on the subway; urban alchemy is the art of urban transformation. Guides can hope participants will take their tour content and spin off their own ideas, questioning tales and developing their own investigations of the city long after a tour. Maybe someone will tell that story about the hidden Jewish history of Harlem or about the missing grazers at Sheep's Meadow, or the ceiling mural of Grand Central Terminal. In doing so, the free culture of New York City is transformed, reinterpreted, and then spun off back into the crowds again, and again, and again.

Quizzes, Tests, and Dissertations

Locating Research, Locating Researcher

I remember the first moment of really reflecting on my position as an urban researcher studying other students of the city. It was on a warm summer evening in 2003 on a tour with Justin Ferate, as he took a Cooper Union continuing education class through Cobble Hill, Brooklyn. The group was a mixture of guides and history buffs, and we were in a gentrified area that was rarely, if ever traveled by a tour group. We learned the neighborhood was "invented"—which is to say labeled—in 1961, and we were treated to a few lessons on architecture (e.g., that oriel windows jut out but do not continue down to the ground like bay windows) which Justin is well known for. He paused on quaint Verandah Place to ask if anyone had any questions. Someone gestured to a rooftop, and asked almost absent-mindedly, "What's going on there?" A flock of pigeons circled over the street before arching out of view beyond the cornice of a typical Brooklyn three-story apartment building. They swooped around again and again as if tied on invisible strings, reflecting the bronze early evening light off their wings. Justin said, "You know, in all my years, I've never figured out what that's about. Does anyone know?" The group looked at each other, and finally, from my usual position at the edge of the group, I looked up from my notebook and said, "I do."

The group pivoted and I moved from the back of the group to the front. I folded my pen in my notebook and said, "Someone raises pigeons up there," starting a little too obviously. "See, if you have two people—called 'mumblers'—who have coops of pigeons, they can play this game: each waves a flag or a shirt on a stick in the air to rouse the birds into flight. The more they circle the more the two groups intermingle. It's called 'rolling' or 'action,' I think." I pointed to a man on this roof coaxing his birds higher, with a makeshift flag made of a t-shirt on a stick. In truth, I wasn't sure where I picked up these bits of information. There were a few coops in my neighborhood of Williamsburg, and I remember reading an article about it in an alternative newspaper, *The Brooklyn Rail*, and learned a bit from a tour guide, somewhere. "Now," I went on hesitantly, "the idea is that the pigeons will switch coops if they are successfully lured by the other group. At the end of it, the mumbler with more pigeons wins. It's up to the owners on whether or not they keep the new residents or hold them for ransom."

"Whether they play this game," I continued, "or just get the birds up in the air, most birders do this around the same time of evening, a little before dusk—theoretically because the setting sun reflects off of the birds' wings." I stopped there. And that was it. The group nodded, and Justin smiled at me. Two people linger as everyone else moves down the street. Two asked followup questions I didn't know the answers to.

The sudden shift made me the bearer of knowledge. This small thing, this trivial bit of urban ephemera, gave me a chance to add something to the group, however timidly. It was a simple exchange of information. Within the span of four minutes my role changed from observer to participant back to observer. As we walked away I wondered: Did I provide accurate information? How certain was I? Will the guides then go off and tell others this questionable bit of information? Back at school, typing up my fieldnotes, I checked out what I had stated as fact. To my surprise, I was pretty accurate.

This wasn't the only time I participated in the field, but it serves as a reminder of the reflection upon one's position as a researcher that is something of a tradition among ethnographers (see Whyte 1955, Liebow 1968, Kornblum 1974, Duneier 1999). Perhaps it is because the methodology requires a balance between engaged participation and distanced observation that reflexivity such as this is a necessity.[1] Chipping in a few bits of information on tour is fairly modest involvement when compared to other ethnographic work. There are those who were deeply engaged in their field: Fred Davis worked as a cab driver (1959), Kornblum worked as a factory foreman

(1974), Bromley and Shupe attempted to convert to the Unitarian Church (1995), and Wacquant apprenticed as a boxer for three years (2005). And there are others who tried their hands at a particular craft: Bennett "became" a rock musician (1980) while Grazian joined an open mike night at a blues club (2005), Duneier took up a vending table on Sixth Avenue as a part of his research on homeless street vendors (1999), and Lankeneau tried his hand at panhandling (1999). There were a number of factors that kept me from plunging into the field as a full participant, which will be addressed in the following section, but I did participate in the field in a few ways, including by giving a walking tour myself.

A Walking Tour about Walking Tours (Murray Hill Tour, May 2004)

My tour group is comprised of eighteen of my colleagues from the City University of New York, the New School, and NYU, and the two administrative assistants from my program. I volunteered to give an end-of-the-semester walking tour as a part of our brown-bag series. The tour is all my own design: to share a little bit about the neighborhood around the school: from 34th Street and Fifth Avenue to Grand Central to the New York Public Library, and then to a picnic lunch in Bryant Park.

Drawing from my years as an architecture student, from walking around the area, and from the tours of a few guides, I collected materials on the area (the preponderance of art deco buildings—the ubiquitous blend of ancient Egyptian, cubist, futurist, and machine aesthetics that arose between the two world wars that has left its lasting imprint on the Empire State, Chrysler, Rockefeller skyscrapers—was a theme tied in to a serendipitously timed special exhibit on art deco in the library), and about the tricks of the trade ("I must say that I am proud to come from the second school at this location, the City University of New York. Any questions?" "Wait, what was the first school?" "Oh, it's good that you asked! You see, B. Altman's Department Store had a school right here for its workers and . . ."). The tour is reflexive: a walking tour about walking tours. Throughout, I detail on the jokes, the cultural goods transmitted, and my own tentative formulations on public culture and tourism.

Intended to be a fun excursion as well as an outline of my research to date, people laugh at the experience as much as at anything I say. On 41st Street I mention a quote that I had read that reminds me of the perspectives of walking guides: "The universe is made of stories, not of atoms." I asked if anyone could think of which poet said that. When no one answers, I move my feet to reveal a plaque embedded in the sidewalk as a part of the New York Public Library's Literary Walk with that very quote, and the name of its author. "Oh, that's right, Muriel Rukeyser. Okay, and on this corner . . ." A few easy jokes like that are working on the sympathetic crowd but there are also a couple of things I forget, and others that I get flat out wrong (I realize later, for example, that I perpetuate the common misconception that the 1929 height competition was not between the Chrysler and Empire State buildings, but rather the Chrysler and the Manhattan Company Building at 40 Wall Street), necessitating a follow-up email—something I cannot imagine a guide doing.

How I Ended Up Giving a Walking Tour

I stacked the audience with colleagues for my first walking tour. There were no kids, no buffs, no fellow guides. They were all academics and friends. A number of factors led me to this more measured level of engagement in the field. For one, the tourism market was very fragile at the time of my research. This made it a significant and valuable moment for study, but it also made me feel it would be inappropriate to fully enter into the field despite slow improvements to the industry's economic health. Just as cooks were suspicious that Gary Alan Fine's presence in their kitchens was because he was penning a newspaper exposé or participating in some advanced employee surveillance program (1996, 234), guides were often intensely curious about why I would be so interested in their tours and their lives. In the times of an economic downturn, guides felt many people were trying to enter the informal sector of the tourism trade and often developed a healthy dose of suspicion. Early on I realized I could not fully participate as a guide without jeopardizing my relationships with guides.

Although it was hardly the first time these concerns presented themselves to me, a good example of this was in my correspondence with two guides that occurred when I was finishing up my research. Going through rewrites, I needed more data—a common enough occurrence when transforming a dissertation into a book—and wanted to contact a few guides to follow up on their lives and their work. When I made a request to take a few final tours I received two very negative responses. One guide wrote back to me: "To what ends? I am having severe troubles with people copying tours/excessive notetaking." Another wrote: "Excuse me, but why should I allow you to rip off my carefully developed tour for your personal profit? What's in it for me if you 'tag along'? I am talking cash here. You are looking to exploit my intellectual property and I will not sell it cheap." Both needed renewed clarification on my research method and explanation of how their tours would be represented and, once they were made plain, the guides happily invited me back on tour. Both independently cited their deep reservations about journalists and students who take their tours as a way to do research for articles on a neighborhood as reasons for their initial reactions. Furthermore, both admitted to having not closely read my requests.

These concerned communications dramatize the very real issue of any ethnographer profiting from the research he or she conducts. I doubted any guide would find it acceptable for me to take the information and tricks from my research and make money as a guide. Even if I was to take the role of the independent guide and publicly list a free tour, it could siphon off business (i.e., would a tourist be more likely to take my free tour over another guide's $10 tour?), and just as important, my listing would take up a coveted place in a publication. If I worked at a tourism company the situation would not improve. Seth Kamil, in fact, asked me if I would ever work for Big Onion. The notion was tempting: I would know what it was like to be a BOWT guide and, just like the rest of his employees, I needed to make money to pay the high cost for graduate school and living in New York City. At the time I felt like I learned a lot, and my fervor for learning more had even eclipsed my interest in sociology. I was awash in the books guides recommended and was eager to learn more. The thought of consuming binder after binder of historical data Seth and Big Onion had compiled over the years enticed my inner amateur historian, but I had to balance these feelings with knowing that such employment would negatively impact interviews with non–Big Onion guides and would confirm their fears that anyone taking notes is out to steal their material, possibly for the benefit of a competitor. I had to decline.

In spite of these concerns, I knew I had to participate in the field in ways that I hoped would provide insight into the practice of tour guiding and verify many of the things guides were reporting to me, while at the same time honoring the trust I had worked to cultivate. The first way I tried to strike this balance was by leading a handful of free tours to friends, family, and colleagues like the one highlighted here. In all, I led only six tours—including a tour of the East Village for an art class at the Parsons School of Design. A seventh tour—a walking tour and pub crawl about walking tours and urban nightlife coauthored for the Eastern Sociological Society with Lower East Side nightlife scholar Richard Ocejo—afforded me the chance to feel the sting many guides have felt over the years: after hours of careful research

and negotiation, the tour was canceled due to inclement weather. In addition, by dint of my having interviewed and tagged along on multiple tours,
some guides began to treat me as a quasi-assistant, bouncing ideas off me,
asking which stories I thought would work best in a given situation, serving
as the straight man for a few jokes on tour, and even carrying books for a
guide as he gave his shtick. One even introduced me as his "amanuensis."

Second, in spring 2005 I was approached to write a 1,800-word article
for *Time Out New York*, a weekly magazine that also provides free listings for
walking tours. The experience was challenging. On the one hand, I wanted
to promote the community in a fair fashion, and on the other I was placed
in a position of granting consecration to only a handful of guides and doing
so on the terms of the publication's editors. Expectedly, there were a few
struggles regarding content. I balked at the editor's request for a "Top 10
Best and Top 10 Worst Guides" article and settled on what I saw as the least
problematic title offered: "New York's Most Interesting Tours." I then had to
fight for the inclusion of one guide while another was imposed to "balance
out the article." Overall, it was an opportunity to share my findings with a
wider public: *Time Out* has an average weekly press run around 160,000. The
editing process created a number of small firestorms with guides who had
agreed to be included—ranging from concerns over their pictures to the editing out of more positive anecdotes and descriptions from earlier drafts—as
well as a half-dozen emails from guides who were disappointed or angry
their tours had not been included.[2] As far as the legitimating force of such
an act, it was only days before clips from the article appeared on guides' Web
sites.

Publishing this article provided an additional wrinkle to the research
and its re-presentation in this book: the article required real names and real
tours, and would compromise the anonymity to any careful reader of my
planned book. The biographical details in the magazine article could con-
ceivably match up with the ethnographic detail within *The Tour Guide*. Even
though there are strong methodological and theoretical arguments for gar-
nering waivers from participants for using their real names (see Duneier
1999 and Marwell 2007), in this case my own participation in the field made
it a practical requirement. Starting in 2007, I began requesting waivers to
use real names only to find out that most of the guides had already presumed
their names were being used (despite signing the original Human Subjects
Review Form that assured anonymity). The process of contacting them included setting up a meeting, explaining the overall structure and emphasis
of the book, and allowing them to read each and every mention of them in it,
particularly emphasizing the context in which they are presented. Almost all

were excited to engage with the process and a few, including Justin Ferate, scanned every single page out of deep interest and amusement. No guide withdrew his or her participation, no guide balked at his or her representation, even the less flattering elements. Only one guide worried about a quote that he told me being attached to his real name and in that single case I made this comment anonymous.

My third engagement in the field returns to the very beginning of the book: I took the new licensing exam. A few things changed about the test after the city hall incident. Because of a low pass rate, the passing grade dropped from 120 out of 150 to 97—the average grade of the first 100 exams taken—and anyone with a 120 now receives a special commendation and notification on the DCA Web site. (In addition, the city government made it mandatory for out-of-town groups to employ a New York City Licensed guide rather than bringing in their own, effectively generating a greater pool of jobs for hometown guides—something GANYC had perpetually been lobbying for.) Here I was faced with another interesting choice: to either study diligently, perhaps taking the recommended preparation course, or take it with the information I already had, which is to say, I would test what I had learned from the walking tours themselves. Either way, if I failed it would underscore the rigor of the exam (or that I wasn't paying close enough attention). If I passed handily, it would either prove the test to be easy, demonstrate that the information guides provide resonated in my memory, or that guides hew closely to the content of the test. I decided to take the test armed only with a number 2 pencil and the information presented to me over three years of research. The 150-question, 1.75-hour exam was rigorous. There were several moments when I was greatly helped by a place memory of a particular building or intersection that jogged me enough to remember exactly where I was when I learned something. I found myself saying, "Okay, so-and-so corner is too far away from that neighborhood, and if it's not near there, then . . ." Other answers and sites were in my fieldnotes (and eventually in this book). When I turned the test in I had no inkling whether or not I passed. There were a dozen or so questions on taxation for self-employment and what the legal bus routes in New York City were, and I simply guessed at those (just as, in turns out, many guides with no interest in bus tourism do). I strolled around Lower Manhattan for the hour it took to take to grade my exam. I wondered: How much do I know about this city? Will a failure on the exam be a failure of my belief that places and experiences can serve as important aspects of learning? I revisited one of my favorite sites in this book, the U.S. Customs House, and recounted its venerable architect and various attributes I learned on tours—Cass Gilbert, French,

Belgium, Micmac, and so on. Upon my return, I was happy to find that I had passed by all of four questions. Eking out this grade, in a way, gets through the knot of participant and observer, master and novice. Like George Plimpton limping off the football field in *Paper Lion*, I was happy to demonstrate one of the difficulties guides go through with a little dignity intact.[3] I would have failed had the passing grade remained at 120 and yet, when a guide I was interviewing teased me about it, I retorted, "Do you know what they call the person who graduates med school with the lowest grade? Doctor." I became a Licensed New York City Sightseeing Guide.[4]

The Walking Guide and the Graduate Student

Trust between the guides and I may have required extra care to cultivate, but a certain level of rapport did not. Having coffee and sharing stories out on the sidewalks, either with a group or strolling along in conversation, was easy enough. After all, many of them were much like me: students trying to navigate graduate school, a side job, research, and teaching. Non–Big Onion guides may have been of different ages and with different levels of education, but we still held affinities in juggling our labors and interests in the city. (A few autodidacts, like Mark Levy, were pursuing master's degrees as well.) We shared facts and New York stories. I often enjoyed telling tales I had learned, which made guides feel I had common interests and had a fair amount of currency to exchange. Across dissimilarities we were all willing to put up with informal, suboptimal working conditions to live these lives, whether it was being a graduate student or working a day job. Many saw me as a fellow traveler, or "in a related business," as one told me. We were all aspirants in a fashion. Many were interested in my intended career, just as I was interested in the way that they made efforts to gain a foothold in tourism.

At another level, this in-between quality of the student role resonated with the role of an "unconventional intellectual" (Shils 1972) or Schutz's "well-informed citizen" (1970) that gained conceptual prominence as I moved through the research process. (Similarly, like many of my graduate school colleagues I was drawn to the methodological appendix in C. Wright Mills's *The Sociological Imagination* [1959], wherein he praises serendipity and chance, a theme that I found reflected back to me in my research process and tour content.) The life as a "perpetual student of cities" that was a part of being a walking-tour guide seemed to reflect in the in-between position of graduate student life I saw around me. Graduate school is undoubtedly a "becoming" or "interstitial" space, and I found that the world of guides was one that shared a similar commitment to learning.

Being a graduate student, for me, meant waking up at 6 a.m. to make my morning 6:30–1:30 shift at the Verb Café in Williamsburg, Brooklyn. At the end of my shift I would eat any soup left in the warming kettle and maybe sit at the bar to do some reading before heading to school. The café always had a tilting tower of newspapers, and it was after a shift in January 2001 that I grabbed the *Brooklyn Rail* to read "Beauty in Unexpected Places," the article about pigeons where I had gained the bulk of my knowledge about pigeon wrangling. (I recalled this fact later because I remembered that it was coauthored by Meghan McDermott, a fellow City University of New York graduate student who was juggling work at the weekly while also taking sociology classes with me in my cohort.) Then I would head off to classes, at first as a student and later on as a lecturer at Queens College. At night I would transcribe interview data. In good weather, the three-day weekends that graduate school provides were reserved for trailing and interviewing guides, listening to stories and writing up fieldnotes. (Graduate school rarely requires Friday classes, and tour guides mostly give tours Friday through Sunday—a symmetry that worked well for BOWT guides, and for me.) A little later, in spring 2004, I taught an urban ethnography class at Queens College. In addition to the course materials—which included some of the books cited here—the class allowed me to ask questions about my research and share stories I learned on the sidewalk, sometimes from guides who were Ph.D. students themselves who had told their tales to a group simply because the information was central to their own graduate research. Guides' dissertation work and tour material, in turn, became my dissertation work and teaching material.

The research rubbed off in another way, where I became the "tour guide guy," who would always be called upon to draw out an interesting fact or story about a random street-corner. This sort of fusing of research and professional identity is common enough, but it made any stroll with friends, family, or faculty a potential pop quiz. Sometimes I passed. Sometimes I did not. One of those quizzes was at the corner of 23rd Street and Fifth Avenue, with one of my committee members, Mitchell Duneier. I had the chance to talk about my first experience thinking about the field, overhearing an explanation for the term "23 Skidoo," but also fitting in another apocryphal tale, this time about the statue of William Seward that faces the Flatiron Building. I told my professor about how Seward was Lincoln's secretary of state, how he survived Booth's co-conspirator Lewis Powell's murder attempt but is better known for his "folly" of purchasing Alaska, and how it is often said that, due to a lack of funds, the statue only has the head of Seward and the body was a discarded, headless Abraham Lincoln that the sculptor had lying around. These unscripted moments, these "Tell Me About This Block" tests that seemed more like an extension of the oral examination for my Ph.D. requirements, were not always my best outings.

Fifteen blocks north of Madison Square Park, I had the opportunity to piece together a set of stories in a more deliberate fashion, with a "walking tour about walking tours" for my friends and colleagues. I did not want to give a talk in a windowless room where our normal brown-bag seminars are conducted. I did not want to just describe what guides do. I wanted to vividly bring those experiences to mind. This idea of evoking the social context was an idea I carried all the way through my research, to this book: The veracity of this study depending upon the ability of the multiple narratives of ethnographic fieldnotes and analysis to support each other, and for the reader to get the experience of being on tour itself.

Engaging in the Field (Murray Hill Tour, May 2004)

All I can think of is that it's too hot to be wearing a sport coat, and the relief that I didn't wear the bowtie like I had planned. I had memorized as much as I could but, after finishing up teaching two theory courses, I placed a great deal of information on my used, failing, $10 PDA that I bought at a stoop sale in the Village. Most guides work from memory and none with a Palm Pilot, but I've seen some with yellowing three-by-five cards. I found it easy to cut and paste quotes from my interviews and a few facts and download it into my Palm Pilot. It is now my saving grace. I read a few quotes and historic dates verbatim.

Somewhere on 42nd Street, as the group walks behind me, a colleague, Alex says, "I love that we're out here doing this." Others murmur in agreement.

We circle around to Madison Avenue. There I talk about the state of the industry, about how it has largely bounced back from 9/11, and how a few foreign economies have made it favorable to tour in the United States (i.e., the Euro's value against the dollar rose enough in late 2003 to lead to a spike in foreign visitors).

Butterflies in my stomach, I do my best to weave the broader historical and structural issues at hand into the more compelling stories of guides: I offer up the series of tensions between entertainment and education, and tell a few guiding jokes. I schedule the penultimate stop to the side of the grand steps of the New York Public Library, and tell Jennifer's rabbi story. I share a few lines that might contradict the notion that guides are thoughtful histori-

Figure 8 A walking tour of Murray Hill/Midtown, outside of the New York Public Library. Photo by Carla Barrett, 2004.

ans of urban culture (i.e., "Never let the truth get in the way of a good story"), but also couch it in the larger historical and cultural context (i.e., that Egyptian guides would do the same thing in antiquity—"reading" hieroglyphics to travelers despite having lost the ability to read them for millennia—and that they feel participants want to know they've asked a good question).

I gain confidence at the laughs, regretting that I had planned the jokes so late in the tour. On each subsequent stop I convince myself that the group is genuinely enjoying the walk—even Rati and Urania, our program's administrative assistants, seem happy to be along. They're all chatting, mixing with one another. The appreciation surely has something to do with traveling from the classroom to the streets. As we stand behind the library and look over the hundreds of power-lunching and sunbathing bodies of Bryant Park, I talk about how it was once a training ground for Civil War soldiers, the site of the 1853 World's Fair and its Crystal Palace (and I included information that I had read on a plaque on the other side of the park: that it had 4,000 exhibits, and when it went up in flames it was a fire that was possibly set to recoup the $300,000 insurance costs), and talked about how the manicured lawn covers eighty-four miles of books and is a wireless-Internet "hotspot."

In the end, I speak of William H. Whyte's rise to public prominence and his pivotal role in restoring this wildly successful public space. I wrap up with thoughts on intellectual work in the public sphere. Whyte, I say, was a true public intellectual and a passionate critic of the urban world. He used his institutional consecration (although not an academic) to shape the city for the better—particularly through his "Project for Public Spaces." He loathed how urban spaces were walled off and was pivotal in the rehabilitation of the very park where we ended our tour. In the end I talk about his advocacy for urban razzamatazz, "honky-tonk," and anything that would increase the hustle and bustle of the sidewalk—the interpersonal interactions he called "triangulations." I talk about how guides desire to have a similar impact. I talk about how these unconventional intellectuals provide, as de Certeau put it, "miniature gardens" in the minds of their participants. Every once in a while, I say, anyone can see them plugging up a sidewalk, talking about an architectural detail or working class history.

As two or three folks stop and listen to my tour, I think to myself that a walking tour is something Whyte would have just loved.

Cast of Characters

Tom Bernardin: A guide whose primary focus is on immigrant history and is, among his fellow guides, "Mr. Ellis Island."

"Wildman" Steve Brill: An environmentalist who offers tours of the wildlife of city parks, focusing upon edible flora.

Bill Brown: An activist who gives free tours of surveillance cameras and the control of public spaces (highlighted in chapter 6's fieldnotes). He also conducts guerrilla plays in public spaces and maintains an archive of Situationist materials. He currently lives in Ohio.

Gretchen Dykstra: The Commissioner of the Department of Consumer Affairs at the time this research was conducted.

Justin Ferate: One of the most seasoned New York tour guides, who works with several cultural institutions and wrote the Licensing Examination. He is highlighted in chapter 4's ethnographic vignettes.

Brendan FitzGerald: An activist who works in the film industry and offers free walking and biking tours on a variety of public-interest topics, often with his brother. He is in his early thirties and is highlighted in the ethnographic vignettes of chapter 7.

Jennifer Fronc: A former Big Onion guide who has since graduated, and is now an assistant professor of history at the University of

Massachusetts–Amherst. She is highlighted in chapter 5's ethnographic fieldnotes.

Joyce Gold: One of the few guides who makes her living as a guide, but also teaches continuing education courses at NYU and the New School.

Erik Goldner: A former Big Onion guide who has since graduated, and is now an assistant professor of history at California State–Northridge.

Katia Howard: An autodidactic guide who wanted to be an actress but now gives "food" tours and juggles other jobs to make a living.

Seth Kamil: The owner of Big Onion Walking Tours who employs 35–40 Ph.D. students.

Bruce Kayton: A guide who maintains his formal job and offers walking tours throughout the year in his spare time. He is forty-nine years old, has been giving tours for fourteen years and is highlighted in chapter 2's ethnographic fieldnotes.

Mark Levy: A more entertainment-oriented guide who conducts tours with his sons. He is highlighted in chapter 1's ethnographic fieldnotes. He is the director of Levy's Unique New York walking tours.

Matt Levy: The son of Mark, his frequent collaborator, and a guide who focuses on countercultural walking tours and is in his mid-twenties.

Robin Lynn: The programming director for the Municipal Art Society at the time of study and co-editor of *Ten Architectural Walks in Manhattan* with guide Francis Morrone (2010), she currently serves as the director of individual giving at the MAS.

Jane Marx: An autodidactic guide who has been giving tours for thirty years.

Harry Matthews: A GANYC guide who was downsized from his job and entered into guiding while juggling writing gigs in 1997.

Francis Morrone: An architecturally inclined walking guide and author who gives tours for the MAS.

Tony Perrottet: Author of *Pagan Holiday*, who writes nonfiction and historical accounts of touristic experiences.

Annie Polland: A Big Onion guide who now works as the vice president of education for the Lower East Side Tenement Museum in New York City.

Alfred Pommer: An autodidactic, strictly historical guide in his sixties.

Evan Pritchard: A Native American guide who only gives tours for the National Museum of the American Indian and is the founder of the Center for Algonquin Culture.

Darryl Reilly: An aspiring actor who gives tours for the League for American Theaters and Producers (now called the Broadway League) and is a GANYC guide.

Mark Shulman: An autodidactic guide in his forties who makes his living as a children's book author and gives tours for fun.

Andy Sydor: Primarily a bus guide, but also gives walking tours and is the moderator of the popular guiding listserv "Red Menace."

Jeffrey Trask: A Big Onion guide in his early thirties who has graduated since the research for this book was completed, and is now a visiting lecturer at New York University.

Eric K. Washington: An autodidactic guide who came to guiding from freelance journalism. He is an author, was the curator of an exhibit at a public college, and often gives tours for a major cultural institution. He is highlighted in chapter 3's ethnographic fieldnotes.

Catalogue of Tours Taken

	Date	Location	Guide and/or Organization	Hours
1	Sept. 2001	Harlem	MAS	2.0
2	Sept.	SoHo	J. Gold	2.5
3	Oct.	Midtown	MAS	2.0
4	March 2002	Midtown	MAS	2.0
5	April	Central Park	Nature Conservancy	1.5
6	April	Central Park	Nature Conservancy	1.5
7	April	Central Park	Nature Conservancy	1.5
8	Sept.	Financial District	E. Pritchard	1.5
9	Oct.	South Bronx, The Bronx	MAS	2.0
10	March 2003	Financial District	J. Gold	2.0
11	April	Lower East Side/Five Points	M. Levy	1.5
12	May	Lower East Side/Five Points	M. Levy	2.0
13	May	Grand Central Terminal	J. Ferate/BID	2.0
14	May	Brooklyn Heights, Brooklyn	H. Matthews	2.5
15	May	Financial District	J. Trask/BOWT	2.5
16	May	Lower East Side/Five Points	S. Kamil/BOWT	2.0
17	June	Greenwich Village	J. Trask/BOWT	2.0
18	June	Lower East Side	E. Wakin/BOWT	2.0
19	June	Grand Central Terminal	F. Morrone/BID	2.5
20	June	Cobble Hill, Brooklyn	J. Ferate	3.0

	Date	Location	Guide and/or Organization	Hours
21	June	Greenwich Village	J. Trask/BOWT	2.5
22	June	Financial District	E. Pritchard	2.0
23	June	Central Park	B. Kayton	4.5
24	July	Midtown	B. FitzGerald	2.5
25	Aug.	Times Square Theaters	D. Reilly	2.0
26	April 2004	Greenwich Village	J. Fronc/BOWT	2.0
27	April	Upper West Side	BOWT	2.0
28	April	Financial District	BOWT	2.0
29	April	Midtown	B. FitzGerald	2.5
30	April	South Street Seaport	Austrian Cultural Forum	3.0
31	May	Upper West Side	B. Brown	3.0
32	May	Greenwich Village	B. Brown	3.0
33	May	Harlem	E. Washington	2.5
34	May	Lower East Side/Five Points	J. Fronc/BOWT	2.0
35	May	Bowery	New Museum	2.0
36	May	Manhattanville, Harlem	E. Washington	3.0
37	May	Greenwich Village	Broadbent Theatre	3.0
38	June	Greenwich Village	Broadbent Theatre	2.5
39	June	Greenwich Village	J. Marx	2.0
40	Aug.	Midtown	M27 Coalition	2.5
41	Sept.	Lower East Side	J. Fronc/BOWT	2.0
42	Sept.	Times Square	Times Square BID	2.0
43	Sept.	34th Street	34th Street BID	1.5
44	Oct.	Sunset Park, Brooklyn	Green-Wood Cemetery	2.0
45	Oct.	Greenwich Village	Broadbent Theatre	3.0
46	Oct.	Chelsea	B. Brown	2.0
47	Oct.	Harlem	E. Washington	2.5
48	Oct.	Central Park	J. Cardiff audio tour	1.5
49	Oct.	Harlem	B. Kayton	4.0
50	Nov.	Harlem	J. Marx	2.5
51	April 2005	Lower East Side	Tenement Museum	2.0
52	April	South Bronx, The Bronx	Soundwalk	2.0
53	April	Chinatown	Soundwalk	2.0
54	May	Brooklyn Bridge	E. Goldner/BOWT	3.0
55	May	Central Park	S. Brill	4.0
56	May	Upper West Side	B. Kayton	4.0
57	May	DUMBO, Brooklyn	Soundwalk	2.0

	Date	Location	Guide and/or Organization	Hours
58	Feb. 2006	Hell's Kitchen	MAS	2.5
59	March	East Harlem	R. Barrett/MAS	2.5
60	May 2008	Lower Manhattan	BOWT	2.0
61	May	Flatiron District	23rd Street BID	3.0
62	June	Lower East Side	K. Howard	2.0
63	Dec.	Central Park	S. Brill	3.5
64	May 2009	Union Square	Union Square BID	2.0
65	June	Gr. Village/ "Before Stonewall"	J. Trask/BOWT	2.0
66	July	Fort Greene, Brooklyn	MAS	2.5
67	July	Astoria, Queens	MAS	2.5
			Total hours	157.5

Note: Guides not named in this book are listed here according to their affiliation.

NOTES

Introduction

1. Pond 1993, 12. See also Sante 1991 and Casson 1974, 100–101, 105.

2. Wacquant (2004) and Grazian (2003, 23) express needing to leave their library settings as the reason for finding their research topics as well.

3. In the summer of 2004, Janet Cardiff distributed CD players so people could listen to her site-specific, ongoing monologue while walking through Central Park, a project called "Her Long Black Hair." As artist-in-residence at the art museum, P.S. 1, another artist used walking tours as a part of his work, and the Austrian Cultural Forum sponsored a third artist's walking tour in 2004.

4. Even estimable research in the field glosses over them: three influential books, Dean MacCannell's classic *The Tourist* (1973), Dennis Judd and Susan Fainstein's edited collection, *The Tourist City* (1999), and John Urry's *The Tourist Gaze* (1990b) cite guides only once between them. The mention of guides is in MacCannell, wherein a guide incorrectly tells his tour group the Liberty Bell was cracked when it was rung too hard (p. 138). Guides are nearly absent from most studies on urbanism and culture, but even looking at the literature that would be most likely to offer such a study on guides, a search of the combined thirty-six volumes of the *Annals of Tourism Research* and *Tourist Studies* revealed that none use the term "walking tour guide," and only eleven articles use "tour guide" (and even then, several are referring to printed material, like *Lonely Planet* and *Baedeker Guides*, rather than actual people). If they are mentioned, guides have almost entirely been examined within non-Western (Graburn 1989) and nonurban settings (Dahles 2002) as the interpreters and packagers of "aboriginal" cultures (Chambers 1999; Nash 1989), although there are some who look at guides through a "glocal" lens (Salazar 2005). This absence may be explained by the academic focus on

the more institutionalized aspects of tourism, culture, and urbanism (Fine and Speer 1985; Holloway 1981; and Pond 1993).

5. From the very beginnings of tourism studies, research has split into "consumption" and "production" perspectives, mostly focusing on the subjective experience or character of the tourist (Cohen 1979; Urry 1990b), or the industry itself (Britton 1991; Hoffman, Fainstein, and Judd 2003; Featherstone 1991; Kearns and Philo 1993). Both are important, yet largely avoid the guide as pivotal in the framing and education of tour participants—save for Cohen (1985). This focus on either the reception of the tourism experience or what Lash and Urry call the more "organized" aspects of an industry, reasserts the separation of the two, a dichotomy found in the culture (1994; see also Schudson 1979) and urban literatures as well.

6. See Demerath and Levinger 2003, Slavin 2003, Adler 1989, Careri 2002, and Solnit 2000. The examples, even the most famous, are too numerous to mention, but an emblematic text may be Rousseau's in *The Reveries of a Solitary Walker* in which he explains that walking provides "the daily fodder for [his] mind" (1980).

7. See Hammett, Hammett, and Cooper 2007, Bryman 1999, Hebdige 2003, Ouf 2001, Nelson 1995, Ritzer and Liska 1997, Rojek 1993, Ward 1998, and Warren 1994.

8. For studies on these examples of "urban alchemy," see Becker 1984, 260; Schmelzkopf 1995; Reynolds 2008; Snyder 2009; Gowan 2000; Duneier 1999; Flusty 2000; Tanenbaum 1995; and Bywater 2007.

9. Answer: The White Horse.

10. Suttles, so irked by the heavy emphasis on large-scale urban processes in the academic literature, was prompted to make an explicit reminder of the importance of these kinds of interpersonal relations in *The Man Made City* (1990). This was to be an indictment of the field in general, but more specifically Logan and Molotch's *Urban Fortunes* (1987).

11. Respectfully: Anderson 1923, Park 1925, Cressey 1932, Donovan 1920, Shaw 1930, Sutherland 1937, Gold 1952, Davis 1959, Becker 1951, Duneier 1999, Rupp and Taylor 2003, Grazian 2003, Bearman 2005, Wacquant 2004.

12. Similar presentation methods are used in other ethnographies. For comparative use of data presentation, see Hochschild's *Second Shift* (1989), in which each chapter is organized around the struggles of a particular individual, Grasmuck's discussion of her use of fieldnotes in her book *Protecting Home*, which illustrates themes that "crisscross" chapters to create a presentation "with the goal of drawing on the strengths and limitations of representing the swirl of social life" (2005, 14), and Bourdieu's collage-style of presentation-in-boxes, which appears to recall the layout of contemporary introductory textbooks (1984). One could also look at the photographs in Mitchell Duneier's *Sidewalk* (1999), which float in and around the text rather than existing to explicitly address the text he writes. Howard Becker's *Telling about Society* (2007) also provides a rich discussion of the multiple ways of presenting evidence in sociology.

Chapter One

1. MacCannell (1973, 593).

2. Famous rubberneckers included Frances Milton Trollope (mother of novelist Anthony Trollope), Davy Crockett, and Charles Dickens, who wrote that the Five Points area was bustling with every imaginable individual "as if the judgment hour were near at hand, and every obscene grave were giving up its dead" (quoted in Allen 1993, 22).

3. Sante 1991, 128-29. See also Asbury 1980, 298–99, and Anbinder 2001.

4. Fronc 2009. As to not confuse presentation of the "ethnographic present" too greatly, it should be noted that, from the time of research to the publication of *The Tour Guide*, Fronc was, in fact, a Big Onion guide (highlighted in chapter 5), who has gone on to serve as an assistant professor of history. Her book, *New York Undercover* (2009) includes much of the information she honed on her tours.

5. Cocks continues: "Turn-of-the-century Americans saw in rationalized recreation the possibility of stable, amicable social relationships requiring no personal knowledge and thus better suited to an industrial, urban, and heterogeneous republic" (2001, 5–6).

6. See World Travel and Tourism Council (WTTC) 2009. Since the impact of tourism reaches other sectors of the U.S. economy, the WTTC separates the "U.S. Travel and Tourism Economy" from the "U.S. Travel and Tourism Industry." The WTTC's numbers are based upon the "industrial activity defined by the diverse collection of products (durables and non-durables) and services (transportation, accommodations, food and beverage, entertainment, government services, etc) that *are delivered to visitors*" (WTTC 2004, 11).

7. NYC & Company (2009). See also Gladstone and Fainstein 2001, 2003b; Fernandez 2006; and Rauh 2008.

8. Through careful planning, city culture has become "aimed at attracting a mobile public of cultural consumers" (Zukin 1995, 19; see also Zukin 2003; Hall 2000; MacCannell 1977; Ryan and Glendon 1998; Featherstone 1991; Kearns and Philo 1993).

9. Boyer continues to describe it as "an outdoor advertisement that narrates a story about trade and commodities and these narratives of adventure and conquest fill out the more intangible nostalgic desires of the consumer" (1992, 198-202; see also Mele 2000; Smith 1996; Crawford 1992; and Hoffman 2003, 292). Gates finds evidence of at least 150 years of commodification of New York's ethnic communities for touristic purposes (1997). *Places* are the goldmines for what David Harvey calls a "speculative construction" that binds local symbols, image, and memory into a consumable package (1989, 8; see also Gottdiener 2001, 15–40; Zukin 1991, 23 and 1995, 17, 45; Lloyd and Clark 2001; Eeckhout 2001; Lash and Urry 1997, 215; Hayden 1996; Kirshenblatt-Gimblett 1998, 167; Boniface and Fowler 1993; Chang, Milne, Fallon, and Pohlmannet 1996; Craik 1997; Ley and Olds 1988; Kearns and Philo 1993; Hall and Zeppel 1990; Greenwood 1989; Nuryanti 1996).

10. See du Gay and Pryke 2002; Delany 1999; Gottdiener, Dickens, and Collins 1999; Knox 1992; Gotham 2007; Roost 1998; and Ross 2000.

11. See Bauman 1997, 89; Sorkin 1992, 231; Turner and Ash 1975; and Muschamp 1995, respectively.

12. Hoffman 2000. While culturally and economically isolated for half a century, Harlem is now "re-woven into the urban fabric with a capitalist agenda" (Hoffman 2003, 104–8; also Conforti 1996).

13. Recently, bus companies have responded to participants' interest by allowing tourists to step off one bus, walk around, and pick up another bus—further weakening the ties between guides and their participants. But to focus on tour-bus guides—the fixedness, the repetition, the lack of interaction—would provide an all-too-familiar vision of urban culture and tourism that run from the Seven Wonders through MacCannell's "sets."

14. Phil Kasinitz (1988) also examines "house tours," conducted on a particular historical site (e.g., the Lower East Side Tenement Museum, or the Astor House in Beachwood, N.J.), which can be guided in costume to evoke a particular era.

15. It should be noted that most guides are independent, but that GANYC represents about 15 percent of New York City's 1,700+ licensed guides. As a point of comparison (and not just on local guiding associations), Hong Kong's equivalent association holds 20% of the city's 2,500 guides (Ap and Wong 2001).

16. The under-problemization of the term "tourist" is evident in *Cities and Visitors*, where Hoffman, Fainstein, and Judd—three estimable scholars on tourism—use "tourist," "visitor," and "traveler" interchangeably in an effort to maintain the "common usage" as well as to provide the "most expansive meaning in regard to the tourist's motivation" (2003, 3).

17. Erik Cohen provides a definition of a guide as a pathfinder who leads a group "through a socially defined territory to which they have no access" (1985, 7).

18. A common equation is used by NYC & Company, which defines a "visitor" as an individual who travels fifty miles or more (excluding commuting), or stays overnight in the city. Andronicou demonstrates how out-of-towners often know more than locals do (1979, 251). See also Sherlock 2001; Lloyd 2004, 7; Häussermann and Colomb 2003, 210.

Chapter Two

1. Hotel, amusement, recreation, and museum jobs, for examples, increased from 11 to 16% of the city's employment from 1984 to 1996 (Abu-Lughod 1999, 291; Sassen 2001, 209. See also Harvey 1979, 1988, 1989; Portes and Sassen-Koob 1989; and Gladstone and Feinstein 2003, 90.) On seasonality of tourism see Ball (1988).

2. Peterson and Anand's axiom applies here: "Chaotic careers create orderly fields" (2002, 257). Such new issues over labor led to descriptions of "untidy," "boundaryless," or "chaotic careers" or "career heterogeneity," and guiding is perhaps an activity best understood as existing somewhere within this in-between that is still, nonetheless, "orderly" (Lemmer 1991; Baker and Aldrich 1996).

3. Faulkner explains that this sort of perspective illuminates how "members acquire ways of thinking, feeling, and believing about those arrangements" (1973, 334; see also Becker 1952 and Katz 1977).

4. One out of five Americans works part-time (Kalleberg, Reskin, and Hudson 2000, 257, 260, 273, 343), a steady increase of self-employment and nonstandard work over the last few decades, and Appelbaum, Bernhardt, and Mumane note that "non-standard" and "atypical" jobs account for 30 percent of the employment market (2003, 9).

5. See New York City Economic Development Corporation 2004, Pristin and Eaton 2001, and Berkey-Gerard 2004 for a discussion on the broader affects on the city's labor market.

6. Some estimate up to four-fifths of the United States' part-time workforce—17 out of 21 million—*wants* to work part-time (Tilly 1996 and 1998).

7. This is similar to what Stebbins calls "serious leisure," "the systematic pursuit of an amateur, hobbyist, or volunteer activity sufficiently substantial and interesting for the participant to find a career there in the acquisition and expression of a combination of its special skills, knowledge, and experience" (1993, 23).

8. See Lloyd's chapter, "Making the Scene" (2004).

9. To be a "jack of all trades" is not an insult. The full line is, "Jack of all trades, master of none; though oftentimes better than master of one."

Chapter Three

1. For a full history of the tourism industry see Casson 1974, 264.

2. The section of the law referring to licensing guides is NYC Administrative Code 20–242 et seq.

3. This reinforces Howard Becker's analysis of how support personnel in arts communities are often the invisible, yet pivotal players in cultural production (1984, 76–92), and, although at a larger scale, Logan and Molotch's notion of "auxiliary players" (1987, 75–85).

4. Many U.S. cities have such groups, and the National Federation of Tourist Guides Associations has twelve such groups as members (totaling 2,200 guides), including GANYC's membership. There is also a World Federation of Tour Guides. For an exhaustive review of the 1980s "tour packaging industry," see Sheldon 1986.

5. According to a report by the Congressional Research Service, the language of the original Robert T. Stafford Disaster Relief and Emergency Relief Act was reinterpreted on November 15, 2001. Disaster Unemployment Assistance was for those who were employed or self-employed and left jobless because of a major disaster and who are not eligible for federal and state unemployment insurance, but a new definition of "major disaster" includes unemployment due to a "long chain of events initiated by the disaster" but it also is designed to "exclude those individuals whose unemployment is the result of general economic decline that has been an indirect effect of a major disaster" (Lake 2002).

6. The "Growth Machine" (Logan and Molotch 1987), "Entertainment Machine" (Lloyd and Clark 2001), "Regulation School" (Hoffman 2003; Hoffman, Fainstein, and Judd 2003), and "urban power structure" (Friedland and Palmer 1984) models take this the "top-down" approach to researching tourism and urbanism highlights organizations, gravitating to the corporate capitalists and the "media stars and profiteers in real estate, finance, and culture industries" (Zukin 1995, 260).

7. With intentions similar to the MAS's desire to reach outside common locales and the more apparent intentions of Big Apple Greeters, the Conference Board's Business Enterprises for Sustainable Travel initiative specifically offers tours of more marginal neighborhoods to promote urban culture in low-income communities.

8. According to the Big Apple Greeters Annual Report (2004), the organization's total support and revenue for 2003 was estimated at $1.2 million.

9. Duneier 1999, 232. See also Zukin 1995, 32-47, 128-33; Hannigan 1998; and Wolfson 1992. As in most communities, the municipal government in New York oversees these public-private ventures, first via city council approval and then by Department of Business Services and Department of Finance. In 1981 New York City had three BIDs, in 1991 there were twenty, and currently there are forty-six. There are four major ones: The Alliance for Downtown New York, the 34th Street Partnership, the Times Square BID, and the Grand Central Partnership. For a more critical review see Blakely 1994, Levy 2001, Mitchell 2001, Sussman 1998, Turner 2002, and Council of the City of New York 1995, 1997. The executive director of the Urban Justice Center said BIDs revive a "tradition of non-democracy" (MacDonald 1996).

10. The data provided to me by the NYC Department of Small Business Services states that the 125th Street BID spends 5.3% of its $525,000 annual budget on promotion and tourism, the 34th Street Partnership spends 1.6% of its $8,198,500, the Grand

Central Partnership spends 9.1% of its $11,014,791, Times Square BID spends 13% of its $8,600,000 budget, the Union Square Partnership spends 5% of its $1,189,500 budget, and the Downtown Alliance spends a whopping 40% of its $11,250,000 budget on tourism and promotion. These budgets cannot parse out the tourism and promotions dollars. Data available for the first three were for the 2004 fiscal year, and the latter three were for 2005.

11. The notion of *social capital*—the "resources stored in human relationships, whether causal or close" (Briggs 1997, 112) is worth mentioning. Pierre Bourdieu describes it as "the aggregate of the actual or potential resources which are linked to possession of a durable network of more or less institutionalized relationships of mutual acquaintance or recognition" (1985, 248). Bourdieu (1985, 249) and Robert Putnam (2000) highlight the affirming qualities of social capital (in France and the United States, respectively), which is supposed to provide the beholder an increased sense of solidarity with a larger community and a kind of enforceable trust.

12. Walking guides could fit into various aspects of urban cultural policy (see Griffiths 1995, 255), and studies of how government agencies and cultural institutions use part-time and freelance workers in this milieu is the topic of future research.

13. Each of these findings reinforce what Portes saw as the four negative aspects of social capital: exclusion of outsiders, social control, decreased freedoms of insiders and a degradation of norms (1998, 15). See also Anderson 1992, Baker and Faulkner 1993, Portes and Landolt 1996, Portes and Zhou 1992, Stack 1974, and Wilson 1987.

14. Bourdieu called this "legitimation by contagion," and described as the symbolic consecration in which an institution "presupposes and produces mutual knowledge and recognition" on an individual or group (1984, 250).

15. For de Certeau, "Every authority is based on an affiliation" (1997, 13). Furthermore, Bourdieu offers three versions of legitimacy (1993, 50–51): recognition by one's peers ("specific legitimacy"), by the larger public of ordinary consumers ("popular legitimacy"), and from those who have power outside the field ("bourgeois legitimacy"). Guides can look for legitimation from the community of guides as well as from their participants (happy customers who offer "popular legitimacy").

Chapter Four

1. The use of "tricks" is not to imply guides are con men, but is similar to Hughes's explanation of the "dirty work" that occurs in every trade (Hughes 1962).

2. See Fine and Speer 1985.

3. See Lofland on "historical layering" and juxtaposition (1998, 84–85).

4. Jacobs 1961, 129; Careri 2002, 50; and Whyte 1958, 7.

5. Tuan 1980, 463. See Anderson and Gale 1992; Boyer 1992; and Casey 1998.

6. According to a report for the New York State Department of Transportation, New Yorkers are likely to take more and longer trips outside of the house than the rest of the United States, and the difference is "largely due to the predominance of walking trips in New York City" (Hu and Young 1999). New Yorkers walk four to five miles a day (Powell 2003). See Blackmar 1979. Park also noted the importance of wandering (1925, 132).

7. See Boyer 1992, 188. Hans Joas claims *action* plays a formative role in our understandings of the social world, that our bodies "capabilities, habits and ways of relating to the environment . . . form the background to all conscious goal-getting, in other words, to our intentionality" (1996, 158).

8. On the ways her fellow academic historians treat their material, Halttunen writes that few of her peers experiment with multiple voices and perspectives and are willing to "abandon unified closure for open endings, highlight gaps and contradiction" (1999, 167).

Chapter Five

1. Hochschild calls this *emotive dissonance*: the "maintaining a difference between feeling and feigning" (1983, 90; see also Leidner 1993 and 1999). Emotions themselves have received theoretical attention and empirical research (see Ducey, Gautney, and Wetzel 2003; Hochschild 1975 and 1979).

2. Hannigan describes how museums are making efforts to become entertaining, and that the desire for "edutainment" plays out in the tourist realm in that tourists "by and large, prefer romanticized and fictional representations of history and geography" (1998, 98).

3. Davis 1959, 162-63. As is the case with the Davis study, ethnographic evidence for these characters is hard to come by, and it is important to note that the following sections are much more concerned with guides' own impressions of how these types act on their tours.

4. For Richard Caves, interestingly, the presence of "buffs" in a cultural field contributes to its definition of being "high culture" (2000, 18).

5. See Boorstin 1961, 99; Hobsbawm and Ranger 1983; and MacCannell 1973, 592.

6. Mass tourism appears to undermine the perceived authenticity of the city these guides work within (Greenwood 1989). Walking guides have certainly felt the pressure of cultural expectations from their participants.

7. "Cultural experience," according to Van Mannen (who claims to follow MacCannell's lead), "implies the transformation of an original emptiness, vagueness, or skepticism on the part of an individual or group into a feeling or belief that is based on direct involvement" (1992, 7). See Edensor 2001, 74–78, on the assumptions of tourists writ large. Tourism, in general, is largely about such *differential* knowledge between the everyday and the exceptional (see Urry 1990a). This could also be related to what has been called the "massification hypothesis" (Macdonald 1957; DiMaggio and Peterson 1975). See Wacquant 2004, 15; Debord 2006, 93-99; and Seigworth 2000. For a broader, Weberian tale of rationalization and McDonaldization, see Ritzer 1993.

8. In Grazian's *Blue Chicago*, musicians talked about not being "blue enough"—with "blue" serving as a euphemism for "black" (2003, 178).

9. See Goffman on props (1959, 22-24, 59), footholds (1981, 128), and symbolic armor (1967). Richard Peterson, for example, found country singers fashioning new "signifiers of authenticity" in reaction to expectations of dress, speech, and song content (1997, 223).

10. Van Mannen and Kunda 1989. These could also be considered "contrived performances" (Goffman 1959, 70). While Goffman's *Relations in Public* documents the great lengths that people will go through to maintain the rituals and ceremonies that people play in the urban world, many tour groups form a "collusive net" or "alignment" (1971, 338) wherein all participants form a bond around the educational or entertaining experience.

11. Recall Goffman's definition of a *performer*, as "a harried fabricator of impressions involved in the all-too-human task of staging a performance,"—and a *character*, someone

"whose spirit, strength and other sterling qualities the performance was designed to evoke" (1969, 244). Furthermore, concerns over authenticity have something to do with experience, but also the *lack* of experience (Grazian 2003, 12). Grazian notes that blues consumers "expect to be entertained by performances that conform to dominant stereotypes of the setting, with attention given to local dialect, styles of interaction, dress, and so forth" (2004, 138). In regards to tourism see also Stewart 1984, 133; Häussermann and Colomb 2003.

Chapter Six

1. Larson 2003, 253.

2. See Goffman 1974, 45, 49, 79. Goffman notes that "rekeyings" are dependent upon "primary frameworks," and this conceptual wrinkle is a worthwhile reminder that guides in fact rely upon the rise of commercial and mass tourism as a way to garner income, and also as something to actively push against in their own narrative takes on urban culture.

3. This is a good instance of an incorrect quotation being bandied about. While Picasso might have said this as well, the more attributed quote is, "Good artists copy, great artists steal."

4. Through conducting this research, I was always seen as being suspicious for taking notes. Even after guides read the consent forms I provided and I had explicitly stated my research agenda, many were still uncertain. During several interviews, respondents were reluctant to disclose an example from their tours, or a favorite story, despite probing and assurances. Such concerns led to conflicts of positioning myself in the field, a topic for discussion in the Appendix. See Duneier's thoughtful appendix on the morally ambiguous tensions in ethnography (1999).

5. "Every time I describe a city," Polo states ambiguously, "I am saying something about Venice" (Calvino 1974, 86).

6. This is not mere paranoia. See Lee, Yu, and Xu's article on "modeling human walking trajectories" (2003).

7. This sort of "local fetishization" can be understood in relation to "place character" (Molotch, Freudenburg, and K. Paulsen 2000, 793).

8. See Ritzer 1993; MacCannell 1973; Judd 1999.

9. Homogenization scenarios "commercialize and thus trivialize culture by reducing its relevance to something that is bought and sold and thought to be fully under the control of a few and exported to many" (Van Mannen 1992, 8).

10. In the words of de Certeau, this kind of mobile classroom "'escapes' from the domination of a sociocultural economy, from the organization of reason, from the grasp of education, from the power of an elite and, finally, from the control of the enlightened consciousness" (1984, 158).

11. See Wynn (2010). Guides reinforce Bourdieu's description of an educational system monopolizing the distribution of scholarly certification, but not the acquisition of cultural capital or the means of reproducing cultural capital via teaching (1984, 80).

12. Such a binary is pervasive. Griswold, for example, proposed a clear distinction between *academic specialists* and *local informants* (1987, 24), rather than seeing a large gray area between.

13. There are other models for such characters. De Certeau talks about the "Third Man" who tells the "tales of the unrecognized" (1984, 68–69), and Gramsci's organic

intellectual is someone who engages in "active participation in practical life, as con-structor, organizer, 'permanent persuader' and not just a simple orator" (1971, 10). For Bourdieu, "the autodidact constantly betrays, by his very anxiety about the right classification, the arbitrariness of his classifications and therefore of his knowledge—a collection of unstrung pearls, accumulated in the course of an uncharted exploration, unchecked by the institutionalized, standardized stages and obstacles, the curricula and progressions which make scholastic culture a ranked and ranking set of interdependent levels and forms of knowledge. . . . The apparent heterogeneity of his preferences his confusion of genres and ranks, operetta and opera, popularization and science, the unpredictability of his ignorance and knowledge, with no other connection than the sequence of biographical accident, all stem from the particularities of a heretical mode of acquisition" (1984, 328).

14. Goffman 1967, 109.

Chapter Seven

1. To preface his famous exegesis on spatial rationalization, Foucault describes how the bureaucratic ordering of cities has its very foundations in the response to the plague—at the end of the seventeenth century wherein cities attempted to control the chaos of contagion with the utopian plan of a "perfectly governed city" (1977, 198). See Weber 1958, 42; Park 1925.

2. The notion of alchemy as a way to understand how people transform themselves and their environments is not particularly new. Walter Benjamin (1999) was taken by Baudelaire's alchemic ability to use the pieces of the city to uncover a cultural uncon-scious and dreamworld, and even Carl Jung believed alchemy was a kind to understand-ing how one's unconscious is more of a process (1973, 202–4).

3. The Howling Mob Society, http://howlingmobsociety.org.

4. For Goffman there are "exploitative fabrications"—those that are intended to manipulate others (1974, 103, 10, 15, and 157), but for the most part, fabrications are everyday occurrences (10, 15). See Feiden 2005 on an example of how the popular press attempts to portray guides as fabricators, and Hughes 1958.

5. See also Lofland's brief discussion on urban whimsy and unexpectedness (1998, 81–82).

6. To further extend the point, many have turned a profit from claims of what makes a New Yorker a New Yorker. Richard Laermer (2002), for example, includes: "Knows she can cross the street leisurely when Walk/Don't Walk signs are flashing 'Don't Walk,' and can scamper across when the signs bear a solid 'Don't Walk,'" "Pronounces 'Hous-ton Street' properly," "calls Manhattan 'the city,'" "knows what TriBeCa stands for," "Can spot a tourist a mile away," and "Knows what end of the subway to get on so he'll end up at the stairs when he exits and/or knows what door won't open so he can lean on it."

7. Benjamin 1978, 143–44.

Appendix A

1. It should be noted that this is not a perspective exclusive to ethnographers, either. C. Wright Mills once wrote that he felt it "useful . . . to report in some detail how I go about my craft" (1959, 197) and Max Weber wrote that the sociologist should express the position from which he or she writes (1949, 83).

2. The experience of heavy editing was daunting. Hochschild speaks of her own

challenges publishing up to nine different drafts for her series of op-ed articles in major newspapers (Tuchman 1998, 38), and Stacey describes the undesirable effects of one's research being used and potentially manipulated by the media (2004). It was the small things that I had to be satisfied with (e.g., the inclusion of "cultural capital" in the text).

3. An Interpolation on Participation: I admit that I see my own disposition as similar to George Plimpton's, whose participations in sport were always to flesh out the borderlands between the people we watch and those whom we think that we are. Unlike Wacquant's *Body and Soul* where the final page has a picture of the pugilistic professor himself, with the caption "One of Dee Dee's boys" (2004, 256), Plimpton cautiously avoided such assertions, claiming the "participatory journalist" should be akin to the "professional amateur." For example, after a disastrous four downs as the third-string quarterback of the Detroit Lions in a scrimmage, he writes: "I thought about the applause afterward. Some of it was perhaps, in appreciation of the lunacy of my participation, and for the fortitude it took to do it; but most of it, even if subconscious, I decided was in *relief* that I had done as badly as I had: it verified the assumption that the average fan would have about an amateur blundering into the brutal world of professional football. He would get slaughtered" (1966, 202).

4. A review of the test after taking it indicated that only twenty-five of the questions were from the tours that I had taken. Many were from the stories that guides told me in interviews. For obvious reasons I cannot publish which tours presented which questions.

BIBLIOGRAPHY

Abu-Lughod, J. 1999. *New York, Chicago, Los Angeles.* Minneapolis: University of Minnesota Press.

Adler, J. 1989. Origins of sightseeing. *Annals of Tourism Research* 16 (1): 7–29.

Allen, I. L. 1993. *The city in slang.* New York: Oxford University Press.

Anbinder, T. 2001. *Five points: The nineteenth-century New York City neighborhood that invented tap dance, stole elections, and became the world's most notorious slum.* New York: Plume Books.

Anderson, E. 1992. *Streetwise: Race, class, and change in an urban community.* Chicago: University of Chicago Press.

Anderson, K., and F. Gale, eds. 1992. *Inventing places: Studies in cultural geography.* Melbourne: Longman Cheshire.

Anderson, N. 1923. *The hobo.* Chicago: University of Chicago Press.

Andronicou, A. 1979. Tourism in Cyprus. In *Tourism: Passport to development,* ed. E. de Kadt, 237–64. New York: Oxford University Press.

Ap, J. and K. K. F. Wong. 2001. Case study on tour guiding: Professionalism, issues, and problems. *Tourism Management* 22:551–563.

Appelbaum, E., A. Bernhardt, and R. Mumane. 2003. *Low wage America: How employers are reshaping economic opportunity in the workplace.* New York: Russell Sage Foundation.

Asbury, H. 1980. *The gangs of New York: An informal history of the underworld.* New York: Knopf.

Baker, T., and H. E. Aldrich. 1996. Prometheus stretches: Building identity and cumulative knowledge in multiemployer careers. In *The boundaryless career,* ed. M. B. Arthur and D. M. Rousseau, 132–49. Oxford: Oxford University Press.

Baker, W. and R. Faulkner. 1993. The Social Organization of Conspiracy: Illegal Networks in the Heavy Electrical Equipment Industry. *American Sociological Review* 58: 837–860.

Ball, R. M. 1988. Seasonality: A problem for workers in the tourism labour market. *Service Industries Journal* 8 (4): 501–3.

Bateson, G. 1949. *Bali: The value system of a steady state*. New York: Institute for Intercultural Studies.

Bauman, Z. 1997. *Postmodernity and its discontents*. Cambridge: Polity Press.

Bearman, P. 2005. *Doormen: Fieldwork encounters and discoveries*. Chicago: University of Chicago Press.

Becker, H. S. 1951. The professional dance musician and his audience. *American Journal of Sociology* 57 (2): 136–44.

———. 1952. The career of the public school teacher. *American Journal of Sociology* 57 (5): 470–77.

———. 1963. *Outsiders: Studies in the sociology of deviance*. Glencoe, Ill.: Free Press.

———. 1984. *Art worlds*. Berkeley: University of California Press.

———. 1998. *Tricks of the trade*. Chicago: University of Chicago Press.

———. 2007. *Telling about society*. Chicago: University of Chicago Press.

Becker, H. S., and J. W. Carper. 1956. The development of identification with an occupation. *American Journal of Sociology* 61 (4): 289–98.

Benjamin, W. 1978. *Reflections*. Translated by E. Jephcott and edited by P. Demetz. New York: Schocken Books.

———. 1999. *The Arcades Project*. Translated by H. Eiland and K. McLaughlin and edited by R. Tiedemann. Cambridge: Harvard University Press.

Bennett, H. S. 1980. *On becoming a rock musician*. Amherst: University of Massachusetts Press.

Bennett, J. 2001. *The enchantment of modern life*. Princeton, NJ: Princeton University Press.

Berkey-Gerard, M. 2004. Tourism and jobs. *Gotham Gazette*. May 31.

Big Apple Greeters. 2004. *Big Apple greeters annual report 2003*. New York: Big Apple Greeters.

Blackmar, B. 1979. Re-walking the "Walking City": Housing and property relations, 1780–1840. *Radical History Review* 21:131–48

Blakely, E. J. 1994. *Planning Local Economic Development: Theory and Practice*. 2nd ed. Thousand Oaks: Sage Publications.

Boniface, P., and P. J. Fowler. 1993. *Heritage and tourism in the global village*. London: Routledge.

Boorstin, D. J. 1961. *The image: A guide to pseudo-events in America*. New York: Vintage.

Bourdieu, P. 1984. *Distinction: A social critique of the judgment of taste*. Cambridge: Harvard University Press.

———. 1985. The forms of capital. In *Handbook of theory and research for the sociology of education*. ed. J. G. Richardson, 241-58. New York: Greenwood.

———. 1993. *The field of cultural production*. New York: Columbia University Press.

Bourgois, P. 1995. *In search of respect: Selling crack in El Barrio*. New York and Cambridge: University of Cambridge Press.

Boyer, M. C. 1992. City for sale. In *Variations on a theme park: The new American city and the end of public space*, ed. M. Sorkin, 181–204. New York: Hill and Wang.

Braudel, F. 2002. *The wheels of commerce*. Vol. 2 of *Civilization and capitalism, 15th–18th century*. London: Phoenix Press.

Briggs, X. 1997. Social capital and the cities: Advice to change agents. *National Civic Review* 86:111–17.

Britton, S. 1991. Tourism, capital, and place: Towards a critical geography of tourism. *Environment and Planning D: Society and Space* 9:451–78.

Bromley, D. G., and A. Shupe. 1995. Anti-cultism in the United States. *Social Compass* 42:221–36.

Bryman, A. 1999. The Disneyization of society. *Sociological Review* 47 (1): 25–47.

Burrows, E. G.,M. Wallace. 1999. *Gotham: A history of New York City to 1898*. New York and Oxford, UK: Oxford University Press.

Bywater, M. 2007. Performing spaces: Street music and public territory. *Twentieth-Century Music* 3:97–120.

Calvino, I. 1974. *Invisible cities*. Translated by W. Weaver. London: Vintage.

Careri, F. 2002. *Walkscapes: Walking as an aesthetic practice*. Barcelona: Gustavo Gili.

Casey, E. S. 1998. *The fate of place*. Berkeley: University of California Press.

Casson, L. 1974. *Travel in the ancient world*. Toronto: Hakkert.

Caves, R. 2000. *Creative industries: Contracts between art and commerce*. Cambridge: Harvard University Press.

Chambers, E. 1999. *Native tours: The anthropology of travel and tourism*. Long Grove, Ill.: Waveland Press.

Chang, T. C., S. Milne, D. Fallon, and C. Pohlmann. 1996. Urban heritage tourism: The global-local nexus. *Annals of Tourism Research* 23 (2): 284–305.

Chauncey, G. 1994. *Gay New York*. New York: Basic Books.

Cocks, C. 2001. *Doing the town: The rise of urban tourism in the United States, 1850–1915*. Berkeley: University of California Press.

Cohen, E. 1972. Toward a sociology of international tourism. *Social Research* 39:162–82.

———. 1979. A phenomenology of tourist experiences. *Sociology* 13:179–203.

———. 1985. The tourist guide. *Annals of Tourism Research* 12:5–29.

Conforti, J. M. 1996. Ghettos as tourism attractions. *Annals of Tourism Research* 23 (4): 830–42.

Cooley, C. H. 1902. *Human nature and the social order*. New York: Scribner.

Council of the City of New York. 1995. Cities within cities: Business improvement districts and the emergence of the micropolis. New York.

———. 1997. Managing the micropolis: Proposals to strengthen BID performance and accountability. Staff report to the Committee on Finance. New York.

Craik, J. 1997. The culture of tourism. In *Touring cultures: Transformations of travel and theory*, ed. C. Rojek and J. Urry, 113–36. London: Routledge.

Crawford, M. 1992. The world in a shopping mall. In *Variations on a theme park: The new American city and the end of public space*, ed. M. Sorkin, 3–30. New York: Hill and Wang.

Cressey, P. 1932. *The taxi-dance hall*. Chicago: University of Chicago Press.

Dahles, H. 2002. The politics of tour guiding: Image management in Indonesia. *Annals of Tourism Research* 29:783–800.

Davis, F. 1959. The cabdriver and his fare: Facets of a fleeting relationship. *American Journal of Sociology* 65 (2): 158–65.

Debord, G. 2006. *Society of the spectacle*. New York: Zone Books.

de Certeau, M. 1984. *The Practice of Everyday Life*. Berkeley: University of California Press.

———. 1997. *Culture in the plural*. Minneapolis: University of Minnesota Press.

Delany, S. 1999. *Times Square red, Times Square blue*. New York: NYU Press.

Demerath, L., and D. Levinger. 2003. The social qualities of being on foot: A theoretical analysis of pedestrian activity. *City and Community* 2 (3): 217–37.

DiMaggio, P., and R. Peterson. 1975. From region to class, the changing locus of country music: A test of the massification hypothesis. *Social Forces* 53:497–506

Donovan, F. 1920. *The woman who waits*. Boston: Badger.

Douglas, M. 1975. *Implicit Meanings*. London: Routledge.

Ducey, A., H. Gautney, and D. Wetzel. 2003. Regulating affective labor: Communication skills training in the health care industry. *Research in the Sociology of Work* 12:49–72.

du Gay, P., and M. Pryke. 2002. Cultural economy: An introduction. In *Cultural economy: Cultural analysis and commercial life*, ed. P. du Gay and M. Pryke, 1–19. London: Sage.

Duneier, M. 1999. *Sidewalk*. New York: Farrar, Strauss and Giroux.

———. 2004. Scrutinizing the heat: On ethnic myths and the importance of shoe leather. *Contemporary Sociology* 33:139–50.

Edensor, T. 2001. Performing tourism, staging tourism. *Tourist Studies* 1 (1): 59–81.

Eeckhout, B. 2001. The "Disneyification" of Times Square: Back to the future. *Research in Urban Sociology* 6:379–428.

Eisenstadt, Jill. 2003. My brother, the licensed know-it-all. *New York Times*, May 11, B1.

Essig, L. 2002. Fine diving. http://www.salon.com/mwt/feature/2002/06/10/edible_trash.

Faulkner, R. R. 1973. Career concerns and mobility motivations of orchestra musicians. *Sociological Quarterly* 14:147–57.

Featherstone, M. 1991. *Consumer culture and postmodernism*. London: Sage.

Federal Writers Project. 1982. *The WPA Guide to New York City*. New York: Pantheon.

Feiden, D. 2005. Takin' tourists for a ride: News puts city's tourist guides to the truth test, and guess what? *New York Daily News*, September 25.

Fernandez, M. 2006. 44 million tourists and counting. *New York Times*, December 28.

Fine, G. A. 1996. *Kitchens*. Berkeley: University of California Press.

Fine, E. C., and J. H. Speer. 1985. Tour guide performances as sight sacralization. *Annals of Tourism Research* 12 (1): 73–95.

Flusty, S. 2000. Thrashing downtown: Play as resistance to the spatial and representational regulation of Los Angeles. *Cities* 17 (2): 149–58.

Fodor's. 2004. *New York City*. New York: Fodor's Travel Publications.

Foucault, M. 1977. *Discipline and punish: The birth of the prison*. Translated by A. Sheridan. New York: Vintage.

Fried, J. P. 2006. It's not a tour. It's a stroll with your new "Aunt Tilly." *New York Times*, May 25.

Friedland, R., and D. Palmer. 1984. Park Place and Main Street: Business and the urban power structure. *Annual Review of Sociology* 10:393–416.

Fronc, J. 2009. *New York undercover*. Chicago: University of Chicago Press.

Gates, J. A. 1997. Strangers in New York: Ethnic tourism as commodity, spectacle, and urban leisure in three Manhattan neighborhoods. PhD diss., New York University.

Ginzburg, C. 1992. *The cheese and the worms: The cosmology of a sixteenth-century miller*. Baltimore: Johns Hopkins University Press.

Gladstone, D. L., and S. S. Fainstein. 2001. Tourism in US global cities: A comparison of New York and Los Angeles. *Journal of Urban Affairs* 23 (1): 23–41.

———. 2003. The New York and Los Angeles economies. In *New York and Los Angeles: Politics, society and culture*, ed. D. Halle, 79–98. Chicago: University of Chicago Press.

Goffman, E. 1959. *The presentation of self in everyday life*. Garden City, NY: Anchor.

———. 1963. *Behavior in public places: Notes on the social organization of gatherings*. Glencoe, Ill.: Free Press.

———. 1967. *Interaction ritual: Essays on face-to-face behavior*. Garden City, NY: Anchor Books.

———. 1969. *Strategic interaction*. Philadelphia: University of Pennsylvania Press.

———. 1971. *Relations in public: Microstudies of the public order*. New York: Basic Books.

———. 1974. *Frame analysis*. Boston: Northeastern University Press.

———. 1981. *Forms of talk*. Philadelphia: University of Pennsylvania Press.

Gold, J. 1988. *From Trout Streams to Bohemia*. New York: Old Warren Road Press.

Gold, R. 1952. Janitors versus tenents: A status-income dilemma. *American Journal of Sociology* 57:486–93.

Goodlad, S., and S. MacIvor 1998. *Museum volunteers: Good practice in the management of volunteers*. London: Routledge.

Gotham, K. F. 2007. *Authentic New Orleans: Tourism, culture, and race in the Big Easy*. New York: NYU Press.

Gottdiener, M. 2001. *The theming of America: American dreams, media fantasies, and themed environment*. Boulder, Colo.: Westview Press.

Gottdiener, M., D. R. Dickens, and C. C. Collins. 1999. *Las Vegas: The social production of an all-American city*. Oxford: Basil Blackwell.

Gowan, T. 2000. Excavating "globalization" from street level: Homeless men recycle their pasts. In *Global ethnography*, ed. M. Burawoy, 74–105. Berkeley: University of California Press.

Graburn, H. N. N. 1989. Tourism: A sacred journey. In *Hosts and guests*, ed. V. L. Smith, 21–36. Philadelphia: University of Pennsylvania Press.

Gramsci, A. 1971. *Selections from the prison notebooks of Antonio Gramsci*. Translated and edited by Q. Hoare and G. Nowell-Smith. New York: International Publishers.

Grasmuck, S. 2005. *Protecting home: Class, race, and masculinity in boys' baseball*. New Brunswick, NJ: Rutgers University Press.

Gray, C. 1999. Streetscapes/Henry Hope Reed: An architecture critic who still loves the classics. *New York Times*, September 19.

Grazian, D. 2003. *Blue Chicago: The search for authenticity in urban blues clubs*. Chicago: University of Chicago Press.

———. 2004. Opportunities for ethnography in the sociology of music. *Poetics* 32: 197–210.

Greenwood, D. 1989. Culture by the pound: An anthropological perspective on tourism as cultural commoditization. In *Hosts and guests*, ed. V. L. Smith, 129–39. Philadelphia: University of Pennsylvania Press.

Griffiths, R. 1995. Cultural strategies and new modes of urban intervention. *Cities* 12 (4): 253–265.

Griswold, W. 1987. The fabrication of meaning: Literary interpretation in the United States, Great Britain, and the West Indies. *American Journal of Sociology* 92 (5): 1077–1117.

Hall, M., and H. Zeppel. 1990. Cultural and heritage tourism: The new grand tour. *Historic Environment* 7:86–98.

Hall, P. 2000. Creative cities and economic development. *Urban Studies* 37 (4): 639–49.

Halttunen, K. 1999. Cultural history and the challenge of narrativity. In *Beyond the cultural turn: New directions in the study of society and culture*, ed. V. Bonnell and L. Hunt, 165–81. Berkeley: University of California Press.

Hammett, J., K. H. Hammett, and M. Cooper, eds. 2007. *The suburbanization of New York: Is the world's greatest city becoming just another town?* Princeton, NJ: Princeton Architectural Press.

Hannerz, U. 1980. *Exploring the city: Inquiries towards an urban anthropology.* New York: Columbia University Press.

———. 2004. *Foreign news: Exploring the world of foreign news correspondents.* Chicago: University of Chicago Press.

Hannigan, J. 1998. *Fantasy city: The pleasure and profit in the postmodern metropolis.* London: Routledge.

Harvey, D. 1979. Monument and myth. *Annals of the Association of American Geographers* 69:362–81.

———. 1988. Voodoo cities. *New Statesman and Society* 1 (September 30): 33–35.

———. 1989. *Conditions of postmodernity.* London: Blackwell.

Häussermann, H., and C. Colomb. 2003. The new Berlin: Marketing the city of dreams. In *Cities and visitors: Regulating people, markets and city space*, ed. L. M. Hoffman, S. S. Fainstein, and D. R. Judd, 200–218. London: Blackwell Publishing.

Hayden, D. 1996. *The power of place: Urban landscapes as public history.* Cambridge, Mass.: MIT Press.

Hebdige, D. 2003. Dis-gnosis: Disney and the re-tooling of knowledge, art, culture, life, etc. *Cultural Studies* 17 (2): 150–67.

Hedges, C. 2003. So many street corners, so many stories. *New York Times*, April 9.

Hobsbawn, E., and T. Ranger. 1983. *The invention of tradition.* Cambridge: Cambridge University Press.

Hochschild, A. R. 1975. The sociology of feeling and emotion: Selected possibilities. In *Another voice: Feminist perspectives on social life and the social sciences*, ed. M. Millman and R. M. Kanter, 280–307. Garden City, NY: Anchor Books.

———. 1979. Emotion work, feeling rules, and social structure. *American Journal of Sociology* 85:551–75.

———. 1983. *The managed heart: Commercialization of human feeling.* Berkeley: University of California Press.

———. 1989. *The second shift: Working parents and the revolution at home.* New York: Viking.

Hoffman, L. 2000. Tourism and the revitalization of Harlem. *Research in Urban Sociology* 5:207–23.

———. 2003. The marketing of diversity in the inner city: Tourism and regulation in Harlem. *International Journal of Urban and Regional Research* 27 (2): 286–99.

Hoffman, L. M., S. S. Fainstein, and D. R. Judd. 2003. Introduction. In *Cities and visitors: Regulating people, markets and city space*, ed. L. M. Hoffman, S. S. Fainstein, and D. R. Judd, 1–20. London: Blackwell Publishing.

Holloway, J. 1981. The guided tour: A sociological approach. *Annals of Tourism Research* 8 (3): 377–402.

Howe, I. 1989. *The world of our fathers.* New York: Houghton Mifflin.

Hu, P. S., and J. R. Young. 1999. 1995 New York nationwide personal transportation survey: A comparison study (revised). Prepared for New York State Department of Transportation.

Hughes, E. C. 1958. *Men and their work*. Glencoe, Ill.: The Free Press.

———. 1962. Good people and dirty work. *Social Problems* 10 (1): 3–11.

Jacobs, J. 1961. *The death and life of great American cities*. New York: Vintage.

Joas, H. 1996. *The creativity of action*. Chicago: University of Chicago Press.

Judd, D. R. 1999. Constructing the tourist bubble. In *The tourist city*, ed. D. R. Judd and S. S. Fainstein, 35–53. New Haven: Yale University Press.

Judd, D. R., and S. S. Fainstein, eds. 1999. *The tourist city*. New Haven: Yale University Press.

Jung, C. 1973. *Memories, dreams, and reflections*. Edited by A. Jaffé and R. Winston. New York: Pantheon Books.

Kalleberg, A., B. F. Reskin, and K. Hudson. 2000. Bad jobs in America: Standard and nonstandard employment relations and job quality in the United States. *American Sociological Review* 65 (2): 256–78.

Kasinitz, P. 1988. The gentrification of "Boerum Hill": Neighborhood change and conflicts over definitions. *Qualitative Sociology* 11 (3): 163-82.

Katz, J. 1977. Essences as moral identities: Verifiability and responsibility in imputations of deviance and charisma. *American Journal of Sociology* 80 (6): 1369–90.

———. 2007. Sensitizing concepts and current themes: NSF REU Group, March http:// www.sscnet.ucla.edu/nsfreu/CurrentThemesMarch2007.pdf (accessed September 22, 2008).

———. 2010. Time for new urban ethnographies. *Ethnography* 10 (2-3): 285–304.

Kayden, J. S. 2000. *Privately owned public spaces: The New York experience*. New York: John Wiley and Sons.

Kearns, G., and C. Philo. 1993. *Selling places: The city as cultural capital past and present*. Oxford: Pergamon Press.

Kellogg, C. 1960. Women are ardent fans of city walking tours. *New York Times*, August 4, 13.

Kelner, S. 2010. *Tours that bind: Diaspora, pilgrimage and Israeli birthright tourism*. New York: NYU Press.

Kilgannon, C. 1999. Urban tactics; sights unseen from a bus top: Marilyn's grate and gay Harlem *New York Times*, November 14, 3.

Kirshenblatt-Gimblett, B. 1998. *Destination culture: Tourism, museums, and heritage*. Berkeley: University of California Press.

Knox, P. L. 1992. The packaged landscapes of post-suburban America. In *International perspectives*, ed. J. W. R. Whitehead and P. J. Larkham, 207–26. London: Routledge.

Kornblum, W. 1974. *Blue collar community*. Chicago: University of Chicago Press.

Kusenbach, M. 2003. Street-phenomenology: The go-along as ethnographic research tool. *Ethnography* 4 (3): 449–479.

Laermer, R. 2002. *Native's guide to New York: Advice with attitude for people who live here—and visitors we like*. New York: W. W. Norton & Company.

Lake, J. E. 2002. Congressional research service report for Congress: Disaster unemployment assistance. Washington, DC: Congressional Research Service.

Lankeneau, S. E. 1999. Stronger than dirt: Public humiliation and status enhancement among panhandlers. *Journal of Contemporary Ethnography* 28 (3): 288–318.

Larson, E. 2003. *The devil and the white city*. New York: Crown.

Lash, S., and J. Urry. 1994. *Economies of signs and space*. London: Sage.

———. 1997. *The end of organized capitalism*. London: Polity Press.

Lee, D. 2002. Neighborhood report: New York up close; voices stilled, Gray Line guides battle their former employer. *New York Times*, September 15.

Lee, K. K., M. Yu, and Y. Xu. 2003. Modeling of human walking trajectories for surveillance. *Intelligent Robots and Systems* 2 (October): 1554–59.

Leidner, R. 1993. *Fast food, fast talk: Service work and the routinization of everyday life*. New York: Oxford University Press.

———. 1999. Emotional labor in service work. *Annals of the American Academy of Political and Social Science* 561:81–95.

Lemmer, E. M. 1991. Untidy careers: Occupational profiles of re-entry women. *International Journal of Career Management* 3 (1): 8–16.

Levy, P. R. 2001. Paying for the public life. *Economic Development Quarterly* 15:124–31.

Ley, D., and K. Olds. 1988. Landscape and spectacle: World fairs and the culture of heroic consumption. *Environment and Planning D: Society and Space* 6:191–212.

Liebow, E. 1968. *Tally's corner: A study of Negro streetcorner men*. Boston: Little Brown.

Lloyd, R. 2004. *Neo-Bohemia: Art and commerce in the post-industrial city*. New York: Routledge.

Lloyd, R., and T. N. Clark. 2001. The city as entertainment machine. *Research in Urban Sociology* 6:357–78.

Lofland, L. 1998. *The public realm*. Hawthorne, NY: Aldine De Gruyter.

Logan, J., and H. Molotch. 1987. *Urban fortunes: The political economy of place*. Berkeley: University of California Press.

M27 Coalition. 2004. http://www.m27coalition.org/directaction_locations.html (accessed July 3, 2005).

MacCannell, D. 1973. *The tourist: A new theory of the leisure class*. Berkeley: University of California Press.

———. 1977. The tourist and the new community. *Annals of Tourism Research* 4:208–15.

Macdonald, D. 1957. A theory of mass culture. In *Mass culture*, ed. B. Rosenberg and D. M. White, 59–73. Glencoe, Ill.: Free Press.

MacDonald, H. 1996. BIDs really work. *City Journal* 6 (2): 29–42.

Marcus, G. 1998. *Ethnography through thick and thin*. Princeton, NJ: Princeton University Press.

Marwell, N. P. 2007. *Bargaining for Brooklyn: Community organizations in the entrepreneurial city*. Chicago: University of Chicago Press.

Mele, C. 2000. *Selling the Lower East Side culture, real estate, and resistance in New York, 1880–2000*. Minneapolis: University of Minnesota Press.

Mills, C. W. 1959. *The sociological imagination*. New York: Oxford University Press.

Mitchell, J. 2001. Business improvement districts and the management of innovation. *American Review of Public Administration* 31:201–17.

Moeran, B. 1983. The language of Japanese tourism. *Annals of Tourism Research* 10 (1): 93–108.

Molotch, H., W. Freudenburg, and K. Paulsen. 2000. History repeats itself, but how? City character, urban tradition, and the accomplishment of place. *American Sociological Review* 65:791–823.

Morrone, F. 2005. How Henry Hope Reed saved architecture. *New York Sun*, August 1.

Morrone, F., M. A. Postal, and R. Lynn, eds. 2009. Ten Architectural Walks in Manhattan. New York: W. W. Norton & Company.

Muschamp, H. 1995. A flare for fantasy: "Miami Vice" meets 42nd Street. *New York Times*, May 21, sec. 2, pp. 1, 27.

Nash, D. 1989. Tourism as a form of imperialism. In *Hosts and guests*, ed. V. L. Smith, 37–52. Philadelphia: University of Pennsylvania Press.

Nelson, S. 1995. Broadway and the beast: Disney comes to Times Square. *TDR* 39 (2): 71–85.

NYC & Company. 2009. NYC statistics. http://www.nycgo.com/?event=view .article&id=78912 (accessed December 3, 2009).

New York City Economic Development Corporation. 2004. *2004: Economic snapshot*. New York: New York City Economic Development Corporation.

New York Times. 1857. No more rioting. July 7.

———. 1892. Spend your vacation walking. August 22.

———. 1938. Informal era ends for street barker. January 25.

Nuryanti, W. 1996. Heritage and postmodern tourism. *Annals of Tourism Research* 23:249–60.

Oder, N. 2005. Tourism troubles: It's not just the buses, but the guides too. *Gotham Gazette*. http://www.gothamgazette.com/commentary/appletours.shtml (accessed May 20, 2005).

Ouf, A. M. S. 2001. Authenticity and the sense of place in urban design. *Journal of Urban Design* 6 (1): 73–86.

Perrottet, T. 2002. *Pagan holiday*. New York: Random House.

Peterson, R. A. 1997. *Creating country music: Fabricated authenticity*. Chicago: University of Chicago Press.

Peterson, R. A., and N. Anand. 2002. How chaotic careers create orderly fields. In *Career creativity*, ed. M. A. Peiperl, M. Arthur, R. Goffee, and N. Anand, 257–89. Oxford: Oxford University Press.

Pressentin Wright, C. von. 1991. *The Blue Guide to New York*. New York: W. W. Norton & Company.

Plimpton, G. 1966. *Paper lion*. New York: Pocket Books.

Pond, K. 1993. *The professional guide: Dynamics of tour guiding*. New York: Van Nostrand Reinhold.

Portes, A. 1998. Social capital: Its origins and applications in modern sociology. *Annual Review of Sociology* 24:1–24.

Portes, A., and P. Landolt. 1996. The downside of social capital. *American Prospect* 16:18–21.

Portes, A., and S. Sassen-Koob. 1987. Making it underground: Comparative material on the informal sector in Western market economies. *American Journal of Sociology* 93 (1): 30–61.

Portes, A., and M. Zhou. 1992. Gaining the upper hand: Economic mobility among immigrant and domestic minorities. *Ethnic and Racial Studies* 15:491–522.

Powell, M. 2003. Licensed to drive? Fuhgeddaboutit!: Most New Yorkers do without wheels. *Washington Post*, August 19, A01.

Pristin, T., and L. Eaton. 2001. A nation challenged: The unemployed; disaster's aftershocks: number of workers out of a job is rising. *New York Times*, September 26.

Putnam, R. 2000. *Bowling alone: The collapse and revival of American community*. New York: Simon and Schuster.

Rajchman, J. 1994. Thinking big—Dutch architect Rem Koolhaas—interview. *Artforum*, December 1.

Rauh, G. 2008. City in record territory as a tourist destination. *New York Sun*, January 14.

Reynolds, G. 2008. Stand by your beds. *Guardian UK*, April 25.

Rich, A. 1986. *Blood, bread and poetry: Selected prose, 1979–1985*. New York: W. W. Norton & Company.

Ritzer, G. 1993. *The McDonaldization of society*. Thousand Oaks, Calif.: Pine Forge Press.

Ritzer, G., and A. Liska. 1997. "McDisneyization" and "post-tourism": Complementary perspectives on contemporary tourism. In *Touring cultures: Transformations of travel and theory*, ed. C. Rojek and J. Urry, 96–112. London: Routledge.

Rojek, C. 1993. Disney culture. *Leisure Studies* 12:121–35.

Roost, F. 1998. Recreating the city as entertainment center: The media industry's role in transforming Potsdamer Platz and Times Square. *Journal of Urban Technology* 5 (3): 1–21.

Ross, A. 2000. *The Celebration chronicles*. New York: Ballantine Books.

———. 2003. *No collar: The humane workplace and its hidden costs*. New York: Basic Books.

Rousseau, J.-J. 1980. *The reveries of a solitary walker*. New York: Penguin.

Rupp, L. J., and V. Taylor. 2003. *Drag queens at the 801 Cabaret*. Chicago: University of Chicago Press.

Ryan, C., and I. Glendon. 1998. Application of leisure motivation scales to tourism. *Annals of Tourism Research* 25 (1): 169–84.

Sadler, S. 1998. *The situationist city*. Cambridge, Mass.: MIT Press.

Salazar, N. B. 2005. Tourism and glocalization: "Local" tour guiding. *Annals of Tourism Research* 32 (3): 628–46.

Sante, L. *Low life*. 1991. New York: Vintage.

Sassen, S. 2001. *The global city*. 2nd ed. Princeton, NJ: Princeton University Press.

Sassen-Koob, S. 1989. New York City's informal economy. In *The informal economy: Studies in advanced and less developed counties*, ed. A. Portes, M. Castells, and L. Benton, 11–37. Baltimore: John Hopkins University Press.

Schmelzkopf, K. 1995. Urban community gardens as contested space. *Geographical Review* 85 (3): 361–81.

Schudson, M. 1979. On tourism and modern culture. *American Journal of Sociology* 84:1249–58.

Schutz, A. 1970. *Alfred Schutz on Phenomenology and Social Relations*. ed. H. R. Wagner. Chicago: University of Chicago Press.

Seigworth, G. J. 2000. Banality for cultural studies. *Cultural Studies* 14 (2): 227–68.

Sennett, R. 1990. *The conscience of the eye*. New York: Knopf.

———. 2005. Capitalism and the city. In *Cities of Europe*, ed. Y. Kazepov, 216–24. London: Blackwell.

Shaw, C. 1930. *The jack-roller: A delinquent boy's own story*. Chicago: University of Chicago Press.

Sheldon, P. J. 1986. The tour operator industry. *Annals of Tourism Research* 13:349–65.

Sherlock, K. 2001. Revisiting the concept of hosts and guests. *Tourist Studies* 1 (3): 271–95.

Shils, E. 1972. *The intellectuals and the powers and other essays*. Chicago: University of Chicago Press.

Slavin, S. 2003. Walking as spiritual practice: The pilgrimage to Santiago de Compostela. *Body and Society* 9 (3): 1–18.

Smith, N. 1996. *The new urban frontier: Gentrification and the revanchist city*. London: Routledge.

Snyder, G. 2009. *Graffiti lives: Beyond the tag in New York's underground*. New York: NYU Press.

Solnit, R. 2000. *Wanderlust: A history of walking*. New York: Penguin.

Sorkin, M., ed. 1992. *Variations on a theme park: The new American city and the end of public space*. New York: Hill and Wang.

Stacey, J. 2004. Marital suitors court social science spinsters: The unwittingly conservative effects of public sociology. *Social Problems* 51:131–45.

Stack, C. 1974. *All of our kin: Strategies for survival in a black community*. New York: Harper and Row.

Stansell, C. 2001. *American Moderns*. New York: Henry Holt and Company.

Stebbins, R. A. 1993. Social world, life-style, and serious leisure: Toward a mesostructural analysis. *World Leisure and Recreation* 35:23–26.

Stewart, S. 1984. *On longing: Narratives of the miniature, the gigantic, the souvenir, the collection*. Durham, NC: Duke University Press.

Sussman, M. 1998. New York's facelift. *TDR* 42 (1): 34–42.

Sutherland, E. H. 1937. *The professional thief*. Chicago: University of Chicago Press.

Suttles, G. 1984. The cumulative texture of local urban culture. *American Journal of Sociology* 90:283–304.

———. 1990. *The man made city*. Chicago: University of Chicago Press.

Tanenbaum, S. 1995. *Underground harmonies: Music and politics in the subways of New York*. Ithaca, NY: Cornell University Press.

Tilly, C. 1996. *Half a job: Bad and good part-time jobs in a changing labor market*. Philadelphia: Temple University Press.

———. 1998. Part-time work: A mobilizing issue. *New Politics* 6 (4): 19–26.

Tuan, Y.-F. 1980. The significance of the artifact. *Geographical Review* 70 (4): 462–72.

Tuchman, G. 1998. Interpreting media reviews. *Contemporary Sociology* 27 (1): 35–39.

Turner, L., and J. Ash. 1975. *The golden hordes: International tourism and the pleasure periphery*. London: Routledge.

Turner, R. S. 2002. The politics of design and development in the postmodern downtown. *Journal of Urban Affairs* 24 (5): 533–48.

Urry, J. 1990a. The consumption of "tourism." *Sociology* 24:23–35.

———. 1990b. *The tourist gaze: Leisure and travel in contemporary societies*. London: Sage Publications.

Van Mannen, J. 1992. Displacing Disney: Some notes on the flow of culture. *Qualitative Sociology* 15 (1): 5–35.

Van Mannen, J., and G. Kunda. 1989. "Real feelings": Emotional expression and organizational culture. In *Research in organizational behavior*, ed. L. L. Cummings and B. M. Staw, 43–103. Greenwich, Conn.: JAI Press.

Vowell, S. 2005. *Assassination vacation*. New York: Simon and Schuster.

Wacquant, L. 2004. *Body and soul: Notebooks of an apprentice boxer*. New York: Oxford University Press.

Ward, S. V. 1998. *Selling places: The marketing and promotion of towns and cities, 1850–2000*. London: E. F. and N. Spon.

Warren, S. 1994. Disneyfication of the metropolis: Popular resistance in Seattle. *Journal of Urban Affairs* 16 (2): 89–108.

Washington, E. 2002. *Manhattanville: Old heart of West Harlem.* Charleston: Arcadia Publishing.

Wasik, B. 2006. My crowd, or, phase 5: A report from the inventor of the flash mob. *Harper's Magazine* 312 (March): 56–66.

Weber, M. 1949. *From Max Weber.* Edited by H. Gerth and C. W. Mills. New York: Oxford University Press.

———. 1958. *The city.* Glencoe, Ill.: Free Press.

White, N., and E. Willensky. 1967. *The American Institute of Architects Guide to New York City.* New York: Macmillan.

White, E. B. 1949. *Here is New York.* New York: The Little Bookroom.

Whitehead, C. 2003. *The colossus of New York.* New York: Doubleday.

Whyte, W. F. 1955. *Street corner society: The structure of an Italian slum.* Chicago: University of Chicago Press.

Whyte, W. H., Jr. 1958. Introduction. In *The exploding metropolis,* ed. W. H. Whyte, 7–22. New York: Doubleday.

———. 1980. *The social life of small urban spaces.* New York: Project for Public Spaces.

———. 2000. New York and Tokyo: A study in crowding. In *The essential William H. Whyte,* ed. A. LeFarge, 227–45. New York: Fordham University Press.

Wilson, W. J. 1987. *The truly disadvantaged.* Chicago: University of Chicago Press.

Wolfe, G. R. 1975a. *New York: 15 Walking Tours.* New York: New York University Press.

———. 1975b. *New York: A Guide to the Metropolis.* New York: New York University Press.

Wolfson, H. 1992. New York bets on BIDs. *Metropolis* (April): 15–21.

World Tourism Organization. 2001. Commission of the European Communities 2001, Organization for Economic Co-operation and Development, United Nations, and World Tourism Organization. *Tourism satellite account: Recommended methodological framework.* (ECD/UN/WTO).

World Travel and Tourism Council (WTTC). 2003. *Progress and priorities 2003/04.* London: World Travel and Tourism Council.

———. 2004. United States travel and tourism: Forging ahead. 2004 Travel and Tourism Economic Research. London: World Travel and Tourism Council.

———. 2009. Progress and priorities 2008/2009. Travel and Tourism Economic Research. London: World Travel and Tourism Council.

Wynn, J. 2010. City tour guides: Urban alchemy at work. *City and Community.* 9 (2): 145–164.

Zemon Davis, N. 1983. *The return of Martin Guerre: Imposture and identity in a sixteenth-century village.* Cambridge: Harvard University Press.

Zukin, S. 1991. *Landscapes of power: From Detroit to Disney World.* Berkeley: University of California Press.

———. 1995. *The cultures of cities.* Cambridge, Mass.: Blackwell.

———. 1998. Urban lifestyles: Diversity and standardization in spaces of consumption. *Urban Studies* 35 (5–6): 825–39.

———. 2003. *Point of purchase.* London: Routledge.

Zukin, S., and P. Kasinitz. 1995. A museum in the Berkshires. In *The cultures of cities,* ed. S. Zukin, 79–108. London: Blackwell.

Zukin, S., and E. Kosta. 2004. Bourdieu off Broadway: Managing distinction on a shopping block in the East Village. *City and Community* 3 (2): 101–14.